J.Y.M. Seated, 1996, oil on canvas, 28 x 26 in., 71.1 x 66 cm.

FRANK AUERBACH

Recent Works

9 January through 15 February

MARLBOROUGH FINE ART LONDON

6 Albemarle Street London W1X 4BY 0171.629.5161

MODERN

Contributors to this Issue

Founded and edited by Peter Fuller
1987–1990

Modern Painters
Universal House
251 Tottenham Court Road
London W1P 9AD, UK

Editorial Assistants
Penny Clark, Helen Hobbs,
Sophie Mackley, Georgia Mazower
Tel: +44 171 636 6058
Fax: +44 171 580 5615

Advertising
Celia Bailey Tel: +44 171 636 6305/580 5618
Fax: +44 171 580 5615

Design and production
Catherine Fryett Tel: +44 1225 783432

Reprographics
D.P. Graphics, Holt, Wiltshire

Printing
Southemprint Ltd., Poole, Dorset

Subscriptions
are available by post or phone
at the following prices:
UK: £18; USA: $36;
Europe/Eire/rest of the world:
£44 (air mail) £26 (surface).
Institutuional rates on request.

For UK/Eire/Europe/rest of the world,
please make cheques payable to 'Fine Art Journals'
and send to: Central Books, 99 Wallis Road
London E9 5LN, UK
Tel: +44 181 986 4854

For USA and Canada
please make cheques payable to
'Modern Painters' and send to:
Modern Painters, c/o Mercury Subscription Services
2323 E-F Randolph Avenue, Avenel, New Jersey 07001
(US Mailing Agent)
Periodicals postage paid at Rahway, N.J.
2nd class postage permit number: 003524

Buying direct from newsagents
Modern Painters can be ordered across the counter from any
UK/Eire newsagent. If you have any problems call Time Out
Distribution on: 0171 813 6060

Distribution
UK Newsagents
Time Out Distribution, Universal House
251 Tottenham Court Road
London W1P 9AD, UK

UK/Eire/Europe/rest of the world
Galleries and bookshops
Central Books, 99 Wallis Road
London E9 5LN, UK

USA and Canada:
Eastern News Distributors, Inc.
2020 Superior Street, Sandinsky
Ohio 44870, USA

New Zealand:
Propaganda, CPO Box 582
Auckland 1001, New Zealand

South Africa:
Intermag, PO Box 10799
Johannesburg 2000, South Africa

Modern Painters does not assume responsibility for
unsolicited manuscripts, photographs or illustrations.
Copyright worldwide of all editorial content is held
by the publishers, Fine Art Journals Ltd.
Reproduction in whole or part is forbidden
save with the express permission
in writing of the publishers.

Published quarterly by
Fine Art Journals Ltd.
England
ISSN 0953-6698

William Boyd's
latest book, *The Destiny of Nathalie X,* a collection of short stories, is published by Penguin.

Patrick Carnegy,
a Leverhulme Research Fellow, 1994–96, his books include Faust as Musician: a study of Thomas Mann's 'Dr Faustus' and, forthcoming from Yale University Press, *Wagner and the Art of the Theatre.*

Matthew Collings
is an artist and writer. His forthcoming book, *From Bohemia to Britpop: The London Artworld from Francis Bacon to Damien Hirst,* will be published in 1997.

Peter Davidson
teaches English and comparative literature at the University of Warwick. As well as academic books and verse translations, he has published Word/Image pieces, most recently with Alan Powers, *Five Gates for England.*

David Elliott,
Director of MOMA Oxford since 1976, is now Director of Moderna Museet, Stockholm, and working on contemporary art in Europe and South East Asia.

Lance Esplund,
a painter who lives in New York City, is a faculty member at Parsons School of Design.

Boris Ford,
Editor of the *New Pelican Guide to English Literature,* the *Cambridge Cultural History of Britain* and *Benjamin Britten's Poets,* was Professor of Education at the University of Bristol, now retired.

Martin Gayford
writes on jazz and the fine arts. He is a regular contributor to *Modern Painters, The Daily Telegraph* and *The Spectator.*

Jonathan Glancey
writes on architecture for *The Independent* and other publications.

Piers Gough
is the G of CZWG Architects, and architect of the recently reopened Victorian and Modern Galleries at the National Portrait Gallery.

John Haldane
is Professor of Philosophy in the University of St Andrews. He has published widely in art, philosophy and religion. His most recent book is *Atheism and Theism* with J J C Smart, in the 'Great Debates in Philosophy' series (Oxford: Blackwell).

Philip Hensher's
first novel was Other Lulus (Hamish Hamilton and Penguin). His new novel, *Kitchen Venom,* was published in 1996, also by Hamish Hamilton.

Michael Hofmann
is a poet and translator; his new translation of Kafka's *America* will be published by Penguin in February.

Merlin James
will be showing his work at the Francis Graham Dixon Gallery, 23 January–8 March, and a touring exhibition 'Critical Pictures', organised by Kingston University, will be at Edinburgh School of Art, 6–20 January.

Lisa Jardine's
latest book is *Worldly Goods: A New History of the Renaissance,* from Macmillan.

John Lessore
is a painter. His next exhibition at the Theo Waddington Gallery will be from 8 March to 5 April.

David Lister
writes for *The Independent* and *The Independent on Sunday.* Before helping to launch *The Independent,* he worked on *The Times* and *The Times Educational Supplement.*

Norbert Lynton,
author of *The Story of Modern Art,* is a critic and art historian. His most recent book is Ben Nicholson from Phaidon.

Tom Lubbock
is a free-lance writer and illustrator.

Ian MacMillan
is a documentary film-maker.

Julian Mitchell
is a playwright. He is currently working on a film, *Wilde,* starring Stephen Fry as Oscar Wilde, and due for release in 1997.

Blake Morrison's
new book, *As If,* about children, childhood and the Bulger case, will be published in February.

Jed Perl
is art critic for *The New Republic.* He is the author of *Paris Without End: On French Art since World War 1* and *Gallery Going,* a selection of his essays from periodicals, including *Vogue, The New Republic, The New Criterion* and *Modern Painters.*

Bryan Robertson
is a broadcaster and writer, whose books include Jackson Pollock and Sidney Nolan.

David Sylvester
is currently editing a collection of his interviews, mostly with Americans, recorded between 1960 and 1996.

Glynn Williams
is a sculptor and Professor of Sculpture at the Royal College of Art. He exhibits internationally and is represented by the Bernard Jacobson Gallery.

Trevor Winkfield's
work will be the subject of a monograph with text by John Ashbery and Jed Perl, to be published later in 1997 by Hard Press, New York. He is represented by Donahue/Sosinski.

PAINTERS

Winter 1996

Editor
Karen Wright

Associate Editor
Linda Saunders

Editorial Board
David Bowie
William Boyd
Martin Gayford
Martin Golding
Grey Gowrie
Jeremy Isaacs
Howard Jacobson
William Packer
Jed Perl
Michael Podro
Bryan Robertson
Richard Wollheim
Patrick Wright

COVER: Ellsworth Kelly, *Red Curve 1V*, 1973, oil on canvas, 254 x 254 cm., detail
Reproduced by kind permission of the Musée de Grenoble

BERNARD JACOBSON GALLERY

The leading dealers in modern British art

William Scott, 'Still Life with Onions', 1950, oil on canvas, 25 ¹/₂ x 34 ¹/₂", 64.7 x 87.6 cm

Ivor Abrahams
Maurice Cockrill
Ivon Hitchens
Ian McKeever
Ben Nicholson
Stanley Spencer
William Tillyer

David Bomberg
Stephen Finer
Peter Lanyon
Richard Smith
William Scott
Graham Sutherland
Glynn Williams

14a Clifford Street London W1X 1RF Tel: 0171-495 8575 Fax: 0171-495 6210

New York   London   Madrid   Santiago   Tokyo

Marlborough Gallery New York
40 W 57th Street New York NY 10019 212.541.4900

Paula Rego
Recent Work
Through January 1997

Magdalena Abakanowicz
"Mutants"
15 January through 11 February

Neil Welliver
Recent Work
13 February through 8 March

Marlborough Gallery Madrid
Orfila 5, 28010 Madrid, Spain 34.1.308.4345

Roots of Contemporary Spanish Sculpture
Through February 1997

Marlborough Gallery London
6 Albemarle Street London W1X 4BY 0171.629.5161

Frank Auerbach
Recent Works
9 January through 15 February

Steven Campbell
Recent Works
19 February through 27 March

THE GOODMAN GALLERY
SOUTH AFRICA

Celebrates
the launch of our new space
with

LIFT
OFF

Artists:
Willie Bester
Norman Catherine
Kendell Geers
Robert Hodgins
William Kentridge
Pat Mautloa
Zwelethu Mthethwa
Penny Siopis

Opening Thursday 6th February 1997

New address:
The Galleries, 163 Jan Smuts Ave. Parkwood 2193
Johannesburg, South Africa.
Tel: 27 11 788-1113 - Fax: 27 11 788-9887
E MAIL: goodman@iafrica.com

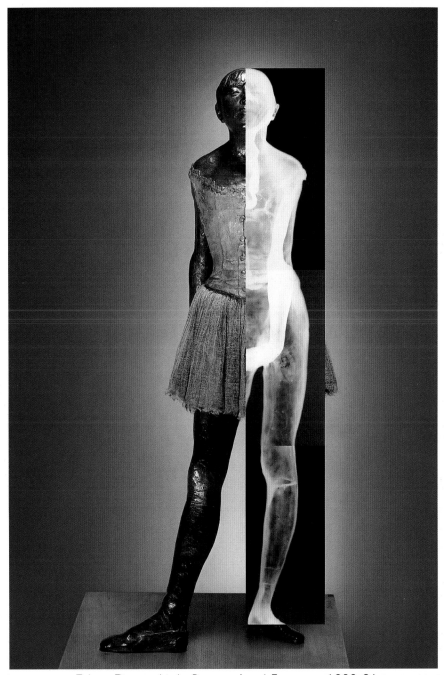

Edgar Degas, *Little Dancer Aged Fourteen*, 1880-81

Thanks to BP the Tate has given her a clean bill of health.

116 years after its creation and 73 years after casting, no-one quite knew the state of health of Degas's *Little Dancer*.

His original wax version caused a scandal when she was first seen with her strained stance and real clothes. But there's no controversy about the fact that she is now one of the world's most important sculptures and vital to preserve.

And thanks to BP, the Tate's conservators were able to use X-rays and other technologies to make a complete examination of her. It revealed that she is in remarkably good condition and at the same time gave the Gallery's experts vital insights about how this masterpiece was created.

Now the *Little Dancer* is up and about and ready to see you after her major check-up.

You'll find the visiting hours below.

TateGallery Millbank, London SW1. Tel: 0171 887 8008. Open Mon-Sat 10am-5.50pm, Sunday 2pm-5.50pm.

ODD NERDRUM

MARTINA HAMILTON FINE ART

Exclusive Management of Odd Nerdrum

Sales, Domestic and International Exhibitions

Phone 212-722-3311   Fax 212-996-3198

NEW YORK

'Buste de Setsuko', pencil on paper, 15³/₄ x 19¹⁵/₁₆ in. (40 x 50.6 cm)

An Exhibition of Works on Paper

by

BALTHUS

2nd – 20th December 1996

Monday – Friday

10 am – 5 pm

THE LEFEVRE GALLERY

(Alex Reid & Lefevre Ltd)

30 Bruton Street,
London W1X 8JD
Tel: 0171-493 2107
Fax: 0171-499 9088

DAVID HEPHER

Streets in the Sky
26 November - 31 December 1996
museum of
LONDON

Two Triptychs
29 November - 19 January 1997
Flowers East

A new monograph
on the artist
written by
Edward Lucie-Smith
will be available

Flowers East

Angela Flowers Gallery PLC
199-205 Richmond Road
London E8 3NJ
Tel 0181 985 3333 Fax 0181 985 0067
Tuesday - Sunday 10.00am - 6.00pm
e-mail: 100672.1903@compuserve.com

'A Tower Block For Lovers' (detail) 1995
Acrylic, plaster and PVA on canvas
37 x 50 cms

PHILIP HARRIS

5th – 29th March 1997

'Figure At Nightfall' 1996. Oil on canvas 54 x 36 ins

Catalogue available

BEAUX ARTS LONDON
22 Cork Street, London W1
Tel: 0171 437 5799   Mon-Fri 10-6 Sat 10-2

Inaugural exhibition of

Contemporary Painters and Sculptors

in association with

Davies & Tooth, Jeremy Hunt Fine Art and Victoria Collomb-East

December 10th - 20th 1996

32 Dover Street London W1X 3RA
Tel: 0171-409 1255
Monday to Saturday 10.00 -5.30

including work by

Bolan Chen - Jenny Franklin - Balraj Khanna - Brian McCann
Bruce McLean - Derek Morris - Hock-Aun Teh - Richard Winkworth

Worry on, Virginia

by David Lister

The star of *Art*, a marvellous new play in London's West End, is a gleaming and entirely white canvas. It is, says its proud purchaser, who has paid a small fortune for it, actually white lines on a white background. The terrain of the excesses of the art market and gullibility of its consumers seems at first familiar, and not just from real life. The West-End stage has explored it before in Timberlake Wertenbaker's deft satire, *Three Birds Alighting On A Field*. But *Art* takes us on an even more compelling trip. It goes beyond the arguments of representational versus abstract art to probe (with laughter and poignancy) how personal relationships can be hurt, even shattered, by conflicting opinions over a work of art; how two people's judgements of a painting can turn rapidly and violently into judgements of each other, and conversely how a renewal of affection between friends can change the sceptic's visual and intellectual judgement. The previously laughable con trick of the all-white canvas is now a full-blown narrative. A man has walked through the snow and disappeared. 'There is a system to it. A journey has taken place', says one of the characters about the canvas early on, to much laughter. Yet so touching is the eventual reconciliation of the friends brought about by their wrestling over the ultimate abstract painting that one is almost inclined to agree with this verdict by the final curtain.

The name of the fictional artist in *Art* is Antrios. And Antrios, one suspects, could yet figure in a speech from the Secretary of State for National Heritage, Virginia Bottomley. Art imitates life and life had a shot at imitating *Art*. Within a few days of the play opening, Mrs Bottomley gave a lecture entitled 'Our Heritage, Our Future' to the Royal Society of Arts in which the supposed embodiment of home counties cultural conservatism paid tribute to the unholy conceptualist trinity. She said:

A disproportionate number of world-renowned sculptors and painters of the younger generation are British. Anthony Gormley, Damien Hirst and Rachel Whiteread are just three with an international reputation, and these follow an established generation of artists of world standing: Anthony Caro, Lucien Freud and Howard Hodgkin. It is part of my role [she went on] to create a framework in which the experimental will be supported. Georges Braque said 'all art is meant to disturb'... Whilst work which sets out merely to shock or be a sensation is unlikely to endure, when artists simply reflect consensus we should worry for the state of our arts.

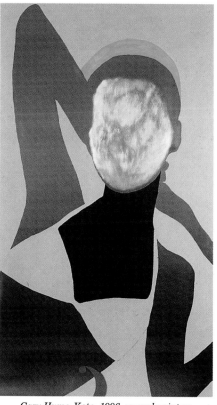

Gary Hume, Kate, 1996, enamel paint on aluminium panel, 208.5 x 117 cm. Courtesy Jay Jopling, London

Her championing of Hirst and co. got her into the headlines and on to Radio 4's Today programme. But one aspect of this which has gone unremarked is that a Cabinet minister now demonstrates street cred by praising contemporary artists. For the last few decades it has tended to be the name of a rock band or just occasionally a young turk of the theatre or perhaps a daring and cultish movie like *Trainspotting* (though Mrs Bottomley had already used that one earlier in the year). For a Conservative Cabinet minister with responsibility for the arts to go out of her way to give honourable mention to three contemporary artists is a moment worth noting for the record.

Before getting too carried away it is also worth noting that the three are all previous Turner Prize winners, so have some establishment standing in spite of themselves; that their proximity to the cutting edge is a matter of argument; and that Mrs Bottomley is not quite the devotee of their work that her speech suggests. Her office told me that she had in mind as much their earning power abroad as their artistic talent, and had not seen a great deal of their work. In that case she also should not get too carried away. Damien Hirst cuts the mustard in New York more or less, but no amount of formaldehyde will put him in the Andrew Lloyd Webber or Oasis league as far as the balance of payments is concerned.

Nevertheless, having started the debate, Mrs Bottomley should continue it. This does not mean a debate on the intrinsic worth of contemporary artists selected either at random or from civil service briefs. Not only is that debate shackled by subjective judgements inappropriate for ministers of the crown to utter on public platforms, it also suffers from the fact that the vocabulary of current artistic discourse is a minority sport. As one of the characters in *Art* memorably scoffs when the purchaser of the all-white canvas offers to 'deconstruct' it for him: 'Deconstruction!' he retorts haughtily. 'In order to convince me that some work of art is comprehensible you pick a word from *Builders Weekly*.'

No, Mrs Bottomley might make her last few months as minister memorable by extending her chosen debate. 'When artists simply reflect consensus we should worry for the state of our arts.' But what is true for artists is also true for gallery directors, Arts Council advisers and Turner Prize judging panels. The cross pollination of a small group of people among the various key advisory bodies and directorates in the visual arts has been detailed many times. And perhaps this year's mediocre shortlist for the Turner Prize demonstrates how stultifying the consensus is becoming. When a senior curator of the Tate shows a group of journalists round the Turner exhibition and explains that Gary Hume's portrait based on the supermodel Kate Moss left her face blank because he could not convey his experience of such beauty, then one worries either for the ability of the one figurative painter on the shortlist or the judgement of the Tate's curators, or both. When much of another room is taken up by Simon Patterson's rendering of a London Underground map (a fine design but not his) with the names of film stars replacing the names of stations, then one can only note that even the critic Waldemar Januszczak, a vehemently voluble champion of the Turner Prize when he worked for its sponsors Channel 4, is provoked into going into print to condemn it, saying that Patterson is '29 going on 13'. It is a small but interesting breach in the consensus. And consensus, Mrs Bottomley please note, has never been a sin of artists (or only at a remove, when they are seduced by it into banality) but of patrons, curators and critics. □

Ellsworth Kelly

Bryan Robertson *considers the strengths and vulnerability of the work of Ellsworth Kelly in the context of a major new show at the Guggenheim, New York, which travels to London and Munich in 1997.*

The retrospective exhibitions staged in New York this October for Jasper Johns, aged 66, at the Museum of Modern Art, and for Ellsworth Kelly, 73, at the Guggenheim Museum, are the largest surveys of the work of these artists ever assembled. Do they deserve this valedictory treatment? Yes, they do: Johns and Kelly, with true independence of spirit and in ways quite different from each other, revitalised the scope and the possibilities of painting at a moment in the late '50s when art everywhere began to suffer from a surfeit of Abstract Expressionism, before Pop Art or Minimalism got into their stride. Both artists contributed indirectly and in an uninvolved way to these developments along wholly original lines, although the central energy of their aesthetic and imaginative powers (if somewhat problematically in the past decade with Johns) was to extend far beyond them.

Both of the shows in New York are exemplary in choice and range of work; the catalogue for each event has detailed and expertly researched information with excellent reproductions, weighs a ton and is well worth its hefty price. Both shows have proved very popular, with galleries at each museum swarming with visitors intent upon the twists and turns of an unfolding and nicely plotted chronology. The two exhibitions are partly social events as well as aesthetic demonstrations: in the perception of an American audience these artists have acquired over the last 40 years some-

thing like the status and the historic patina of American icons of uncompromising style and grace. I believe that a European audience would perceive them in much the same way, relishing the sophistication of Johns and the purist zeal of Kelly: two good artists, eminently capable of the long haul, still holding their own at the close of the century. Appraising either of them, one asks how does their work seem, 40 years on from that fresh start?

After two lengthy visits to each show, I felt a certain anxiety about the comparatively vulnerable nature of Kelly's highly individual achievement when his work leaves the studio and appears in the world of museums and presentation. In contrast, the work of Johns in its regular format of paintings and drawings seems almost to take care of itself as a conventional installa-

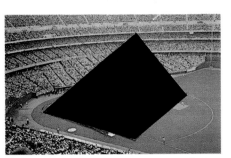

Ellsworth Kelly, Cincinnati Riverfront Stadium, *1980, collage on postcard, 8.9 x 14 cm. Private collection*
Above title: Ellsworth Kelly, *Curve Seen from a Highway, Austerlitz, New York, 1970, gelatin-silver print, 27.9 x 35.6 cm. Private collection*

tion. To explain this anxiety, I should preface anything I have to say about Kelly by pointing to the uncomfortable fact that his art is not seen to its best advantage at the Guggenheim Museum.

The Guggenheim is often an agreeable place to visit for certain kinds of exhibition, but it is a dire venue for painting and most destructive of all to the large-scale abstract painting of this century. The building worked best and indeed came into its fullest life when filled, back in the late '60s, with an exhibition of Calder mobiles which energised and pulled together, through a very modern kind of Baroque exuberance, its interior structure as an actively creative counterpoint to the play of spatial elements. The building should have been retained for ever as a Calder Museum.

As it is, the tilted movement of the Guggenheim's spiralling ramps provides the most continuously intrusive and disruptive background for Kelly's serene work that could ever be devised. The alertly poised or monumentally calm shapes in brilliant colour of his deceptively simple paintings and sculptures require as a support the balance, the *equilibrium*, created between the opposition of absolutely stable and flat vertical and horizontal planes of a normal floor and ceiling. At the Guggenheim, most of Kelly's work is destabilised. The building's distractingly concave walls on which paintings are normally placed have been eliminated by the use of flat panels for this show, but as a spectator you are still walking either uphill or down all the time in

Ellsworth Kelly, Blue Relief with Black, *1993, oil on canvas, 249.6 x 226.1 cm. Private collection, San Francisco*

relation to the paintings, which often appear to tilt or lean themselves in alignment with the sloping floor and ceiling. The strain tells also of continually walking with one leg higher than the other since the floor you stand on has an additional slope of its own, sideways and uphill toward the ramp's balustrade. You walk off the ramp at intervals with tremendous relief to view in normal conditions of floor and wall those works by Kelly that have been removed from the unstable viewing conditions of the main building. It is only here, in these admirably conventional galleries, that Kelly's work can be properly contemplated.

And it is in one of these galleries that a substantial group of Kelly's noblest two-part inventions can be found, dating from the late '80s into the present decade, and perhaps the most beautiful and concentrated works of a lifetime. They are not active dialogues between two shapes so much as formal situations. Kelly's work as a whole seems in its Platonic idealism to have grown further away over the years from any obvious or readily imaginable

starting point in nature – we all gratefully recall the references in early work to his experience of living in Paris, finding in abstract paintings and drawings the suggestion of window blinds lowered at various degrees on buildings, or a bridge over the Seine mirrored by its exact reflection. These new works, though free of such easily detectable references to nature, still seem peculiarly alive: alert and evocative. Each shape is not so much a passive foil as an active partner in a formal situation, which has an odd parallel with the way in which, in choreography, a dancer will not only support but *present* a partner.

In *Blue Relief with Black* (1993), what appears to be a big segment of a blue circular disc, which would have a gigantic dimension if fully achieved, curves downward in front of what might be just exposed parts of a black square, or a black rectangle extending to the same base as the blue segment. Or it could become a far larger black square extending – like the blue segment if transformed into a circle – beyond the right-hand vertical edge that it

shares with the blue, to become a black rectangle in projection as immense as the blue disc. As it is, *Blue Relief with Black* is alertly composed but at rest, mysterious in the stilled potentialities of its interaction between two colours and two shapes, and sensuously beguiling in the interaction between a matt, unfathomable black and a luminous, spacious blue.

In *Orange Red Relief (for Delphine Seyrig)* (1990), an orange rectangle is set diagonally across a bright red square, but the orange rectangle cuts across the red square in such a way that what it conceals could just as readily be taken to be a red rectangle of the same dimensions as the differently inclined orange shape. But this has only minor – if real – interest compared with the outpouring of light triggered off by the juxtaposition of this intense red with that exactly calculated blazing orange. The red square appears to present the orange rectangle rather than support it; the interaction has a mysteriously rich *éclat*, like the memory of glowing light and its afterimage. Delphine Seyrig died in October

Ellsworth Kelly, Cité, *1951, oil on wood, 20 joined panels, 142.9 x 179.1 cm. overall. Private collection*

1990. The dedication in Kelly's title reminds us that the distinguished French actress, who appeared so memorably in films by Resnais and Bunuel, was one of Kelly's earliest supporters from the Paris years in the late '40s and early '50s. Seyrig was one of the group of friends, including Jack Youngerman (to whom Seyrig was married), Robert Indiana, Agnes Martin and James Rosenquist, who, like Kelly, had studios at Coenties Slip in Lower Manhattan for a period in the late '50s.

Scale is crucial to the impact of these works: *Orange Red Relief* is ten feet high and eight feet in width; *Blue Circle with Black* is eight feet high by seven feet across. And these and other wall structures, oils on canvas involving two joined panels, both command and occupy individually a great deal of space – they appear to animate, by implication, far more space around them than any other modern works that I can recall.

Kelly's work in fact raises fundamental questions of space, interaction, scale and installation which most museums would find hard to resolve. His paintings and sculptures present us with formal and sensual essences so utterly fined down to precise dimensions from perception of the

Ellsworth Kelly, Shadows on Stairs, *Villa la Combe, Meschers, 1950, gelatin silver print, 35.6 x 27.9 cm. Private collection*

physical world around us that each work in its concentration really requires, in my view, its own isolated space for it to function properly and to be seen for what it is.

An engrossing and seminal part of the Guggenheim show presents us with a gathering of Kelly's masterly photographs and collages. Here directly or obliquely in sequences of images is a great deal of the inspiration behind Kelly's art. The black shadow splicing diagonally across the open *Hangar Doorway Saint Barts* (1977), the great attenuated curve of the edge of a snow-covered hillside etched sharply against black trees in *Curve Seen from a Highway, Austerlitz, New York* (1970), and also *Shadows on Stairs* (1950), make their point. Collaged postcards of aerial views of cities, beach scenes or stadiums extend Kelly's insights into scale and its occupancy and sometimes surreal disruption. If later paintings and sculptures appear to be more self-sufficient and hard to relate to natural appearances, the link with perception is constant.

To combine a love of morphology with a clear-cut rejection of illusionism is a tough stance for any artist to sustain. But however abstract and apparently near to some form of rarefied geometry, the refer-

Ellsworth Kelly, Orange Red Relief (For Delphine Seyrig)*, 1990, oil on canvas, two joined panels, 306.1 x 250.2 cm. overall*

ences in Kelly's art to something physically, concretely observed, *seen*, is always present. 'It's nothing if it isn't about something you haven't seen before', says Kelly, and goes on: 'The things I'm interested in have always been there'. Yve-Alain Bois has explained Kelly's imaginative editing process very well:

> Much has been made of the fact that Kelly's shapes often derive from things seen, but perhaps not enough attention has been paid to the method of derivation itself. It is a zooming process by which the artist appropriates some unnoticed area of the visual field. He makes a cut out of the area, evacuates it of its substance, lays it flat. Most often, the excerpt in question is interstitial. A part of the ground in our daily perception, it did not call attention to itself until Kelly picked it up, isolating it. Kelly makes it the figure. A shape is born, and this affirmation is based on a negation: it suddenly exists because the rest has been edited out.[1]

The essential drive and ethos of Kelly's mature work and the world of Brancusi which is, of course, a far closer paraphrase of natural forms, cannot really be compared. Brancusi had no interest in the extraction from nature of an interstitial visual event. But there is a parallel in the conditions necessary for the proper appreciation of

either artist, both of whom can at least be said to be reductivist in their feeling for form. Brancusi very sensibly always refused any invitation to show his work with that of other sculptors, although occasionally a piece would appear in a mixed exhibition in circumstances beyond his control. And even in a one-man exhibition, the concentrated nature of a Brancusi sculpture achieves its maximum life only in isolation. In any creative presentation of Brancusi's work as a whole each sculpture is seen in its own singular space because each sculpture fills, imaginatively, big areas of space far beyond its actual presence. The

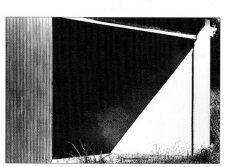

Ellsworth Kelly, Hangar Doorway, Saint Barts, *1977, gelatin-silver print, 27.9 x 35.6 cm.*
Private collection

shapes expand and extend themselves in the mind of the beholder. James Johnson Sweeney, whom Brancusi trusted uniquely, understood this fact very well when he installed so memorably the first great Brancusi show in a sequence of white rooms, each room containing only two or three works, at the Guggenheim Museum's first headquarters in the big New York town house used for housing the collection as well as for exhibitions before the Frank Lloyd Wright building existed.

You either respond to Kelly's art and therefore take it as seriously as the work of Brancusi, as I do, very warmly, or you see and feel nothing beyond the blank impact of simplistic coloured shapes. My own very positive view of Kelly tells me, as an installer of exhibitions, that his paintings and sculptures require equally tough and rarefied conditions really to work as they should. The restrictions have nothing to do with grandeur, or preciosity, or any weakness in the work, but relate only to the special conditions of scale, space and aesthetic identity which Kelly's art creates.

An ideal Kelly show would consist of a sequence of white rooms of carefully selected proportions in which, as in the Musée Picasso at Antibes, only one or two works would be disclosed at a time. The height of each room relative to the work would be as important as its circumference. At the Guggenheim, although the two-part inventions that I have referred to are at least seen in stable conditions in a side gallery, the proportions of the room are not ideal and you see too many works at once. And if you string any of Kelly's paintings in a more or less continuous line, however spaciously, they instantly turn into a sequence of blank logos, or the gaily-coloured flags of mythical nations, or disparate elements in a décor. When you see in this way entire segments of the Kelly show across the ramps at the Guggenheim, his powerful invention is reduced to a sequence of tokens recalling only the later commercial exploitation of his ideas, for Kelly's art in the '50s and early '60s engendered a stylistic revolution in packaging and presentation.

Although Pop artists in the '60s explored a range of commercially designed and packaged subjects, a reverse movement of borrowing and appropriation had been in progress since the early years of the century – and indeed continues – with industrial design and commercial presentation absorbing and regurgitating at an increasingly fast pace the inventions of fine art. The process has accelerated steadily. In the late '20s, the drawings of fashion models in magazines and newspaper advertisements were already influenced by the tapering elongations of Modigliani. Surrealism had begun to affect shop window displays everywhere by the 1940s. The *Skylon*, soaring up by the Thames during the 1951 Festival of Britain could not have been designed without the example of Brancusi's *Bird in Space* – and Brancusi had already had an incisive impact on the 'streamlined' shape of a wide range of manufactured objects, from fountain pens to automobiles.

In 1954, Nicholas de Staël died, and I installed a retrospective exhibition of his work at the Whitechapel Gallery in 1955. In the same week that the show opened, London Transport posters advertising cheap travel rates descriptively designed in unmistakeably de Staël-ish chunky blocks of paint and strong colours were pasted up outside the tube entrance next door to the Gallery, to the wry amusement of his widow and his dealer, Jacques Dubourg. The gap in time between art and commerce had narrowed to practically nothing. Today in film making, high art and low art are practically indistinguishable because so many films are conditioned in their sharp editing, jump-cuts and abrupt dissolves by the only prevalent form of commercial art left: TV advertising. This whole story of relative influence in the twentieth century is a very absorbing one, best summed up by the way

Ellsworth Kelly, City Island, *1958, oil on canvas, 198.1 x 14.8 cm. Collection of Stephen Marsh*

in which the real visual battle in our period has so evidently resolved itself as a fight to the death between Disney and Brancusi.

Kelly was working in a highly personal and reductivist abstract direction in France by 1950, and so of course were a small number of other gifted artists, notably Herbin, Max Bill and other painters and sculptors exhibiting at the Galerie Denise René in Paris. It is of minor but real

Ellsworth Kelly, Wild Grape *(detail), 1961, pencil on paper. Solomon R Guggenheim Museum, New York*

interest, I think, to discover the new-found tailored severity and simplicity of Chanel and the very new and severely minimal shapes and cut of Courrèges appearing so strikingly through the '60s. Kelly had himself designed in 1950 some excellent silk fabrics which were used by Balmain. By the early '70s, Pizza Express in London was using an orange, green, black and white décor of simple shapes in their chain of restaurants in London which would not have been possible without the assimilation, conscious or otherwise, of Kelly's art into commercial awareness . The hanging of Kelly's work at the Guggenheim reduces too many of his formal inventions to emblems. Any abstract paintings hung in this linear, sequential way are similarly reduced because they are viewed as a generalised abstract group before they can be seen individually. This is why Rothko always insisted that each painting in a show should be hung on separate walls or screens so that each work could be encountered in isolation (a condition sadly neglected in the last Rothko show at the Tate).

Conspicuously, among the most original and gifted American artists, Kelly seems to have made a successful personal synthesis between European art and an American sensibility. All his initial insights seem to have come from European art, and his early training as a painter was along European lines in Boston, briefly, and in Paris, at length. By enlarging scale almost in relation to the way in which he reduced form, he arrived at a stage when colour no longer described a form but became the form. The elegance and wit of his work is given another dimension by what seems always to be its weightlessness, the light of early summer and a spirit of boundless optimism, gaiety, insouciance, free of history or any burden of the past. In this, Kelly seems very American, like the purposeful and cheerful elegance of Shaker furniture to be seen in the Shaker Museum not far from where Kelly lives in upstate New York, or the spare formality of traditional American architecture – or a perfect dry Martini, which has after all a trace of French vermouth as a crucial ingredient.

1. *Ellsworth Kelly, Spencertown*, introduction by Yve-Alain Bois and a photographic essay by Jacques Shear, Anthony d'Offay, London.

'Ellsworth Kelly: A Retrospective', until 15 January, Solomon R Guggenheim Museum, New York; 16 February–18 May, The Museum of Contemporary Art, Los Angeles; 12 June–7 September, Tate Gallery, London; November 1997–January 1998, Hans der Kunst, Munich. Sponsored by Hugo Boss. Catalogue edited by Diane Waldman, Guggenheim Museum, New York, $75hb, $39.95pb, £45hb.

Edward Burra, 'Esso' 1952/4, watercolour 29 x 41 inches

**Dealers in 20th Century
Paintings,
Drawings, Watercolours
Sculpture and Fine Prints
Including works by**
Gaudier-Brzeska
Burra
Eardley
John
Moore
Redpath
Spencer
Vaughan
Wadsworth
Wallis
Wood

MERCURY GALLERY

26 Cork Street, London, WIX 1HB
Tel: 0171 734 7800 Fax: 0171 287 9809

— WIGMORE —
FINE ARTS

ALECOS
KONTOPOULOS

PAINTINGS & DRAWINGS

January 10th - February 1st 1997

"Conspirator" 1969   oil on canvas, 110 x 100cm

104 Wigmore Street, London WIH 9DR   Tel.0171-224 1962 Fax 0171-224 1965

The Artists' Artist

Diagnosing an American art scene whose mounting confusion over three decades is a model for our own,
Trevor Winkfield *sees* **Jasper Johns** *as perhaps the sole survivor of a gifted generation of explorers.*

There appears to be neither rhyme nor reason why good art is produced at any given time. Take Russia in 1915: who would have suspected that in the midst of war, in one of the most conservative and repressive societies then existing, a society disintegrating from its own lack of imagination, Kasimir Malevich could have wrenched himself free, ignored his freezing apartment, his dire poverty, his meagre food rations, and settled down to paint the first Suprematist compositions? On the other hand, when all the elements are in place nothing seems to happen. Japan, after 1950, blessed with unparalleled wealth and a curious, acquisitive middle-class lusting after wallcoverings, failed miserably to initiate any contemporary art of value (to the extent of having to import it). All the power of Victorian England, too, only squeaked forth the Pre-Raphaelites and the Royal Academy.

Jasper Johns, who rose to prominence after his first show at Leo Castelli's in New York in 1958, has had a career which at first glance seems a product of the perfected version of the Japanese model. A country (the United States) at the height of its mercantile and military power (1947–65),

secure in its material achievements, with a small but influential and extremely knowledgeable intelligentsia, seeks to legitimise its new wealth by patronising the arts. Of course it helps when there's a bushel of talent awaiting patronage, a bushel moreover firmly ensconced in a city affordable to artists (as New York then was, and alas no longer is). A generation of Abstract Expressionists had somehow managed to survive and fabricate its finest paintings prior to this upsurge of patronage, but it is Johns's generation which reaped its full benefits, and ultimately its poisoned chalice. For around the mid-1960s a new bevy of wealthy collectors (as opposed to middle-class art lovers) muscled into the American art world, their eyes formed by film and television rather than the old masters, and for the most part unable to differentiate good from bad art. For them, Pop Art was an easily assimilated movement, as Bauhaus abstraction had been for an earlier generation. While one doesn't want to denigrate the simplistic liberating effusions of Pop, its legacy (and that of its successor, Minimalism) forms part and parcel of one of the most paradoxical of recent American achievements: the ascent of proletarian

taste by purely capitalist means.

Stylistically, Pop represented a massive surrender of complexity in favour of numskull homogeneity, signalling that great ennui of the imagination now trudging through the West. Financially, the reckless throwing around of huge sums of money which Pop ushered in usurped the old art world and imposed an art market mentality where the relationship between dealer and artist shifted to one between dealer and collector. Art became just another capitalist industry, with aesthetics more or less thrown out of the window. Simultaneously, criticism suffered a massive loss of nerve, refused to take the lead and degenerated into bad journalism, or worse, pseudo-esoteric twaddle. Once this had happened, it was only a matter of time before contemporary art, following on from modern art, could itself be gobbled up by that strange commercial hybrid 'gallery art'. Under this rubric more bad art was churned out – and sold – during the 1980s than at any time since the reign of the nineteenth-century salons. Artists by and large were reduced to mere purveyors to the trade and any art managing to escape its homogenisation tended to be buried by the

Jasper Johns at Pearl Street in 1955, with Flag, *1954–5, and* Target with Plaster Casts, *1955, in the background*
Above title: Jasper Johns, Green Target, *1955, encaustic on newspaper and cloth over canvas, 152.4 x 152.4 cm. The Museum of Modern Art, New York*

dross. Thus, by the early 1990s, New York, its eyeballs exhausted, found itself in the parlous state in which Paris had found itself in the mid-1950s: a plenitude of galleries with nothing much of interest to display and the glum realisation that American art's Golden Age was well and truly a thing of the past.

Through all this dissolution and venal mayhem Jasper Johns has sailed apparently unscathed, a bemused survivor, perhaps the only one, of that gifted slew of explorers gravitating around the Abstract Expressionist/Pop axis. Some had died, still others took early mental retirement, content to endlessly recycle their early formulas (which *were* formidable – nobody can dismiss the sheer visceral impact of early Warhol and Lichtenstein). Those still alive more or less spent their later careers wasting their oxygen. Johns alone has cleaved to his self-imposed role of research painter, one of that endangered band whose password might be Kant's 'I no longer know where I am', and whose first requisite is to be perpetually dissatisfied by the direction their work is taking at any given time.

This discontent is one reason why so many American artists have dedicated a special niche to Johns in their pantheons. He's remained, despite his commercial success, a quintessential artists' artist, on a par with Marsden Hartley and Willem de Kooning, admired at the same time as they are plundered by artists of widely divergent tastes. He is, in fact, one of the least imitated but most influential of American artists (Pollock's work, by contrast, has had

little to offer later generations beyond a concept of what 'greatness' can look like). It's this aspect of John's work – the solitary's dedication to research despite all that's going on around him – which brings us back full circle to Malevich.

Johns's early work – the flags, targets and numerals – were hatched in the same mood of defiant solitude as Malevich's white fields. Few saw them while they were being painted. Only when they emerged as a group in Johns's first show in 1958 did they enter public discourse, and then with alarming rapidity. Johns was obviously the right painter at the right time (unlike all those who emerged in the 1980s, who were the wrong painters at the right time). This ready acceptance was due in no small measure to Johns's ability to render the achievements of Abstract Expressionism comprehensible to an audience more amenable to figuration. This coming together of figurative subject matter with an abstract handling of paint marked a historic breakthrough, and still seems one of Johns's most memorable reforms.

Forty years later, seen in the context of the Johns retrospective at the Museum of Modern Art, these early emblems have only increased their magnetic lustre. One can easily reconstitute their original appeal, a paradoxical union of opposites. Their flat, banal imagery (whose iconic starkness bespeaks America) married to a sensuous, idiosyncratic handling of pigment – a melding of public and private faces – still strikes one as a terrific accomplishment for a young painter. The works vibrate with all

the giddy arrogance of early Seurat and Picasso, when those painters knew they too could and would change the way people looked at the world.

Shorn of their weeping veils of encaustic droplets, the flags and targets might be cast as forerunners of Warhol's masterpieces for morons of the following decade. But retaining the veils signalled Johns's rejection of reductive modernism, which in turn allowed him to bypass the dead-end of Pop and continue along that visionary road he's spent the rest of his life traversing, albeit with many a feint and stumble.

This repudiation of his early success – a triumph based on monolithic imagery confining autobiographical intrusions to the action of the painter's wrist – erupted in 1959 with *Device Circle* and *Out the Window*. In these paintings, the confines of the canvas for once seem too restrictive. The patient, contemplative brush-strokes are ushered away to make room for vociferous pattering wind-bursts looking to spill over onto the wall. The paintings stop being monologues and become conversations, as though Johns had taken to heart Duchamp's insight that it's the viewers, replete with personal histories and their own interpretative skills, who complete the painting. Johns's target surfaces had looked as though they were guarding the images beneath, not only clamping them down but trying to hide them – subsumed violence personified.

From the early 1960s the images bubble to the surface, break free and start parading around, beckoning the viewer to follow. It's

Jasper Johns, Untitled, *1992–5, oil on canvas, 198.1 x 299.7 cm. The Museum of Modern Art, New York, promised gift of Agnes Gund*

little wonder that Alfred Barr, who'd purchased three of Johns's paintings for the Museum of Modern Art from the first show, blanched when he saw the second show in 1960. In place of the secular altarpieces he'd lionised, he found *tableaux* which had the quality of bins into which everything had been tumbled. Many of these later paintings, executed at a time when Johns was claiming 'I don't want my work to be an exposure of my feelings', have literal intrusions: spoons, cups, brooms, a whole pantry of images. They're still bedecked with petrified wax, evoking troops of nerves circulating beneath, as though the paintings' real lives, as ever, took place out of sight. Here Johns (a ravenous reader of poetry, whose work contains numerous references to poets such as Frank O'Hara, Hart Crane, Ted Berrigan and Tennyson) consciously or unconsciously succumbed to that well-worn but still potent Mallarméan notion of painting not the thing itself but the effect which it produces. Seen in this light, are the targets surrogate self-portraits, as some have hinted? Are the body parts, corpses, skulls, sleeping soldiers, wooden beams and bloodied bandages evidence of the strangest religious painter of our time? Has Johns's life work been a struggle to erect a crucifixion without painting one?

Johns's own intentions have remained skilfully shrouded in ambiguity. In the interviews and remarkable sketchbook notes published to coincide with the current retrospective, we're supplied with elliptical clues rather than the hard facts that lazybones crave. There's no simple 'Yes' or 'No' to Jasper Johns, it's always overlaid with 'Either/Or'. He himself asserts: 'I don't put any value on a kind of thinking that puts limits on things'. His mercifully reticent biography offers few clues as to how to

Jasper Johns, Voice 2 *(detail, 1st panel), 1968–71, oil and collage on canvas, three panels, each 182.9 x 411.4 cm. Öffentliche Kunstsammlung Basel, Kunstmuseum*

approach the work. At one point in the chronology running through the Museum of Modern Art catalogue (one of those unnecessary rib-crushers so beloved of contemporary curators) the compilers are so stumped for interesting tidbits they're reduced to such small potatoes as the entry for October 7, 1983:

> From Stony Point, Johns writes to Castleman denying rumours he has broken his leg. He adds that the monotypes are being cleaned by Bill Goldston, and that he will soon decide on how to tear these prints' margins.

One can, I suppose, dismiss these non-events. But reading between their lines we can detect that the important part of Johns's life has been lived on the canvas, not in the world outside – which gives his inert slabs of encaustic a terrible poignancy.

A problem which such a devotion creates is the sheer boredom and loneliness many artists experience when confined to their studios for hours at a time, day in and day out, decade after decade. It's the main reason so many abandon the task, or start talking to themselves. Johns, about the time his paintings stopped being monologues and became conversations (1960), with studio fever mounting, adopted the clever strategem of taking up a team activity in the form of printmaking. The revivifying impact apart – manoeuvring raw lithographic ink jolted his paint into chromatic overdrive – it led, by the end of the decade, to an increased flattening of the paint surface.

With his passionless 'Screen Pieces' of 1967–8 one suspects he no longer meant what he painted. As their titles suggest, the 'Screen Pieces' were more about flatness than hidden depths, more about print than paint. By the time he came to paint *Decoy* in 1971 he'd become a moody topographer of atmosphere, but little else.

It's clear he'd simultaneously run out of ideas of what to paint and how to paint. The three interchangeable panels of *Voice 2* (1968–71) illustrate the colour crisis he was experiencing at the same time. It's often been said – Johns has tacitly agreed – that he has at best a rudimentary grasp of colour. I beg to differ. He's a wonderful colourist. While it's true he rarely puts us in a lather with cunning arrays of tints the way Matisse does, he's always used colour so it doesn't overpower his ideas. When we leave Matisse, on the other hand, often we're left with a stunning crimson glow, and an empty head. *Voice 2* does, however, betray Johns's lack of self-confidence in his innate colour sense to an alarming degree. Originally, each panel was painted primary red, yellow and blue (remnants of these colours act as *mementi mori* along the edges of the canvases). In this primal state – still visible in slides taken in 1970 – the whole ensemble was a prismatic riot. Alas, Johns lost his nerve and felt compelled to tone it down by reverting to his usual monochromatic grey overlays; so what we perceive now is very much a shadow of its former self, still a masterpiece, not ruined but muted.

At this impasse (impasses occur regularly at the turn of each decade in his career), Johns was driving on Long Island and saw a car coming towards him. Covered in cross-hatchings and glimpsed only for a second, its fortuitous dazzle supplied subject matter sufficient for a decade's mining. This ability to capitalise on apparently trivial occurrences (witness his dream of painting the stars and stripes, or the casual suggestion by a friend that he paint a pet) marks him not only as a willing sponge but draws attention also to his relative lack of imagination. Not that there's anything wrong with that – many find Picasso too overpoweringly protean. And besides, painters by and large aren't the most imaginative creators; compared to musicians and poets, they come pretty low on the imaginative totem. Mainly it's a matter of finding and refining a few subjects, and Johns slots into this scheme of things perfectly.

The range of his subject matter may be narrow but it runs deep, sparking endless shufflings and myriad interpretations. Just as Cézanne's apples, contemplated long enough, take on the gravity of planets in their orbits, so Johns can transform a green target into a whirlpool, one which becomes a bird's-eye view of the roof of a tower, its multiple floors receding into the wall behind. This awareness that what we are seeing is not all that we can get (*Voice 2*'s buried spectrum being this concept's most tangible archaeological evidence) is made explicit in the works from 1980 onwards.

Jasper Johns, Mirror's Edge 2, *1993, encaustic on canvas, 167.6 x 111.7 cm.*
Robert and Jane Meyerhoff Collection, Phoenix, Maryland

Thanks to paint's ability to depict and disguise at the same time, previously secret layers are hauled to the surface yet retain their unfathomable ambiguities. Autobiographical elements such as the floor plan of his grandfather's house are carpeted by ladders, body shadows, segments of sidereal space, stick men and Picassoid eyeballs. It's as though Johns is finally declaring his life to be an open book .. if only we can find him on the shelf.

Labouring under the label Greatest Living American Painter (a burden which should be returned to the Guinness Book of Records) cannot have been easy for Johns. He must often have felt he'd been transformed into one of his alleged self-portraits,

a target. Certainly he's received more than his fair share of brickbats when he's failed to deliver a Great Painting. Much better to think of him as a Remarkable Painter, a maverick isolationist who has never stopped painting his best work.

Jasper Johns: A Retrospective, sponsored by Philip Morris Companies, until 21 January 1997, Museum of Modern Art, New York; 7 March–1 June, Ludwig Museum, Cologne; 28 June–17 August, Museum of Contemporary Art, Tokyo. Kirk Varnedoe, *Jasper Johns: A Retrospective*, distributed by Harry N Abrams, $32.50US/$65US; *Jasper Johns in His Own Words*: Writings, Sketchbook Notes and Interviews, compiled by Christel Hollevoet, distributed by Harry N Abrams, $24.95US.

Rubens's Landscapes

Martin Gayford *walked round the exhibition of Rubens's landscapes*
at the National Gallery with painter **John Lessore**.

Martin Gayford: Shall we take a look at the first room?

John Lessore: That's absolutely marvellous, isn't it, the *Self Portrait with Friends*? Especially his own head and shoulders, but all of them really. He must have been looking at Titian and the Venetians.

MG: Why do you say the Venetians?

JL: It's the treatment of the head, those very subtle gradations making such a grand shape. He's done it especially with his own head. The one on the right is much more Nordic; it looks almost Dutch, with all that detail. His own head is very simple and grand; it's a brilliant piece of painting.

MG: It's not a modest picture, though, is it? He comes out of it much more strongly than anyone else.

JL: He must have been good at self-promotion. And of course he did make his way in life.

MG: That little landscape in the middle of the lake at Mantua is rather Venetian, too, in a stormy, Giorgione sort of way.

JL: Absolutely. When was it done? 1602. Well, he'd been seeing Italian paintings and it shows.

MG: Yes, but independent landscape paintings were really a Flemish speciality – the catalogue quotes Michelangelo sneering at them as an inferior form of art. Real art depicted people – and gods, I suppose. What this room really documents is that in the

Peter Paul Rubens, Self-Portrait with Friends,
c.1602 oil on canvas, 77.5 x 101 cm.
Wallraf-Richartz-Museum, Cologne, on loan from
the Federal Republic of Germany

sixteenth-century Flemish artists concentrated on two basic landscape formulae – both invented by Breughel, who, like Rubens later, was based in Antwerp. One was the World View, or God's Eye View. That Joos de Momper over there is quite a good example.

JL: It's a marvellous feeling, looking down on the world like that.

MG: I suppose it's more or less the view that Christ was given by Satan when he was taken up on the mountain top and shown the world spread out at his feet. I like the other type, the forest landscape, where you're looking into dense woodland, with knotted tree trunks and mysterious depths.

JL: That forest painting there by Abraham Govaerts really has a lot of the feeling of Rubens. It's much softer in fact than most of the Breughel family. And you've got these great sweeping gentle rhythms. And the torn tree.

They had a system, didn't they, of using brown in the foreground, green in the middle distance, and blue in the distance. But actually they worked all of the colours

Peter Paul Rubens, Peasants with Cattle by a Stream in a Woody Landscape ('The Watering Place'), *c.1620, oil on oak, 99.4 x 135 cm. The National Gallery*
Above title: Peter Paul Rubens, A Shepherd with his Flock in a Woody Landscape, *c.1620, oil on oak, 64.4 x 94.3 cm. The National Gallery*

into all of the stages, with the possible exception of the blue that they didn't put in the foreground. I mean the brown has green in it, the green has brown in it. It's much more subtle than the catalogue makes it sound. They are all like that, more or less. That was their interpretation of aerial perspective, and it wasn't a bad one. You go from the red end in the foreground to the blue end in the distance, roughly speaking.
***MG: The Govaerts is actually like a series of stage flats, one behind the other. The next room shows Rubens playing around with those two formulae, doesn't it, varying them, and making them more subtle. These are the landscapes he did in his 30s and early 40s, after he had returned from Italy to Antwerp, and settled down to making his fortune from art.* The Watering Place,** *for example, is basically derived from pictures like that Govaerts, with its gnarled trunks, but it's got a misty distance on the left, and it's dominated by that great mound of rocks and roots in the middle.*
JL: I think if you look at the earlier Flemish landscapes in the first room, you can see that it was traditional to have a space in the middle, and to have the piles of rock and stuff on the side. But you can see from a number of pictures here, that Rubens liked

to have a large mass in the middle, then let the eye go away on each side of it.
 This arrangement with the chap on the horse, and the cows and the girl with the jug and so on, is the same shape as the rock. So the rock reflects the shape of the group underneath. It's an amazing design, an extraordinary pyramid of movement, shooting up, and then exploding in these tree trunks at the top. He must have been looking at pictures of volcanoes or something.
MG: It's got tremendous vitality.
JL: It really has – volcanic.
MG: It's very striking how much subsequent landscape painting – or its starting point – you can find in these.
JL: One thinks of Gainsborough, but also one thinks of van Gogh. If Frans Hals is the natural ancestor of van Gogh as far as the portraits go, one feels that Rubens has to be the natural ancestor as far as landscape is concerned. Van Gogh had that same love of rather tortured things, twisted trees and so forth, plus amazing precision with small brushes, not unlike Rubens's.
MG: And also the galvanising energy he puts into inanimate objects.
JL: Yes, although that I think he got from himself. I don't feel he got it from Rubens. It's similar certainly: van Gogh liked the pastoral life, the way Rubens did, and he also liked great open spaces. You feel that van

Gogh really went from the writhing forms which dominate the earlier work, to the later pictures where there are more peaceful expanses. Though there are exceptions, Rubens was a bit the same. He kept up his interest in twisted trees and so on, but the landscapes get bigger and grander, and he goes in more and more for wide horizons.
MG: Leading up to the great, late Autumn Landscape with Het Steen.
JL: That's what I was thinking of, but there are several of them.
MG: I thought that the theory put forward about* The Watering Place *here and* A Shepherd with his Flock in a Woody Landscape *beside it was very convincing. Did you read it? The suggestion is that the* Shepherd *was painted first, then Rubens either did another version himself, or got someone in the studio to do one. And from that* The Watering Place *slowly evolved, and as it did so Rubens had more and more bits of wood attached to the original panel.
JL: It's quite possible. He certainly added bits of panel to the larger painting, and that was something he was clearly in the habit of doing. If you look at *Peace and War* upstairs, he'd obviously started with the rectangle in the centre, which actually makes a wonderful picture on its own, and

Peter Paul Rubens, Landscape with a Cart Crossing a Ford: 'La Charrette Embourbée', *c.1620, oil on canvas (transferred from panel), 86 x 126.5 cm.*
The State Hermitage Museum, St Petersburg

then added bits – though this in fact is canvas sewn together. Of course, one of the things you get is that marvellous woman on the left, turning. She wouldn't have been there if he'd stuck to the original size, nor would the lovely figure flying at the top. He must have been more modest in his intentions than he found he was in his execution. The idea grew on him and he needed more space. I can easily go along with the idea that *The Watering Place* was developed from the *Shepherd with his Flock*.

MG: It's almost unfolded like a baroque architectural design, say for a church façade, throwing out arches and columns.

JL: You can see where the shepherd once was in *The Watering Place*. He's started to come through again. Obviously Rubens didn't need him once he had these other figures; he didn't want the eye being pulled over to the left.

MG: Oh yes, the ghost of a shepherd. Shall we look at the Landscape with a Cart Crossing a Ford, over there? That's one of the pictures Catherine the Great bought from Walpole, so it's in the Hermitage now.

JL: That's a lovely picture, and absolutely unspoilt. No restorer has got his hands on this. It's just about the masterpiece of the exhibition. I don't mind that you can see with the naked eye where he's added strips on. It's just sheer joy. You go from one

beautiful area to another without any interruption, without any jumping of tones because someone's been wiping away too much, or anything like that.

This again has a rock in the middle, and diverging views. It's almost as if he wanted you to have a divergent squint, to be looking in both directions at once. Titian sometimes did that: he split the focus up into two directions so that you don't ever rest or settle. Your eye is kept on the move the whole time. This cart, with the most lovely curving of its rail, sends you in both directions. It's a brilliant idea.

MG: Yes, the design's got a good deal in common with The Watering Place.

JL: Judging by this room, Rubens liked to have a high horizon on the right and a low one on the left. It's the same in virtually every picture. By the way, have you noticed that the moon has a little face, like a picture in a children's book? Rather sweet.

MG: Oh yes, the Man in the Moon. I agree that this is in marvellous condition; it's got that bloom, like a perfect fruit, that an untouched picture has.

JL: All their desire for gaudiness and gloss has gone into the frame, thank God, and not into the picture. It's been wonderfully looked after.

MG: Do you think other pictures in the exhibition have suffered from over-cleaning, which has disturbed the relationship of the tones?

JL: Yes, certainly. That one on our left for example, *Pond with Cows and Milkmaids,* is a case where much of the connection with Rubens has been severed. Which is a pity, because you can see that it would have been a marvellous design and a beautiful picture. Getting up close, you can see a lot of Rubens in it, but somehow it's difficult not to believe other people have been having a go at it.

MG: Because the transitions between tones are so sharp?

JL: It jumps about; it's difficult to know where things are, and that's most uncharacteristic of Rubens. Normally you get an entirely solid feeling of where everything is.

MG: These drawings in the next room are stunning.

JL: They really are, aren't they?

MG: The drawing of a Tree-trunk and Brambles over there puts me in mind of Ruskin.

JL: I see what you mean, but Rubens's drawings are enormously more virile than anything I've seen by Ruskin. They've got that robust power that van Gogh has. I don't find Ruskin robust, and there's something mean about his shapes. This one, which is not a very promising subject in itself – it's just a tangle – is actually made into something powerful and magnificent.

And this *Study of a Tree* is beautiful, too. You can see that the work with chalk has been done in a great hurry, then he's taken it home and worked on it. I think he's

Peter Paul Rubens, An Autumn Landscape with a View of Het Steen in the Early Morning, *probably 1636, oil on oak, 131.2 x 229.2 cm.*
The National Gallery, London

gone over it with ink to make it more substantial. Not only was the chalk obviously put on fast, but even the pen was done pretty quickly too, and he hasn't overdone it at all. Just enough to make it look solid. You get the feeling it was done by someone who didn't have much spare time.

MG: I'm sure he didn't. But it gives you an amazing feeling of the light, and the different textures of the foliage.

JL: *Landscape After a Storm* over there is an extremely beautiful painting, I think.

MG: It's thinly painted.

JL: I think actually that Rubens often painted more thinly than survives today. People obviously felt his pictures needed filling out, and I've read that through the centuries all sorts of people have had a go. I wouldn't be surprised if an awful lot of his paintings started out like that. Maybe some of the ones we've been looking at in the other rooms.

MG: You don't think it's unfinished?

JL: I wouldn't really have thought so. If you think about some of his sketches for compositions there's really no more paint on them than that, and sometimes there's less. I suppose that they are unfinished by some standards, and maybe some patrons wouldn't have wanted anything quite so broad and lightly touched in as that. But I don't think Rubens would have felt it necessary from his own point of view to do much more. After all it's very full: you can see everything you want, everything's in its place.

MG: Let's go through into the big central gallery. What do you think of this full-scale colour photograph of the Landscape with a Rainbow from the Wallace Collection that's been framed

and hung opposite Het Steen?

JL: It's a monstrosity. It's the biggest mistake of the exhibition in my opinion. It really spoils the room, spoils the exhibition to some extent.

MG: It's an interesting demonstration though, don't you think, of how unlike an oil painting a colour reproduction actually looks?

JL: Yes. In fact, having seen this, I went round to the Wallace Collection to have another look at the original. And it is much better than this suggests, although it's been badly overcleaned. But this is even more flayed-looking than the real painting.

MG: Do you think a black and white photograph would have been better?

JL: Yes, and a smaller black and white photograph at that. I suppose this is full scale.

MG: The theory is that it must have hung opposite Het Steen, since they would not make topographical sense side by side.

JL: Both this painting and *Het Steen* have been cleaned, and neither looks as good as it used to. All the same, they're both pictures that one can still enjoy a lot of beauty in, especially *Het Steen*. If they think that they can include a photograph that looks like this in the exhibition, you begin to suspect there's an unconscious ideal, in the museum world, of making old paintings look like colour reproductions. They obviously feel that this is how paintings ought to look, just as they make you see them by electric light. All these paintings are about outdoor light: Rubens painted them by daylight, and they should be seen by daylight. This gallery is a mistake for this show – or indeed any show

of painting.

MG: What do you think of that large painting called Summer that belongs to the Queen?

JL: I think that one looks a mess – completely bitty. If you think how beautiful the wheelbarrow of vegetables in *The Farm at Laeken* was, and compare it with that cart in *Summer*....

MG: It's not so exciting, is it? But this one's considered to have large passages by members of the studio, especially in the centre. Though the added sections on the left, right and bottom are supposed to be by Rubens.

JL: All the same, the old woman on the right is beautifully painted; but she looks as if she's in mid-air. That's so uncharacteristic of Rubens. Someone's interfered with the ground she should be standing on. This is a frustrating picture. There are lovely passages in between, like this bit of pink land, but all the figures, houses and animals are very unworthy.

MG: It's also got a very glossy varnish on it.

JL: I'm less bothered by varnish in Rubens's case than I am in many cases. I mean, the last exhibition I saw here was the Degas exhibition, which was ruined by the fact of the pictures being varnished – the *Portrait of Hélène Rouart*, for example. Degas obviously meant them to be matt, and varnishing them screws up his tones completely. But I feel that Rubens probably intended his pictures to have some shine on them. He was obviously someone who painted wet into wet, and liked there to be a skin – the complete opposite of Degas.

MG: Let's turn and look at the Land-

Peter Paul Rubens, Study of a Tree, *c.1615, pen and wash on paper, 60 x 50.1 cm.*
Départment des Arts Graphiques, Musée du Louvre, Paris

scape with Het Steen?

JL: That's always a pleasure.

MG: *Despite cleaning, this is still a staggering painting.*

JL: But there was a time when it had even more space in it, and you were more aware of the sun on the right, which I'm sure used to look different. Now you hardly notice it; when you look at it from a distance you can't really see it at all. The whole thing was more mysterious and it was a better unity, but it's still very beautiful. I just remember the light moving across it in a more mysterious way.

MG: *It captures that feeling we were talking about earlier of it being absolutely marvellous to be alive in the early morning, but even more strongly.*

JL: Yes, but all Rubens's pictures are about that, aren't they? There's a joy in them that is quite consistent all through his work. He never depicts misery. Or even poverty – he's unlike van Gogh in that respect. He always goes for opulence, and for affluence. I can't think of anything depressing in Rubens. And it's not just the subject matter. His handling is always joyous, full of energy. He touches the paint with life.

MG: *It has the feeling of an early*

Summer day, with soft sunlight.

JL: Looking at it you feel everything's great, not only is it a wonderful day, but life is rich.

MG: *There's something tremendously moving about this light casting long shadows across rolling grassland, with clumps of trees. That's Rubens and his wife over there on the left, isn't it? Taking an early morning stroll through his estate. Of course, by this stage he'd made enough of a pile from painting to buy this country house and become lord of the manor. He was actually styled the Lord of Steen.*

JL: Early morning and evening can look very similar, but they don't feel the same; and this picture feels like morning. Dawn, and the world waking up was obviously a time that Rubens really loved. I expect he got up early and went out to enjoy himself a bit before the cares of the day set in.

MG: *The composition of this has got the dual focus we were talking about earlier, but it hasn't got the big mound in the middle.*

JL: The trees have moved over to one side.

MG: *You've got the sun on the extreme right and the building on the extreme*

left. *I take it that's one reason why you get this tremendous feeling of expansiveness.*

JL: And of liveliness. If you can carry it off, a picture with a spread of focal areas is much more exciting than a picture with only one. Somehow, it keeps your eye flickering everywhere.

If you look at *Landscape in Flanders,* there's an interesting technical point to be made that has implications for *Het Steen.* The wood on the horizon is much too dark, and that is something I think that's happened to the paint with age. In the catalogue there's a reproduction of an engraving which was done when the picture was quite fresh, and the trees nearer to you are much darker than the ones on the horizon. You can see the gradation of tone, and how they disappear into the distance.

If you apply that idea to *Het Steen,* you can imagine that the trees bang in the middle, at the top, might once have been much lighter. If they were, the eye would travel much more happily away into the distance. You can't exactly blame the restorers for that. You have to blame Rubens's materials. In Antwerp there's a trunk which contains Rubens's colours, and you can see that the white lead, ultramarine, madders and the earth colours have kept their strength, while all the others have just faded away. It seems that a lot of Rubens's colours were not that good, and that people have felt the need to repaint them through the centuries. And that's a pity: the painting should have been allowed to age, even to decay.

MG: *Shall we take a look at the carpentry display next door?*

JL: It isn't really interesting, is it?

MG: *Well, it's got a diagram showing that the panel* Het Steen's *painted on is an absolute mosaic of small pieces of wood, glued and dowled together.*

JL: On second thoughts, that is sort of interesting, because it doesn't look as if *Het Steen* could have grown from a smaller picture.

MG: *No, the argument is that he had the panels for pictures he did for his own satisfaction made up of odd bits and pieces of wood, perhaps because it was cheaper that way.*

JL: Well, we know he was sharp about money, don't we? He drove a very hard deal. In this case, if he didn't intend to sell the picture, perhaps he didn't want to invest much money in it. That sort of thing does affect one's attitude. I use better materials on a commission than I do normally. But when you think about it, it shows a touching sort of modesty in a painter of Rubens's stature; you might have expected him to use only the best materials. Did you know, by the way, that van Gogh and Rubens both felt they had to work extra hard to make up for lack of talent!

'Making & Meaning: Rubens's Landscapes', until 19 January 1997, the 1996 Esso Exhibition at the National Gallery, London. Catalogue 10.95.

The Nest, 1996, Acrylic on canvas, 76" x 50"

GALERIE DE BELLEFEUILLE
1367 GREENE AVENUE, WESTMOUNT, QUEBEC, CANADA H3Z 2A8
TELEPHONE: (514) 933-4406 FAX: (514) 933-6553

Kiefer in French?

Michael Hofmann *appraises new work by* **Anselm Kiefer***, observing the influence of the German artist's recent migration to France.*

Exhibition openings in December and press dates in November meant that I wasn't able to look at Anselm Kiefer's new paintings in Dering Street or on the Peckham Road, but instead saw a smaller and quite possibly different show just ending at the Galerie Yvon Lambert in Paris. Five enormous canvases, two workbooks and two rubbery photo-books in a room and a half. The physicality of the work, its enormous scale and the pressure of its details force me to write about what I've seen, rather than conjecture from transparencies.

But then contingency is the mother of coincidence: in Paris, I learned that Kiefer had left Germany and taken up residence in France. He has exchanged his brickyard at Buchen in the Oderwald, south of Frankfurt, for a former silkworks near Barjac in the Gard. As to when this happened, the catalogue is discreetly silent; and I suppose Kiefer must have 50 hermeneuts for one biographer. Still, we are to think of him, astoundingly, as remaking himself – perhaps – as a French artist, now scrawling French words on his paintings, addressing themes from French history, using French materials in his compositions. His new works, four pictures from 1996, one from 1995, include two – *Les Reines de France*, if you please, and *Maginot* – on explicitly French themes; even the cosmic paintings, like *Cette obscure clarté qui tombe des étoiles* (I don't know whose the

line is, if indeed it is anyone's), seem more French- than German-cosmic, more Verlaine than Novalis. Certainly, the work seemed as though made to be looked at where I happened to be looking at it: it seemed rooted and local. The colours of the pictures, predominantly white and off-white, were everywhere in evidence outside: in the winter Paris sky, the stone hotels, the peeling façades and shutters of the Marais, the coarse sand of the boules pits. You can look at them and be reminded of – I don't know – Dufy. Or Braque. Or Tati.

The last time Kiefer exhibited at the Galerie Lambert five years ago, his works were fashioned from lead, glass, brick and fire. A French critic, the late Jean-Noel Vuarnet – in the French manner more a rhapsode than a critic – anatomised his greys:

> iron-grey, grey-white, silver-grey, silver-white, the greys of clouds and sauerkraut ... an elemental, so to speak, *technological* colour ... evocative of film, of the cathode ray tube and of radar and VDU screens, of aeroplanes and rocketry.

Now, though, there is this mild and subtle and variegated off-white, not modern, not cutting-edge, not fearsome. One thinks, not of technology but of nature, of clays and shales. Or if of something man-made, then of buildings, and then not new buildings but things time has got its teeth into – a dirt road, crumbling plaster, cement dust on a

workman's overalls. The French catalogue speaks of the 'violence' in Kiefer, but I feel this is no longer true. There is a kind of serenity or acquiescence in the new work. His endlessly resourceful and undesigning processes mimic time in the way they bring things to beauty or beauty to things. Something similar, I think, has happened to Kiefer's use of history and mythology: it seems less impersonal, less minatory, less imposing. France, historically equated with such values as lightness, grace and pleasure, offers these qualities to Kiefer, their unlikeliest recipient. On top of everything else, his recent work seems to be autobiographical.

The most explicit of the paintings – the one on its own in the half-room – is *Maginot*. The name of the French system of fortifications, built following the 1871 defeat by Prussia and simply bypassed in 1914 by the Schlieffen Plan, it is written across the whole width of a large canvas in Kiefer's spindly capitals. The whitish canvas, treated, distressed, slathered and gouged, built up and peeled off, aged and watchable, is pierced by scores of asparagus stems, which come out of the painting at the viewer. The initial effect is bewildering, a sense of feeble bristling – especially out of the letters of the word 'Maginot' – a suffusing of a dry yellow colour over the white, perhaps some illegible alternative script. Then, when one recognises the withered, straw-coloured, agonised, practically

Anselm Kiefer,
Cette obscure clarté
qui tombe des étoiles, *1996,*
emulsion, acrylic, shellac
and sunflower seeds,
520 x 560 cm

Above title:
Anselm Kiefer,
Les Reines de France, *1996,*
mixed media on canvas,
280 x 500 cm

All photos courtesy
Anthony d'Offay Gallery,
London

crucified forms as asparagus, the effect is terribly moving. This is asparagus-abuse: these twisted, inedible, unsucculent, unphallic forms have become the antithesis of asparagus, a kind of anti-asparagus! You stand in front of *Maginot*, and grapple with what you're given. The thing itself – green, epicurean, spear-shaped, luxurious, slick – but then countermanded, as it were, by its withered condition, by the individuality and anguish – the personality – of each dead stem, not least by its being levelled pathetically against you, and then it sets up a sort of inconsolable vibration with the word 'Maginot'. Is 'Maginot', with its historical fate – an irrelevance, first and foremost, a sternly practical measure turned uselessly quixotic, like the erecting of a row of windmills – to be equated with those stalks; or did they pierce it; are we to understand something of the Germans' motivation for trying to conquer France (they wanted to eat it: Brecht, from East Berlin, saw in a French cheese platter with 70 cheeses the acme or definition of civilisation; the German proverb for the good life is '*wie Gott in Frankreich*', like God in France)? Or do we see in the painting, with the one-dimensional historical resonance of its title, and the one-dimensional asparagus sticking out of it, twisting in space, some oblique reference to the painter's own move to France? A curving arrow like the German infantry in World War I, like the asparagus? What

does it do when a German painter paints 'Maginot'? What if instead he'd called it 'Spargel'? Or '*ceci n'est pas une asperge*'? I suppose the painting is a voicing of historical guilt. Like his teacher Beuys, Kiefer uses inanimate things to register trauma. His tragicomic asparagus is a notable addition to his expressive repertoire.

Les Reines de France is in a far more straightforward relation to its also less fraught title. It too can be read as an announcement of or a commentary on Kiefer's change of address and allegiance, and this time in a frankly romantic way. At the foot of the painting a man lies on his back, in white trousers, stripped to the waist. He looks a little like Lenin, a little like Gary Numan, but is perhaps Kiefer himself – I have no idea what he looks like, and of course the catalogue doesn't offer anything so vulgar as a photograph of the artist. He is resting or dead or dreaming or tanning. The ambiguity is not troubling, a reliable tranquillity goes out from the painting. Above him, in a cloud of history, is the entire distaff side of the French monarchy. Along the top of the painting, which is made up of nineteen hinted concave vertical panels, goes the march of time: '*4ième, 5ième siècle, 6ième*' through to '*21ième, 22ième*', for which there is predictably as yet no demand. In between the supine male figure and the chronometric scale are the names of the queens, scribbled

on businesslike buff cards and stapled to the painting, one hundred and twelve of them in all, from Clotilde and Basile to Marie-Amélie de Bourbon-Sicile, in Kiefer's slapdash hand. The fantastic schoolboyish cataloguing zeal of the thing and its inescapable scruffiness are better conveyed by the work-book version: here the names are more legible for a start, the cards are numbered, the dates of the queens are included and even, in some cases, the names of their kings. In addition, the work-book has vertical ledger-like columns for each decade, and this shows you, as again the huge painting doesn't, the eccentric accuracy of the enterprise: each little card trimmed to the length of the queen's life, stuck down in precisely the correct position, and – a crowning weirdness – where there is doubt about the date of birth or death, the left or right edge of the card is trimmed in a pennant-like zigzag. Seen from a distance, the picture reminds me of the naming of mountain peaks in a panorama, but the strongest impression is that of schoolboy ardour and out-of-hours pedantry. It reminds me of our real and fictional teamsheets, of the defunct cricket game 'Howzat', of our perfectionist but ultimately unimpressive semi-practical 'projects', and, most specifically, of a piece of wrinkly pseudo-parchment I was bought in America at eight or nine, with the names and dates and (*sic!*) photographs of all the presidents on it, and also, before long, in biro

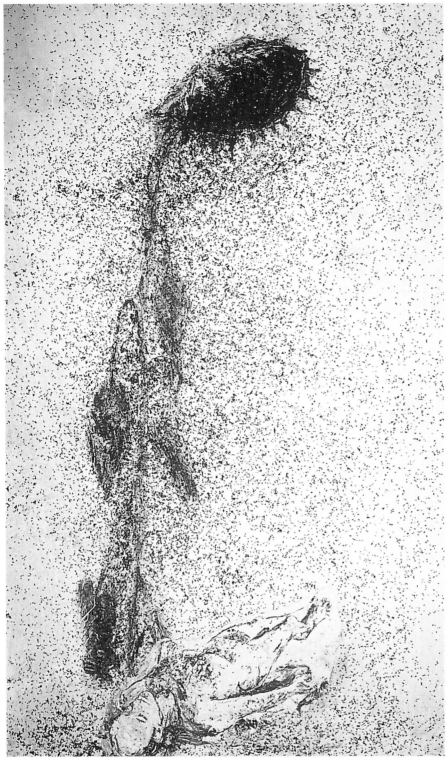

Anselm Kiefer, Sol Invictus, *1995, mixed media on canvas, 476 x 280 cm*

that's above – one would read the picture as expressive of heart, vulnerability and affect. The caking, cracking ochre mortar and the bent, almost corrugated panels – as though taken from old 2CVs – make this an almost overly French picture.

However, the most arresting piece in the exhibition, for me, is *Sol Invictus*, 'Undefeated Sun', another huge and lofty painting, with the same recumbent man, this time lying head to the fore, feet diminished by perspective, naked this time, and under a gigantic and – thrillingly – real sunflower. The man is irredeemably banal – another painting, in the catalogue though not in the show, which has the sunflower sprouting in lieu of a penis, a thoroughly ill-judged idea in my view, does nothing to change this – but the sunflower is absolutely splendid. This one reminded me of Blake – not his poem *Ah Sun-Flower*, but the final image of *A Poison Tree*: 'my foe outstretched beneath the tree'. One of the photo-books has a sequence of photographs of sunflowers, first a whole field of them, then moving closer and closer to their 'heart of darkness' till it ends with cosmic spatter, debris, very tiny or very distant matter: a rather hackneyed idea, I have to say, though it looks better in the two remaining paintings, *Cette obscure clarté* and *Homme sous une pyramide*. But the sunflower itself is wonderfully potent: left to stand in square fields until September or October when everything else has long been harvested, its yellow and green a memory, a ragged spine supporting a stricken face, massed, statuesque, anthropomorphic, a form and a face, a triffid. There seems to me something religious about it, in the way it is basically left to die in order to be reborn in its seeds, in the shape of it, a bell on a tower or again perhaps a crucifix, in its extended suffering the opposite of the fig in Rilke's Sixth Elegy, which fruits before it leafs. (As indeed I think there is something religious about the scale and the height of Kiefer's paintings, of which you can only see a half or even a third at all closely: the workings and details and textures of the top part you have to take on trust.) Here, Kiefer has nailed or smashed or glued an actual sunflower to his painting, subtly working it in with paint and varnish and other materials. Above all, with a wonderful seething, swirling, brewing mass of sunflower seeds – you can practically hear them buzzing on the painting. They are sinisterly beautiful, death-in-life or life-in-death, disposed with wonderfully natural randomness singly or in clusters, little flying wedges, both singular and 'incorrigibly plural' (Louis Macneice), their shiny insect black softening to brown close to, and bringing out surprising pink and blue tints in the underlying thin and rather glossy white of this painting, falling with delicious ambiguity, like bomblets, like hard rain, like life from the air, on the ambiguous man lying in a field in fair France.

Anselm Kiefer, until 9 February 1997, South London Gallery; until 15 February 1997, Anthony d'Offay Gallery, London.

and in my awful Kieferish hand-writing, my computation of their time in office. This, then, is *Les Reines de France*: a declaration of love to France – the book has a dried lily on its frontispiece and another at the end; Marie-Antoinette gets a yellow rose – and to French history and French womanhood. The names – and Kiefer has always found his prime inspiration in words and names; 'a name', he says, 'contains in itself a presumption, a feeling that conceals and reveals something' – are names to conjure with: Maria Stuart, Catherine de Medici, Anne d'Autriche, and so on and so forth. From the

early names in particular, a historical pity or piety flows: Wisiogarde, Thédechilde, Suavegothe, Radegonde, Brunehaut, Meroflède – to our ears archaic, sexless, barbarous, beautiful names in which the French and the German-Gothic are still entwined (Charlemagne, after all, was also Karl der Grosse, and lies buried in Aachen or Aix). Febrile pencil lines connect the figure on the floor to the names in space, and three clots of an indefinable plant, trailing roots like a hairpiece, are a representation of feeling or longing. Even without the somewhat banal, balding male figure – the recipient of all

FIONA RAE GARY HUME

THE SAATCHI GALLERY

Bold with Beauty

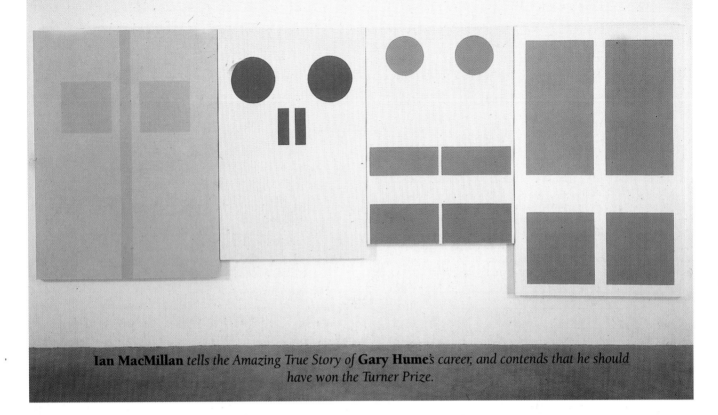

Ian MacMillan *tells the Amazing True Story of* **Gary Hume**'s *career, and contends that he should have won the Turner Prize.*

Everything you are about to read is true, though at times it may seem far fetched and ludicrous and a bit like Kirk Douglas overacting as van Gogh in *Lust For Life*. It is a tale of art-world success, of artistic temperament and failure, of Dulux paint and career crisis and, ultimately, of triumph. Along the way there will be mistakes, bath tubs, has-been radio DJs, hospital doors, bad group shows and a host of stuff that would never in a million years suggest it is in fact also the story of the most inspiring and accomplished painter to emerge from what we are being encouraged to call Young British Art. And we join it at a funeral.

Joshua Compston was a celebrated and maverick young art-world figure who ran a gallery with the fairly ludicrous name Factual Nonsense and an annual summer art party and picnic with the rather better name The Fete Worse Than Death, a title which earlier this year proved to be shockingly prescient when, on his way home from a Serpentine Gallery private view, Compston collapsed and died. Ever leading the high life, drink and drugs were naturally invoked in the splash of broadsheet articles and tributes which followed. Much was made of Compston's erratic personality and his moving and shaking within the British art scene, his desire to shock and generally make his mark whatever that involved. One of his most bizarre but less reported ideas was a series of artists' coffins, where for a fee one could commission a favourite painter or sculptor to design and make a

customised box in which to see off one's life, formaldehyde not necessarily included. By ironic twist, Compston himself had already had a painter friend knock up a prototype, and was laid to rest encased within it. It is the stuff of legend. The coffin was decorated with proto-Matissean swirls and curlicues by the 33-year-old Gary Hume, and he too, in a way, is the stuff of legend. This is his story.

It begins, as do most contemporary British art stories, at the equally legendary 1988 'Freeze' exhibition, the Damien Hirst-curated graduate-fest that launched a score of careers in a manner unheard of since David Hockney discovered peroxide and boys three decades earlier. 'Freeze' waved goodbye to all that ponderous School of Glasgow nonsense which had been cluttering up galleries across the country for too long, and a swift farewell to its accompanying New Imagist tableaux both from here and from its native Germany. It replaced it with a sleek and cool, formal but not formalist art that had its heart in the conceptual and minimal 1960s and its potential market and image in New York's so-called Neo-Geo school of Peter Halley and Jeff Koons. 'Freeze' had wall texts and cardboard sculptures, polythene and bulldog clips, light projections and molten lead, with nary an upside-down farm worker in sight.

There were paintings too, sleekly executed works in oil and, more surprisingly, household gloss paint. Some of these were large canvases in that most drab and nothing of household paint colours,

magnolia; rectangular, reductivist pieces that looked as if Brice Marden had moved to a studio on a Manchester council estate. These were the work of Gary Hume. Closer inspection revealed that they were not quite as empty as first glances suggested. There were symmetrical patterns of circles and squares or rectangles, delineated by a skilful use of re-applied layers of the same base colour, one on top of the other, adding shape and detail to the blank imageless image. Sure, they were minimal, but not in a spiritual 1960s sort of way, perhaps more connected to the painting as object idea. It became quite quickly apparent that these were life-sized depictions of doors, the kind of swing doors you find in hospital wards and operating theatres. Beyond the pat cleverness of taking something normally found on a wall and representing it as a painting hanging on a wall, there was a significant achievement in these simple slabs of colour. Hume seemed to have taken the most empty art of all and imbued it not only with a subject matter but a lightness of touch and, most importantly, a sense of humour. Within a year he was a celebrated art figure, going on to have shows in those paragons of contemporary art culture, Cologne and New York. Always the paintings were big, expansive. Always they were doors. Doors that seemed like an exit from the painterly traditions of the 1980s, no longer heroic and gesturing with thick impastoed oils and neo-expressionist composition, but flat planes of unfashionable colour, and glossy and shiny and smart and enamelled.

There was something astonishing about this high gloss sheen, which it picked up and reflected light in a way painting hadn't done for nearly 30 years, since the textured washes of Rothko or the cerebral calm of Agnes Martin. But Gary was British and Gary did things differently, and these were defiantly modern and unassuming works that seemed to carry with them something of the British reserve. Standing in front of them was no spiritual or heroic gesture, and yet they were insistently attractive and appealing. The gloss seemed to get heavier, the layers and build-up more pronounced, until a series called 'The Dolphin Paintings' culminated in arrangements of several differently sized doors grouped together, wall-length, which positively exuded light and space and reflection and surface in sheer monochrome, and begged the question, where next? More colours: pinks and reds and creams and pale blues. Duochromes, with the door panelling picked out in contrasting colours to the base, and further wall-length arrangements of four of these panels in one long sweep of sugary hued portals. Big paintings, big collectors. Big time.

Big problem. By limiting himself to the door motif Hume had almost literally painted himself into a corner. Sure, the doors could get bigger, more colourful, less (shall we say) door-like, but they were still doors. The galleries probably liked it that way, the collectors were probably still happy with them, but clearly Gary was bored with doors, a potentially disastrous situation, like Lucian Freud becoming bored with fleshy bodies or Robert Ryman finding himself tired of the colour white. Gary Hume, for all his technical skill and careful mastery of a very difficult kind of paint to make art with, had become known as The Man Who Does The Doors. And Gary wanted out.

The art world is a very closely knit, gossipy and insecure place. To be a young and increasingly successful artist surviving within it takes some determination and a lot of playing the game and pacifying people. You do not, under any circumstances, think too hard about leaving the gallery which supported you through your early years. You do not pose for posterity in a Lord Snowdon photograph for *Vogue* magazine with a disastrous attempt at a door sculpture which you will later destroy. You do not, if it can possibly be avoided, abandon your trademark motif and style upon which you have built your reputation, and have a crisis and wonder where to go next. Next year a new fashionable art star will come along to take your place and it will be perceived that you have failed. Play safe, play the game, keep on burning.

All burnt out, Hume did all of this and more. In an act of potential folly, he took part in an influential show of 'Young British Art' at the Barbara Gladstone Gallery by showing a collaged painting of what seemed like a medical diagram of the female reproductive organs, the tubes and

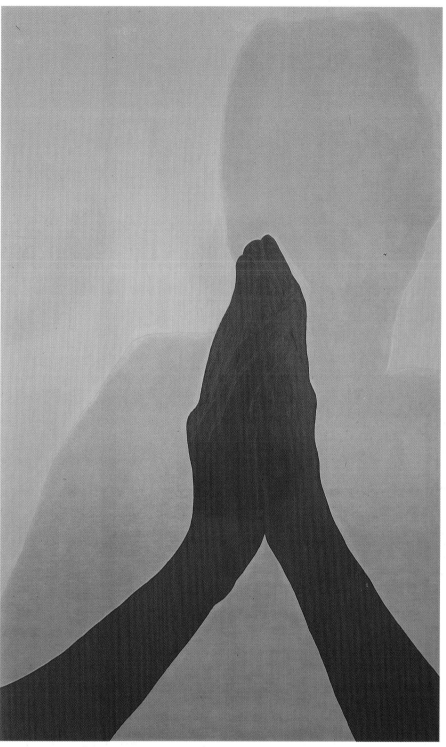

Gary Hume, Begging For It, *1994, gloss paint on panel, 200 x 150 cm*
Above title: Gary Hume, Four Doors (1), *1989–90, gloss paint on four panels, 238.7 x 594.3 cm.*
Both courtesy the Saatchi Collection

ovaries delineated like the details in the door paintings, the pubic hair made up of thousands of streams of shredded pornographic magazines. He may as well have spat on the wall and written 'fuck you' across it. It was a neat, nicely presented, orderly show introducing many 'Freeze' luminaries to the Big Apple for the first time. It was a bad painting. Then Gary disappeared for a while. There was a video of him sitting in a bath tub wearing a cardboard crown from Burger King, *Me As King Cnut*. There was the odd appearance in the odd ensemble exhibition here and there, like

a photo of himself in a plastic facial mask, and odd is the only word to describe these events. He seemed to have gone a bit mad, bereft, maybe even washed up. While stars shone brightly around him and many of the Goldsmiths' gang came to dominate the sharper end of the art world here and in Europe, Gary Hume was nowhere to be seen.

Then the renaissance began. Like Bridget Riley refining her style, colours and mood after abandoning Op once the last Mary Quant shop had shut its doors for good, Hume came back into the limelight. ▷

Gary Hume, Love, Loves Unlovable, *1994, oil on panel, 216.2 x 365.7 cm. Saatchi Collection, London*

It was a slow re-emergence but it was instantly clear that his work had moved on and grown sharper, more focused and ever more pleasing to the eye and mind. Much of the playing around that had been apparent in the video and photographs had found its way into the new paintings. Borders of bright pink and savage yellow, applied with a freshness and looseness in the same shiny enamel paint as before, framing a haloed three leaf clover. In a gesture of free association and like Tony Hancock in his famous parody of the tortured painter, Hume found the perfect throwaway reference point for this work, noticing the uncanny resemblance the image bore to the 1970s radio disc jockey Tony Blackburn. *Tony Blackburn* (1993) became one of the first of a new series of paintings, iconographic and somewhat kitsch representations of popular culture images, from pop music, fashion and the worlds of celebrities and glossy magazines, all with a slightly faded glamour and a touch of the British. A pouting fashion model with a rosette of deep purple bordering her right shoulder; the actress Patsy Kensit looking bereft and vulnerable, her eyes deeply and emptily defined by ghostly layers of carefully outlined gloss and her lips strikingly picked out by deep green lines; a series of heroically posed male models from the 1930s era of masculinity and physical beauty, creepily feminised by a background of delicate, elegant pastel flowers. With

stuff like this, who needed doors? Yet the same kinds of play characterised these pictures as in the earlier, more simplified panels, with surface and light and a use of colour that leaned towards the truly decora-

Gary Hume, Two Three Leaf Clovers, *1994, gloss paint on panel, 241.5 x 155.5 cm. Saatchi Collection*

tive and a cheapened sublime.

The 'Freeze'-ites, as I've noted earlier, seemed to want to take on the 1980s art world, to overthrow and also emulate the dramatic rise and success of the New York artists whom many of them must first have seen at Saatchi's two-part show of his collection in the later part of the decade. With his skilful manipulating of the art world, his flamboyant personality and far-out shock tactics, many saw Hirst as the natural heir to the throne of Bad Boy of Art which Jeff Koons was reluctantly vacating. Vacant to an almost painful degree, Koons talked heartily of embracing banality and using the throwaway to create high art. It was kitsch with a twist, it was cheery with theory. But the comparison always seemed too easy, too much like out with the old and in with the new. If anyone had really learned from Koons it must surely have been Hume, who adopted much of the shallow trash iconography and turned it around by creating luscious, sensitive, abstract yet at the same time figurative paintings using precisely those images of pretty flowers, bunny rabbits, sexy models and childhood toys. Take, for example, Hume's gorgeous painting, *The Polar Bear* (1994), where starkly contrasting green on pink gives us a comforting, humorous and empathetic icon with staring, pleading glossy pools of black for eyes. Please love me, it is saying, and you cannot help but fall for its spell. Hanging among the other delights at Hume's solo show at London's ICA Gallery last autumn it threw a warm glow over the cool, removed world of sharp '90s art. A riotous display of brash colour, pop imagery and sheer exuberance, it marked an insistent return of Gary Hume to the forefront of British painting, with sharp and sexy new dealer, Jay Jopling, in tow. The crisis had more than been averted. Even the spinny, propeller-like works hanging from the ceiling seemed somehow just right. And along with the more literal, imagist pieces there was still room for a cross-breed between the new and the old, the double pools of colour floating on a smooth background that transformed the door paintings into *Two Eggs*, drifting somewhere between Ellsworth Kelley, Peter Halley and the local paint shop.

Yet despite all the cultural reference points and the knowingness of the instantly attractive and recognisable subject matter, the artist claims that there is nothing to the paintings but surface, pure and simple, a line that has been trotted out by artists from Andy Warhol to now. In this case it seems somewhat disingenuous, a pointed tactic from a man who would rather get on with his painting than talk about or dissect it. We are living through a time when the vast majority of current work with paint in this country seems to be totally obsessed with surface, from the stain and splash of Callum Innes to the layer, drag and stroke of people like Jason Martin and Zebedee Jones. By contrast, Hume's works, though master-strokes of surface layering of paint into recognisable forms (note how constant re-applying of white gloss in pools and swirls transforms the monochromatic square that is *Dove* into the bird of its title) have something else. Life, joy perhaps, certainly an expressiveness and a freedom sorely lacking among many of his contemporaries. It's as if, having decided to follow his path, abandon the restrictions of the door format and experiment and grow up in public, he now feels loose and confident enough to take anything from sixteenth-century portraiture to toy animals and make it triumphantly and defiantly his own.

And now Gary is this year's token painter among the Turner Prize nominees. His room at the Turner exhibition at the Tate glows and radiates in a warm splash of colour and form. Not all of his best work is represented, though the free movement and thinning, defined strokes of the painting *Dancer* more than suggest the precision and movement of the feet it depicts, and the brazen simplicity of the tomato-red and chocolate-brown blobs on blue that makes up *Snowman* should have clinched the prize on its own simple merit. Watching the public interact with the work is like seeing children confronted with a new and brilliant surprise for the first time; its beauty registers on their faces, be it the two old ladies in pearls straight out of the Turners in the Clore Gallery or the earnest art students making notes in little black Daler notebooks. We'll pass on decorative and sublime, words destined for evermore to be

Gary Hume, Whistler, *1996, enamel paint on aluminium panel, 201 x 160.5 cm.*
Courtesy Matthew Marks, New York. © the artist

pejorative and unwelcome in contemporary discussion about painting, but beauty we cannot overlook. Hume himself in the catalogue to last year's British Art Show quotes it as the term he most uses to describe art he likes, so I'm saying it here and now. Gary Hume's work is beautiful. Extremely beautiful. It will endure and continue to grow, and will come to represent a very significant moment for British art where truly original and affecting work began to take centre stage internationally.

He deserved to win the Turner Prize, though painting has never been a form which makes a strong showing in this particular charade. Another of the short-listed artists is yet a further 'Freeze' alumnus, Simon Patterson, whose work, though original and interesting, has never quite escaped from its word-play formula into a different level in the way Hume's has. Patterson's newest piece in the Tate show is a wall drawing depicting various states of mental bliss such as Nirvana and Xanadu as spots on a map of the solar system. It seems to suggest they are even more far-

reaching and unattainable than we think, orbiting around us but never to be visited. I don't know where Joshua Compston's spirit is today, his body adorned by, and at peace in, its Gary Hume case, but for the rest of us there is the possibility of achieving some tiny shred of the blissed-out happiness hinted at in Patterson's piece. Go back through the Tate, past the dreary photos and the fuzzy video screens, and there it is. Colour, form, laughter, innocence, attraction, beauty. Gary Hume's room. They should keep it like that, like the Rothko Room. Every now and again in our lives we all find we need something like it.

'Gary Hume and Fiona Rae', 16 January–6 April, 1997, Saatchi Gallery London. Full House: 'Young British Art', until 31 March 1997, Kunstmuseum, Wolfsburg, Germany; Gary Hume, late April–June 1997, Matthew Marks Gallery, Chelsea, New York; 'Treasure Island', 8 February–4 May 1997, Modern Art Centre: Calouste Gulbenkian Foundation, Lisbon, Portugal.
Turner Prize shortlisted artists' works, until 12 January 1997, Tate Gallery, London.
(The winner, Douglas Gordon, was announced on 28 November).

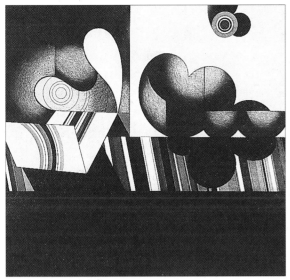

Re-grouping

Merlin James *curates a hypothetical show of intriguing young painters.*

A few times I've been asked what kind of group exhibition of contemporary artists I would curate, given the ideal venue and resources. Partly, I suppose, the question is a rhetorical way of inquiring which current artists I think are good or feel an affinity with, or what interesting directions I discern in present art (specifically in painting and sculpture, since those are the media that really interest me).

To date, my reply has sought to disguise, or make a virtue of, the fact that I have had basically no hot tips, felt no allegiances, seen no particular new trends emerging. The only viable show, I have proposed, would be one built on the premise that all the participants essentially disliked, or disagreed with, or 'had problems with' each other's work. The only believable exhibition, in other words, would be a kind of anti-group show, or anti-theme show. I envisage that its catalogue would have a page-per-artist format (reproduction, c.v., etc.), opposite which would be a series of short statements from each of the other exhibitors, stating exactly what it was they *disapproved* of in that artist's work. Even if there were aspects they liked, the rule would be that they must focus on what they saw as the faults.

I know, it sounds terribly perverse and divisive. Certainly, those to whom I've suggested it (whether or not they may have had any serious thought of commissioning me) have quietly dropped the subject. But the real point – as the catalogue introduction would have to emphasise – wouldn't be mischievous contentiousness. It would be partly, and importantly, an exercise in generating absolutely objective and disinterested criticism which has to be, above all, nothing personal. (And for once the inclusion of the curator's *own* works wouldn't be a self indulgence, it would be a moral obligation.) Just as importantly, the exhibition would be an acknowledgement, almost a celebration, of the fragmentation and confusion within painting and sculpture now. It would be a liberation from all those unconvincing exhibitions that attempt to project some coherence, discern some *Zeitgeist*, detect some significant movement in the contemporary scene. I say *almost* a celebration, because I do not mean a worthy approval of some 'healthy diversity' or 'rich range'. I mean a facing up to actual, irreconcilable divisions and differences within the practice of painting and sculpture. This show would be saying that – yes – some,

maybe all, of the artists here will be absolutely right about each other's wrongness. Imagine the relief: an exhibition of painting and sculpture that isn't, for once, trying to convince you that everything in it is necessarily any good. Rather, it would be saying that the dividedness and intolerance of these artists, however painful, should be valued. It should be valued, for example, for its contrast to the more freely speculative, liberal, *laissez-faire* attitudes that surround other, neo-avant-garde media. It would be proof that painters and sculptors still relate intimately to the history of their activity (for all its heaviness) in ways that oblige them to create imperative, and imperatively *precise,* diagnoses of its present condition and prescriptions for its future direction.

Recently, I thought a similar concept for an exhibition had occurred to someone else, when I received a card for 'Bad Blood' at the Glasgow Print Studio Gallery last May. The title suggested a real embracing of artistic enmities. And indeed the exhibition mixed, without attempting to match, painters of the New Image Glasgow generation (Ken Currie, Adrian Wiszniewski) with a range of other tendencies – a photographic body rendition by Jenny Saville, a near-abstraction by Bruce McLean, a meticulous, contemplative nude by Alison Watt, a gestural *grisaille* of a radio dish by Richard Walker, and so forth. In the event, the show still came over as more of a moderate miscellany than a confrontation of hot hostilities. But it was there that I saw for the first time (aside from in reproduction) the work of the Glasgow-based painter Carol Rhodes. I had missed previous show-

ings of her paintings, at the Fruitmarket in Edinburgh, or in the 'Persistence of Painting' exhibition at Glasgow's CCA gallery in 1995. Her three pictures at GPS (and more were soon to be shown at the Edinburgh City Art Centre's 'Heartlands' exhibition of twentieth-century Scottish landscape) confirmed my suspicion that this was exceptional and fascinating work.

Carol Rhodes paints smallish, oil-on-panel landscapes. She tends to depict environments such as car parks, edges of golf courses, bits of scrub land, service roads and loading bays, forecourts, canals, grassy swards and knolls. There is often a bland nondescriptness about the kinds of views or sites described. Significantly, they are often areas which have been artificially 'land-scaped', or in which such environmental control breaks down or blends into the natural, or at least the untended. The depiction of such places is made resonant partly because their synthetic nature is somehow parallel to that of the paintings which image them. We are continually aware of how, before our eyes as it were, the representation is being 'effected' (and it is this aspect of Rhodes's work that so appropriately lends strength to the current exhibition 'Remaking Reality' at Kettle's Yard, Cambridge). Although – or somehow *because* – there is no obvious 'point' to what is being shown, and certainly no narrative being implied, yet there is a marked fictionality here. These locations, these vicinities, do not read as 'real' places that must exist somewhere in the world, perhaps with some specific significance for the artist that has led her to make 'faithful' records of them. 'Imaginary' would also be the wrong word for them, since that too would suggest they had an authentic pre-existence somewhere (in the artist's head) independent of their extrapolation in the paintings. They read instead as invented, purely painted sites. It is almost as if, should there exist equivalent actual places out there (out here) in the real world, they would owe their existence to having been fictioned in these paintings, rather than vice versa.

What elevates all of this above something that might be experienced in the work purely conceptually, is the precise and nuanced nature of the pictures' execution. They are painted with superbly unobvious finesse. There is usually a single paint layer, with quite a lot of wiping back to a hard white ground. The technique is a delicate wet-into-wet, as if the execution were fairly quick, though this is countered by

Merlin James, Untitled, *1996, acrylic on canvas, 41.6 x 41.6 cm*

evident minuteness of detail (and in fact the artist may sand down and rework whole areas over long periods). There is a subtle use of relative mattness and gloss over the surface, and of the way different directional bristle-tracks in paint catch the light. Paint will be applied with a swish fluency in one area, with a fussy agitation somewhere else, scratched into with a sharp point on yet another feature, dabbed off with a finger or rag somewhere else again. But all this operates at a very miniscule level, with each effect being coerced into describing specific (or deliberately unspecific) planes, surfaces, architectural structures, or the natural organic forms of foliage or cloud.

Precision in Rhodes coexists with a certain softness or intuitiveness of description. There is a very particular looseness of perspective, with the converging lines of a multiple vanishing point system continually being eased toward something more like the continuous, parallel perspective of oriental scroll painting. Occasionally there are even curious reversals of perspective. Frequently the viewpoint is elevated, as in *Airport Hotel and Airport*, 1996, (where the aerial view has obvious relevance to the subject). The high horizon level often increases a feeling of miniaturisation, with associations of architectural models and isometric projections, elaborate train-set or toy-town landscapes. Roads and paths are laid out like circuit-boards.

Colour in the work is again highly synthetic, generally pale and faintly confectionery. The bleached-out quality in turn governs the strange light in which we see the features of this world. It is not a natural light, at the same time it is not sinister or uncanny. Things are not so much lit externally (though cast shadows are important), they have their own cold luminosity. It is important to notice meanwhile that it is not exactly the same light that occurs in each picture. The painter is always, I think, exploring and extending the range of variables that constitute 'a Rhodes'. So the same applies to space, technique, colour, motif – they are all slightly shifting from one work to the next.

These paintings also have what is to me a fascinating relation to art history. Rhodes cites influences from, in particular, early Italian painters like Sassetta and Signorelli. At the same time her work has affinities with certain Dutch paintings – Hobbema's *Avenue at Middelharnis* or the flat landscapes of Philips Koninck – in which the land becomes a kind of socio-topographical diagram spelling out the structure of human interaction with nature. Her pictures also, consciously or unconsciously, relate in unexpected ways to a range of other artists. She shares concerns with William Nicholson's important and still underrated landscapes, and she identifies the interesting moments in artists such as Michael Andrews (his urban architecture paintings, piers, ballooning views) and Wayne Thibaud (the '60s cake-counter period, *not* the kitsch boulevards).

In the end, or rather throughout, there

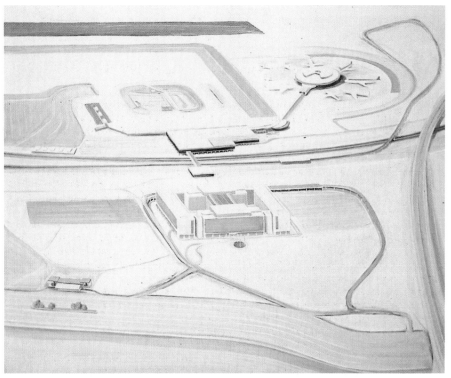

Carol Rhodes, Airport Hotel and Airport, *1996, oil on board, 45.7 x 55.8 cm*

is an emotional neutrality or absence in Rhodes, of which the lack of staffage – human figures – is only the most convenient indication one could cite, not remotely the source. If there is a relation to the experience of dreams, it is interesting only because it is achieved through rigorously conscious process, and without any sense of surrealism or the deliberate conjuring of mystery or menace. Similarly, if the very detachment of the work is significant – the arm's length relationship to subject and the *sang-froid* of execution – this is only because it balances a genuinely engaging counter-pull (a charm, one might be tempted to say, but it is something more substantial and unusual than that) both in the motif and in the way the paintings are formally made and orientated in tradition.

Rhodes is not the only painter whose work has recently elicited in me something other than the usual agreement-to-differ. At the end of last year Francis Graham-Dixon showed paintings by Amanda Thesiger (whose work has since been seen in the Amnesty International touring exhibition, 'Freedom', and the Arts Council purchases anthology at the Hayward).

By rights, I shouldn't have been interested. Thesiger makes frequently quite large, semi-abstract-yet-organically-allusive paintings with earthy, rich colours. That sort of formula would seem to have been done to death; every art school always has a few students drearily doing it. But Thesiger somehow takes the paintings into unfamiliar territory. And far as she is from someone like Rhodes, similar principles distinguish her work. Again, here, there is a sense of conscious fictionality, with shapes and colours suspended at the point where they just begin to create structures of

planes and volumes in illusionistic space, grouping into odd three-dimensional configurations. A form will cast a shadow, and it is as if the shadow itself creates the space for the form to occupy. Shapes may be fruit-like, or have the quality of limp, withering balloons; or they may form irregular, angular box structures with odd flaps and wings. This is not just the standard, non-committal ambiguity of paint churned into a state of semi-representation with default modernist 'physicality'. In the kinds of space and the kinds of identity or presence which are evoked, Thesiger avoids quite consistently the clichés of supposedly dream-like 'spiritual' or 'mysterious' vagueness, or of supposedly psychologically loaded, quasi-erotic 'interior dimensions'.

As, in a different way, in Rhodes, the specific surface qualities of the paintings are crucial. Degrees of dullness and shine are again carefully modulated. Thesiger manages a fairly difficult performance (one which is rarely talked about but very important within modernism, from Courbet onward, as also in much earlier painting), and that is the making compelling of *drabness* as a pictorial quality, in a way that avoids the work itself simply becoming drab, but creates instead a more paradoxical beauty. And Thesiger's paintings have their own interesting reference points in art of the past. They sometimes assume a structure and syntax that recalls seventeenth- and eighteenth-century Italian, or Spanish, still life. Or their luminous forms will recall Pietro Longhi's magically clustered and floating figures in dim, amorphous space. Then suddenly a huge Turneresque recession will open up in one of the pictures, through which a vaporous presence trawls like the *Fighting Temeraire*.

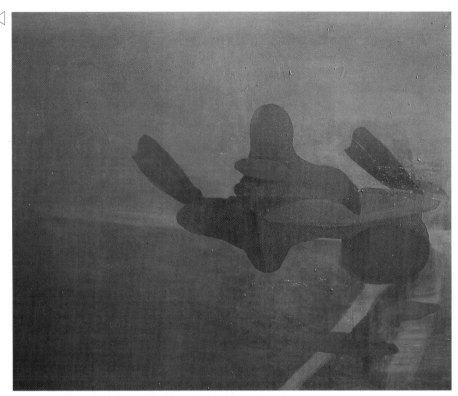

Amanda Thesiger, On Leaving the City, *oil on canvas, 152.4 x 182.8 cm*

Visiting Thesiger's studio a while ago, I was quite disconcerted by the look of these works when they are still in progress. They appeared very much *en route* to being the kind of standard issue, subjectivist, quasi-abstract-expressionism that they finally in fact avoid becoming. (And note: reproduction also makes them look more like that kind of product than they really are.) The artist's way of talking about the work, certainly in a few published statements, can also tend toward usual notions of dreamscape, 'transcendent moments' and artist as 'medium' working between eye and soul. The works so far have achieved something far more interesting than any of that would suggest. Surely their real function involves

some kind of *critique* of familiar ideas of essentialism or transcendence.

That last point – that word critique – needs qualifying. It has to be said that, as with Rhodes, a dryly theoretical take on Thesiger's work misses the mark. If there is a sense of speculative detachment – emotional distance – in both their works, this is only worthy of attention because of an ultimately re-involving, re-engaging complexity and specificity. And it is this that enables the work to be genuinely *about* detachment, and not merely a passive demonstration of it. There is any amount of painting currently around which trades on the ironic quotation and recycling of emptied-out abstract and representational

styles. Both Rhodes and Thesiger avoid that strategy. More particularly, they are not coyly occupying the easily and infinitely ambiguous place *between* knowingness and naivety, which is the refuge of very recent would-be hip painting (the *faux-naïf* landscapes of collaborators Alice Stepanek and Steven Maslin, glimpsable occasionally at Laure Genillard, would be just one example). Young painters seem most often to fall into that sad artistic limbo via the egregious influence of Gerhardt Richter, an influence endemic in British art schools. Richter fans may protest that he is travestied by his epigones (and he himself certainly denies at times any element of ironic detachment). To me his work remains tediously academic in its massive demonstration not just of a numb alienation from, but ultimately an utter *indeterminacy of*, meaning and response. The work reflects a philosophical and emotional non-commitment – almost a *wilful incapacity* – that is the banally familiar orthodoxy of our period.

But other, better artists are certainly in danger of being (mis)used to similarly sanction present styles. One of those would be Alex Katz, increasingly referred to by very young artists here (and elsewhere) who seem oblivious to the subtlety and complexity of his painting, misreading it as a precedent for all kinds of lobotomised and historically estranged figuration. The exhibition at Victoria Miro last year which grouped young graduates around a Katz portrait was certainly in danger of encouraging that reading. The attempts of myself and David Cohen a while ago to encourage certain public galleries in the UK to do a serious Katz show were based on a feeling that his mediation to British audiences needs very careful thought indeed. It will be interesting to monitor the response, when they are exhibited, to the fifteen Katz works that have now been purchased by Charles Saatchi.

Despite my disavowals at the start of this essay, I suppose I have now slipped into the identification of a certain trend in current painting, albeit a negative one – the malaise of this uncommitted hovering before an either/or choice between the empty irony of the post-modern and the perceived redundancy of history. And I suppose I have also begun to identify a notional 'group' of painters who find ways out of that condition. I can think of yet other artists well placed in their work to do similarly. The big names like Richter, and more recently Luc Tuymans (who has certainly made interesting paintings, however), may be obscuring for us significant figures in Germany and Belgium. Michael Bach's paintings of London, shown a while back at the Gilmour Gallery (before David Gilmour became curator of the Delfina Trust Gallery), seem to be breaking out of the quasi-photographic randomness of his old tutor (Richter) to open up genuinely painterly concerns that even begin to link with Canaletto, Pissarro, Morandi. Certain

Charlotte Gibson, Internal State 2, *photograph, 42 x 59.7 cm*

others of his contemporaries in Germany, who are also exploring the possibilities of landscape genres, will be on show at Andrew Mummery's current London gallery space in Great Sutton Street soon after this article appears. That show, devoted to landscape, will also include Carol Rhodes, and possibly Bert de Beul, who is one of the more engaging of the new Belgians. When not applying a token Richteresque blur to his images, he can come close to late Derain.

In this country, meanwhile, several young painters come to mind who could do significant things. Martin Westwood, who recently showed at Delfina, may be finding a way out of merely quirky, interfered-with figuration, through his dark interiors of real visual and art-historical resonance. Joel Tomlin (like Westwood a Chelsea graduate) who showed his B-movie vignettes of sure painterly touch during the last East End Open Studios season, has the right, unlikely enthusiasms – for Watteau and Monticelli. He, too, through nurturing the madeness of the work, has to fight mere contrariness or easy ambivalence (he was pained, not pleased, when he heard that German post-Pop painter Martin Kippenburger 'appropriated' one of Tomlin's canvases as his own work).

On the other side of the equation, there are artists whose task is more to announce complexity within what may seem a conservative performance. The work of both Stuart Parkinson (shown at his concluding exhibition as a 1996 Picker Fellow at Kingston University) and Charlotte Gibson (at Rocket Gallery, through the summer) have qualities in common with Rhodes and Thesiger. Parkinson creates panoramas of mildly fantastical, semi-architectural structures – ribbons, canopies, spindles, spangles – that cannot quite be identified as known objects. His space relates to that of Matta and Gorky, his pictorial elements to Uccello's lances and banners and oranges, and to Duchamp's bachelors and chocolate grinders. If he avoids *too* great a whimsy, and sustains real ambition, he is in a rich area. Gibson paints, and photographs, a doll's house, occupied by and made up of forms that can become as ambiguous as those in Thesiger. She has that soft, Longhiesque space and colour again, but can suddenly also recall Jacques Villon when she imposes a linear structure on her compositions. The Rocket Gallery show (and catalogue) was presented with great refinement – so much so as to be in danger of forcing a premature closure on work that is still very much developing. The potential of its imagery in addressing issues of interiority and internalisation, dwelling and absence, privacy and prying, containments (and discontents?), invitation and exclusion, is enormous.

Only slightly older than Gibson and Parkinson is Peter Jones, a painter who has recently shifted from practising a kind of collaged, mixed-technique figuration associated with certain Central School mid-'80s graduates (Mark Rafter, Sally Meyer, Marcus Vergette) to making big, gestural, drippy landscapes, 'drawn' in mercurial

Bert de Beul, Untitled, *1992, oil on canvas, 45.7 x 53.3 cm*

silvery lines on black grounds. He showed them at the Coventry Gallery in the autumn, and they looked compelling. (Again they evoked late Derain nocturnes.)

There are other more mature painters one could mention. Rob Welch's recent tonal pictures of Deptford creek seem to mark a breakthrough from his earlier still lifes (engagingly Hayden-like though those were). He is showing in the exhibition 'Delight' which was at Manchester Metropolitan University last summer, and is forthcoming at Kingston University's new Picker Gallery. Meanwhile, back in Glasgow, after a solo show of big, scrubby hinterlandscapes at the Mappin Art Gallery in Sheffield, Richard Walker is currently making stunning little studies of the interior of his studio. Like many of his small works, they have the softened crispness of Corot and eighteenth- and nineteenth-century *plein-air* sketchers of Italy, and the fresh rigour of Fairfield Porter. Maybe

Walker's 'studies' will become the substantial centre of his work.

So finally, just at the moment, I could perhaps begin to imagine curating a cohesive collective exhibition, something other than an anti-group show. I even start to sound as if I'm giving some of those hot tips. Of course, the work of most of the artists I have mentioned, even – or especially – if they do pursue solutions to the kind of artistic quandaries I have tried to identify, may be destined for very different, very diverse resolutions. Then we can all go back to affirming our disagreements.

Merlin James will exhibit at Francis Graham Dixon, 24 January–8 March, 1996. Amanda Thesiger is represented by Francis Graham Dixon; Carol Rhodes and Bert de Beul are shown in London by Andrew Mummery. 'Remaking Reality', until 5 January, 1997, Kettle's Yard, Cambridge.

Stuart Parkinson, Untitled, *1996, oil on canvas, 91.4 x 213.3 cm*

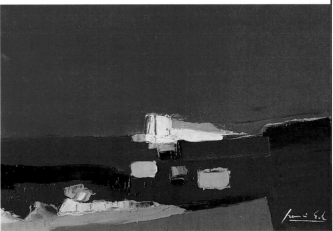

Zsuzsi Roboz   **The New York Blizzard of 1996 II**   Oil on canvas 20 x 30 ins

Caught in New York last winter during the epic blizzard, Zsuzsi Roboz was inspired to create a series of five paintings which capture both the beauty and drama of this spectacular phenomenon. As a prelude to a major exhibition of the artist's work in March, these paintings are to be released and will be available from the gallery during December and January.

War-torn Hungary in the forties ....from England and the Royal Academy Schools to Florence with Pietro Annigoni; she has succeeded with her drawings in capturing the spirit of the ballet, musicians, painters – people famous in the arts. Zsuzsi Roboz now draws from her own life experiences – 'Feelings' – a new exhibition of work presented by the David Messum Gallery.

Exhibition opens 12th-29th March

For catalogue and further details
telephone: +0044 171 437 5545

DAVID MESSUM

—— Fine Art ——

8 Cork Street, London W1X 1PB.
Telephone: 0171-437 5545

GIOTTO
Scenes from a Mystery Play

David Sylvester *contemplates the ideal earthiness of Giotto's subjects in the Scrovegni Chapel at Padua.*

The blue ceiling establishes an enveloping calm that can be disturbed but not disrupted by slaughter, betrayal, scourging, crucifixion, lamentation. Shrieks are muffled by the serenity of the sky.

Nobody is left in isolation. Christ does not go off into the wilderness or pray alone in the garden. At the point of the story where Gethsemane could have been introduced, Giotto retains the setting of the Last Supper, all thirteen actors remain on stage and Christ washes the disciples' feet. Where there might have been a soliloquy, Giotto presents an intimate human contact.

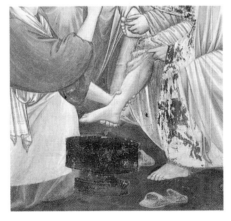

The calm of the atmosphere, the measured way in which every action is performed, the constant presence of several actors – not a crowd, only a chorus – give every event the quality of a ceremony. Nothing that happens seems accidental or unforeseen. The slow succession of episodes no more illustrates reality than the 'humanity' of the participants depends on establishing that they are fishermen, carpenters or whatever. Their 'humanity' comes from their ideal earthiness just as the events presented are like ritualised enactments of moments that have passed into history. They are *tableaux vivants*, scenes from a mystery play. They are more

Giotto, Last Supper, *Scrovegni Chapel, Padua*
Above title: Chancel arch showing, on either side, the Annunciation
Bottom left: Washing of the Feet *(detail)*

like liturgy than scripture. And everything that happens manifestly has its place in a grand design. The rhythm of the forms in the parts and the whole says that everything is inevitable, contributes to the fulfilment of a harsh and optimistic destiny. God has willed it; what God wills is good.

What is new here is that God loves Man means that God is friendly to Man. There's a particular resonance in the juxtaposition of the Ascension and the Pentecost – the flight of God the Son to heaven followed by the flight of God the Holy Ghost to earth, the dove's arrival among that ring of earth-bound seated men. It affirms that God's will is to be done on earth as it is in heaven

through the fact that, after a thousand years of Christian art, the saints are finally seen as terrestrial creatures. Artists can be divided into those who make men light and those who make them heavy: Cimabue and Giotto present an antithesis repeated in, say, Velazquez and Rembrandt. But there is no other cycle of paintings in which the human race is invested with such massiveness.

Nor is there a cycle of paintings in which we are so constantly made aware of the relation of the figures to built settings, now open, now confining. Partly it is because Giotto misses no opportunity to introduce architecture, as when, where the

Angel and the Virgin of the Annunciation are traditionally separated by the real space of the whole width of the arch framing the choir, each of the two figures is given its own architectural canopy. Partly it is because the depicted architecture is exceptional in its inventiveness – more like that of pavilions than of permanent buildings – and in its efficacy as a dramatic divider of spaces. Partly it is because the figures themselves seem to be entities carved from building materials. Giotto insists that, while there's no need to touch on the fact that God on earth was a carpenter, it must not be forgotten that God in heaven is a builder. □

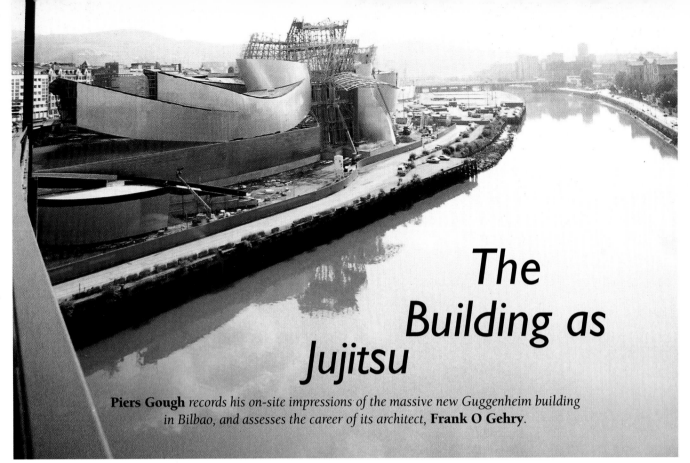

The Building as Jujitsu

Piers Gough *records his on-site impressions of the massive new Guggenheim building in Bilbao, and assesses the career of its architect,* **Frank O Gehry**.

Royal Academy, London, full blown lunch for 50 artists and art writers. Thomas Krens, director of the Guggenheim Foundation, and Juan Ignacio Vidarte, director of the museum project for the Basques, came over to London just to tell us about the new gallery they are building and other projects in Bilbao – a city I certainly wouldn't like to pinpoint on a blank map. The patrician Krens explained that Bilbao had been news to him, too, and he'd visited out of courtesy. The sheer enthusiasm he found there (and $100m) persuaded him to build another Guggenheim satellite in Europe and supply any amount of their existing collection and new work, with a ten million cash-back to acquire some Spanish and European work. Juan Ignacio described how they decided to give post-industrial Bilbao a tube system designed by Foster, a main railway and coach station by Stirling, but before any sensible business parks (by Pelli), to put the city on the map and make a brilliant place for the inhabitants to enjoy.

They invited us to go immediately and see even the half-built building. They simply couldn't hide their feeling that they had a work of genius on their hands. It was palpable. I couldn't even begin to imagine any part of the scenario in reverse: lunch in Madrid, for instance, to announce Architectural fabulousness in London. We may have the Lottery but we don't have Frank O Gehry.

It isn't hard to find Frank Gehry in Bilbao. A walk down the main street looking up the cross streets and diagonals of the city grid. In front of you and behind you at the end of every vista the green of the surrounding hills. Then sure as fate there it is at the end of a street, a tangle of steel looking like

a roller-coaster disaster; not all that high, in fact trees on the hills behind seem to be growing out of the top. It's a street of consistent six-storey buildings of an almost caricature European city which like Barcelona wasn't recently rich enough to ruin itself with vulgar redevelopments. Free now from Franco and looking beyond the EC honeymoon honeypot, Bilbao is the business and post-industrial city to the more professionally oriented Santander.

The grid ends suddenly on a fast-moving cross road running parallel to the city's original reason for existence: the Nervión river. Traffic is streaming down a slip road from a motorway-type bridge that slopes alarmingly down off the hills opposite and across the river. Between the road and the river is a big drop down to a railway marshalling yard coming from the left and not entirely disused. Where the rails hit the buffers, the newest Guggenheim Museum rears up. The tangle of steel turns out to be just the unclad topknot of a huge restless splurge of building where various exterior surfaces are organically creeping up over it. Over to the far right the frame appears again on the other side of the bridge. The building has crawled under the road and embraces it.

Before I can begin to wonder how to deal with my reactions, there he is, Frank himself, and a slew of entourage hopping across the road and onto the site. 'Hi, what are *you* doing here?' – as if I were just passing. It's a major site inspection with Guggenheim people over from NY – Juan Ignacio, Gehry architects, local executive architects, but also Frank's wife and family and now me no problem come along, which is how I got to see the inside first. The main entry to the building is right down at marshalling yard and riverside level. The

ramp, actually an historically correct stepped ramp, is pretty vertiginous. On one side the swelling curves of a submarine-like form are suddenly rolling right over you. Unaffectedly, Berta his wife says simply, 'It's beautiful isn't it?' This main descent is immediately the reverse of the daunting flight of steps up to the front of a monument. Not just politely flat but the absolute opposite – supporting the notion that this is a deliberate anti-monument we are entering. It feels like being a Lilliputian under a Tony Cragg sculpture (one of those recent ones made of ivory dice).

The ramp plunges you right into the central atrium space of the building. It is both fantastical in its size and complication of surface and space, and simple in explaining how the building works. Not unlike the Guggenheim in New York – but that whole building would easily fit into this central space. Looking up, it is hard to understand at first what you are looking at. There are so few normal clues to get a fix on. The exposed structure twists and wriggles via gaps and gashes up to amoeba-shaped openings. The space flows around various vertically elongated forms which may or may not stop short of the top, wherever that may be. For folks used to major structures such as railway stations and gasometers being orthogonally understandable, the present structure is mind-boggling in its spatial audacity and constructional complexity.

The plan of the building is really quite straightforward. Three wings lead off the central space – up river, down river, and back towards the road. This leaves a big view of the sweep of the river straight ahead, an entry through a glass wall and under a framing canopy which is like a hand held over the eyes against bright light.

To the left can be seen a stack of galleries. Beyond them, on part of the first floor, are the bookshop and café, commanding the view down the marshalling yard and over the city. Behind is the wing under whose swelling sides we entered. It has a central spine of rectangular 'classical' galleries surrounded on either side by galleries that have one straight wall and the others ballooning out in plan and section. The scale of all the galleries is huge. Beyond them towards the road are conservation and administration areas.

To the right is the even vaster hangar-like space that disappears in the distance. A curtain of what looks like grey snow is being sprayed onto the massive steel frame. The entourage is already beginning to straggle out as the leaders disappear into the 150 metre-long space that goes right under the road bridge. Above our heads the roof cambers over and zooms away, peeling off twice to form north lights the size of roll-on ferry doors, stopping just short of the bridge through which the traffic can be seen (and vice versa).

This is the gallery for temporary exhibitions of sculpture and installations. It has massive floor loadings to take anything Richard Serra cares to throw at it. The forward party has puzzlingly vanished from what is apparently a dead end. But they are visiting the shell of a sneaky extra temporary gallery café, out towards the river and under another spectacular ramp that careers up to join the road bridge.

Beyond the bridge is the 'High Reader', not as I thought a reference to its lectern qualities, but Gehry's ironic quote of Venturi's prescription for a sign structure, carrying the message for an otherwise dumb box building. Never has a building less needed a sign, except it

turns out that the brief wanted it to be visible from city hall further along the river. So there is a structure; what actually goes in it is undecided, but possibly nothing at all. Frank fancies a Cindy Sherman gallery, though that would be, at the moment, quite separate.

The upper floors are accessed by lifts and stairs in the central space up to the balconies that run around each level. In front of the big window over the river, the balcony gets quite narrow and wiggly – like the film *Metropolis*, says Frank. More like a roller-coaster without the cars, say I, with only some re-bars and orange plastic netting between us and oblivion. Then we all go outside, although actually you can see a lot of the outside from inside. Glass walls in the central space between the wings reveal fabulous oblique views of the exterior skin shimmering over the forms you have memorably just been inside. The exterior is at a fascinating stage akin to a cut-away diagram. The lowest part is clad in its final form; above that is a tide mark of black waterproofing; above that, the backing wall surfaces and insulation, with right at the top the afro of steel coloured with red oxide now going grey. Even Gehry gives me the bit about this is the best time to see the building with the frame exposed. But though it's an unrepeatable thrill to see it, actually the final building will be even better. The frame is extraordinary but not as magical and inexplicable as the final internal and external surfaces will be. All skeletons are interesting, but the human body can be beautiful.

There are three main exterior materials. Flat glass in jaggedy shaped frames which fill the opening between the forms but have a restless life of their own.

Blocks of a marble-like stone form crisp rectangular shapes, laid in a slightly offset pattern over insulation, over plain breeze block walls. The finish to the curved walls is laid in the same pattern. The material finally chosen was titanium (which you will remember from your periodic tables); a couple of years ago it had a price dip in world markets which made it momentarily affordable. However, it does have to be very thin: less than a millimetre. The fixing clips make it crease so that each big tile-like piece has a shallow central dent making it look soft and flimsy. Frank is pleased to aver that it has a 100-year guarantee but will ripple in the wind. Not a claim one hears much from architects. It certainly does even more magical things to light than stainless steel does. It seems softer and more elusive in reflection.

The most spectacular view of the outside is from across the river. There is some dispute over the better café to meet in, the less salubrious one having the best view. Today's problem is that in spite of computer drawings the steel fabricators have somehow managed to get the curve of the canopy slightly wrong. Should it be redone? My problem is to guess which way it's wrong. Frank decides almost immediately that it would be churlish to change it because either way it looks good as it is. The others turn up to hear the verdict and then we all sit and stare at this magnificent animal across the water. It feels as good as being David Attenborough and discovering a whole new species at a watering hole. The conversation turns to what the King and Queen said when they invited themselves to visit halfway through the process. It's one thing to turn up to open a building, quite another to want to enjoy the construction. 'Greatest

Frank O Gehry, house in Los Angeles, east façade

building of the twentieth century', or was that the other King and Queen: Philip Johnson? And then, how they were going to invite their English cousin to show him some real architecture. Meanwhile, Frank is trying to persuade Juan Ignacio to move some parking bays and a street lamp so as not to block the outlook from his important viewing café. I wouldn't be surprised if next time....

Yet another group photo, with the group almost as long as the building and Frank seemingly expansively hugging the whole lot of us. Then it's up in the bridge's lift and a stroll down *over* the building, flashing in the late sunlight. When Frank's in town the entourage rolls on to supper. Tonight it's at a table down the middle of a delicatessen shop. The legs of

the table have been raised by standing them on olive oil cans. The steaks are four ribs of beef charcoal grilled, which arrive in a pile distinctly reminiscent of a certain building. Is this Basque humour? Frank is very happy and they are very happy. There is a real unforced sense of mutual enjoyment and respect, and pleasure in each others' company. Frank is good fun, has a droll humour and carries off being the centre of attention unpretentiously.

The next morning is supposed to be the interview itself, for which I have genned up OK, but any notion of questions and answers is virtually impossible with the guy in such an expansive mood. My questions seem redundant in the flow of reminiscences and ideas. The general drift is how late in the day it is to be having

success just when Berta has got him persuaded at 67 to start taking holidays.

When Tim Street-Porter arranged for me first to meet Frank, he was already 50. We had Mexican brunch in Santa Monica. He'd agreed to show us his new Loyola Law School. But somehow he'd managed to lock his car keys in his yellow beetle. It seems so ridiculous now, but we sat around as if we had any influence in the world and said how are we going to get Frank some more work; he is so down on his luck since his house frightened all the clients away. Not strictly true, of course, but he was doing mostly private houses and that is no way to make a living.

That trip we saw Santa Monica Place, whose parking garage is a sublime essay in chain-link fencing; Loyola in downtown – a village of primitivist buildings set against a long block with Dr Caligari angled escape stairs; and then the trip to the shrine – the famous house which is an explosion of inventive energy in a polite LA suburb. The sheer number of industrial materials, the raw angles, the celebration of construction by revealing it – it was as punk as the Sex Pistols! As decon. as anything since. The bedroom balcony floor was made of sagging chain-link, the kitchen floor of melting asphalt. It was presided over by an impish 50-year-old who delighted in showing it off even for no doubt the zillionth time. The living room was not especially practical at the time since a Larry Bell sculpture filled it completely.

Frank's earlier fame had been as the architect of the Danziger Studio, a dumb box on Sunset, painted (with a pitched roof added) by Hockney. Meanwhile he was successfully putting up biggish modernist

Frank O Gehry, American Centre, Paris, France

Frank O Gehry, Santa Monica Place, 1973–1980, Santa Monica, California

condos. The house blew it. He relied on artist friends who commissioned a bunch of studios where Frank had a few words to say on Post-modernism. One studio had a huge, arbitrary and useless staircase whacked on outside; the other, a useless chimney made of mineral felt.

Frank was influenced by his friends being artists not architects. His training taught him to detail marble, but his clients could only afford balloon frame and crudboard. He thought if Rauschenberg and Johns could use found materials, so could he for architecture. But Gehry draws a distinction between art and architecture. Art is a commentary; architecture is a container of programme. Art can criticise; architecture has to deal with the budget, building codes, gravity, the client. You can make sculptural form, but then you have to punch a window... But he still thinks this gives painting a more difficult problem: that of starting somewhere without a programme.

Then Frank had a flirtation with fish and the underside of Santa Monica Pier. Both were projects against the historicism and borrowing of Post-modernism. The fish, being older than man himself and anthropomorphic by definition, was a counter to every pediment and faux column going. Santa Monica Pier was a celebration of the structure underneath the artifice that no one thought about. Frank liked the crappy overstructured quality of thick bits of wood whacked together as carelessly as, well.. trees. That motif still pops up on the Chiat Day and the Weisman Museum buildings.

It was the last fish that liberated his formal composition. He got a computer – not some CAD line drawer, but something that could handle surfaces, double curves,

triple curves no doubt. A computer that Dassault uses to design fighter planes. This computer, apart from cutting thousands of man hours out of the work, also took thousands of man hours out of puzzling how to build it, how to cut out the structure and the skin. The computer discs can instruct the machine tools direct. This is no client-pleasing fly-around perspective machine, it's the practical way of information provision. The only practical way of building the complex shapes he was now able to embark

on.

Also it gives back to the architect a responsibility which has been ebbing away since the time of master-builders. For everyone else it is as if this architect draws, then sends to the contractor. Contractor tries to figure out what the drawings will need to get them built. Sends copies to subcontractor of each part. They do ditto. Send in estimates (usually so different you can't trust any of them high or low). Then re-draw architect's drawings for manufac-

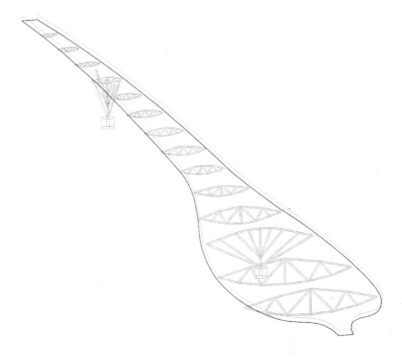

Frank O Gehry, shortlisted proposal for the Millenium Bridge Competition. Photo: Marcus Leith
The winner of the Millennium Bridge competition will be announced on 10 December

ture of their bit – say steel-work structure. Then architect tries to check their drawings, often done by a totally different technique, against his drawings. Always deferring responsibility for missing something back to the subcontractor.

Gehry's office issues 'stone-cutting' discs. He takes responsibility. His insurers freak out. But he also gets the right price and the computer can tell exactly how it should be. And that is why he can build these staggering shapes, not just as models but with every nuance in reality. Post-Barcelona he has dropped fish and started sculpting. As the technique develops, the angular chunks of the Toledo Art School become more muscular at the Minneapolis Museum. Sheet-metal volumes start wrestling up against longer rectangular blocks like a frozen moment from the Eton Wall game. The American Centre in Paris brought stone into the equation, not just for the rectangular bit but the swooping skirt balcony and other Parisian – i.e. sexy, chic – bits. In contrast, in Paris, glass broke free for the first time. Up till then, basically it filled holes to make windows or came in rectangular frames as curtain wall. In Paris it jets out of the building as a *brise soleil* waterfall. The Centre was an obviously contextual building until they demolished the context and built modern next door instead.

Then it looked as if Disney Hall in LA was going to be the big one. In competition with Stirling, it had at that stage a brilliant Scharounish interior but a very iffy outside. But confidence in computerised stone

cutting led to an exuberant collection of stone sails more like a square-rigger than a yacht. Gehry says he was inspired by the moment that a sail luffs, jiggers about between wind on one side and wind on the other. As he tells it, a flat piece of stone cost one dollar, a single curvature two dollars, a double curvature ten dollars. The computer can keep the double curves down to two percent of the surface. But at Disney the money had run out long before, at the top of the sub-ground multi-storey car park. So suddenly Bilbao is the big one (along with a 20,000 square foot house in Ohio called The Lewis Residence).

I ask him what he thinks of Liebskind's V & A. He hasn't had a chance to look at the drawings, so I try does he think it might liberate architecture in Britain. Or sink it forever, is his laconic reply. Frank has a jaundiced view of working in this country not just because of the Prince, who seems more amusing than threatening from a distance, but he was once part of a team on the Kings Cross Regeneration site. SOM, Foster and Tigerman and Gehry were in it together. But Foster secretly had his own totally separate masterplan which eventually won, as it turned out, a pyrrhic victory. So his view of professional ethics over here is not good, to put it politely.

On the matter of public responsibility inherent in building he is however pretty dismissive. Excuses for mediocrity just about sums it up, and that goes for architects' naivety in thinking they can change the world with their ecological, social or political activities. As preposterous as a

child thinking it can break its granny's back when stepping on a crack in the pavement. He wants an architecture that can inspire people, not just solve problems. To inspire is what architecture is in the world for. And he solves any moral dilemma simply by not working for people or organisations he disagrees with. (And that includes organisations where he can't speak to the ultimate boss.)

Then Frank gets up and says well we'd better go and look at the building. I hadn't reckoned on getting my own personal tour on top of everything, and I even get to take some snaps of my own of him polishing the titanium. There's a bit on the top of the ramp where you can touch it: it's going to be a popular spot. I wonder what he is thinking about as he perambulates around the fantastical space. Just the mistakes and missed opportunities, he says, like every other architect.

To get light down into the classical galleries on the lower floors there are lightwells in the middle of the upper floors but with walls around them like square doughnuts of space. Frank won't hear of just using north light, so he has to prove that none of the warmer, sweeter light will directly hit any walls, which means more computer overtime.

We look into possibly the best space, the one behind the submarine shaped exterior. It's a fourteen-metre-high gallery. One wall is straight, the other balloons out. Some complicated rooflights wrestle with the roof. The view from half way up is temporary: it will soon be walled in. Suddenly I would love to be an artist and show in this space. 'Keiffer is getting it', Gehry shrugs....

So don't artists really just want white boxes, aren't they actually the most boringly opinionated clients from hell? No, says Frank, Daniel Buren told him that what artists really want is to exhibit in the most famous of famous galleries. And indeed they are pouring in to check it out. Serra's been, Johns and Holtzer expected any day.

In some places there is quite a gap between the inner and outer walls. Each has its own steel studding either side of the main structure. Gehry knows that architecture critics, with their presbyterian upbringing in worthiness, may get hold of the gap as evidencing some lack of rigour. It seems a reasonable proposition to make, say, a three-storey outside elevation and a single-storey inside one, each as beautiful as possible, while still keeping them relatively close together. The gap between inner and outer Renaissance domes was much greater, and the solution is probably to celebrate it and put in stairs and catwalks and have tours. Meanwhile any suggestion of wilfulness or lack of rigour, is completely dispelled by the exactitude of the forms. They are worked and worked to perfection. Anyway critics can't read drawings and when the gaps are hidden....

One bit of the building is to be rendered and painted. Unfortunately Krens has fallen in love with the red oxide colour of steelwork protection and wants the building that colour. This irks Gehry because, although he is all for freedom, some colours have wrong meanings. So to render with oxide is a *longueur*, and you don't have to be a purist for it to be unsatisfying. So maybe it will be green after all. And there's the matter of the sign across the front. A more redundant item it's hard to imagine, but he's designed it to be nearly illegible and seems more interested in a very big photo out front of the other Guggenheim's Frank [Frank Lloyd Wright] looking disgusted.

Then we join the entourage for another whacking great Basquaise lunch. Deep fried offal for me. Siesta time is back at the project office, which is on a fourth floor overlooking the site with a handy long balcony where you can just sit out and gawp. The office has the most up-to-date model carved out of greeny wood by the computer, but also an early one from the time of the competition, which is quite a shock and looks amazingly primitive. The curvy bits just bump up and over more emphatic rectangles like a diagram of an idea, whereas the later design is integrated and fluid. The rectangles curve a bit. The curved bits have flat passages.

What Gehry has brought back to architecture he calls hand-to-eye coordination. The computer allows him to scrunch up a piece of paper and then build it times a hundred. He can hone his forms. This makes him essentially an Anglo Saxon Arts and Crafts man rather than a Continental or American Beaux Arts Man. 'Graves and Rossi draw just once and so they can't ever capture that redolence in the building. My buildings get better and better and are best when built.'

At last the man has to admit to being too bushed to climb up and look down from the hills. So I go along and what strikes me so forcibly is that the building might seem to have nothing to do with Bilbao in its built form. But in fact it does just what a work of art should do and makes you look anew at the city and its incredible restless energy contained within the surrounding hills. Gehry has a nice description of the building as jujitsu: the energy of the city is turned by a deft flick into a building. No exact epithet

has been coined for the whole building; but it appears like a cubist/vorticist painting of wrestling or sex. But it is also an abstracted view of the surrounding buildings, their quirks of style, their twists on the corners, their colour, their jostling to fill each block. The Guggenheim has little to do with their style, but rather than insult them by its difference, renews enjoyment of the city as expressing the ingenuity of man-made construction. It is, however, disappointing that the rest of the riverside will revert to pretentious Canary-Wharfish Beaux Arts development when Gehry has given such a strong steer on how the post-industrial city might more responsively organise itself. Bilbao may have thought they had chosen a big name, but in fact they are being presented with a big idea. Now they should tear up the other big names and run with the idea.

Most architecture, while necessarily optimistic, is about order, which seemed reasonable when we could only just conquer nature and even when we needed to celebrate democracy. Now Western people take democracy for granted and want freedom. If Graves, Rossi and Meier are about order and idealised democracy, then Gehry says he is really modern – he is about freedom.

These are anti-monumental times. There are more of us going places and we still want and need big places to go. But the Zeitgeist is away from the importance of the monument. The nineteenth century felt it right to express the significance of civic buildings by their imposing qualities. There was an identifying hierarchy to life. State, Church, theatres, railway stations, down to

the apartment. Now the hierarchy has disappeared the house is as important to people as the Town Hall, maybe more.

We need big buildings, but we don't want them to talk down to us. Jim Stirling coined 'the informal monument' for his take on this question: historically informed spaces often with reversed meanings like the voided central rotunda of Stuttgart; visited by people in trainers, sliding in via wavy green glazing, but into formally arranged spaces with a twist. Gehry, however, makes rigorous anti-monuments. The spaces are large, spectacular, inspiring, dramatic and beautiful. But the whole refuses to impose. A voluptuous building invites the enjoyment of art – through a kind of muscular generosity, so that although amazed the visitor is not dominated.

Then down from the hills for another celebratory dinner. Lots of invitations to return again before it's finished. And now it turns out that we are on the same flight out to London, but if this article chats on about that much more it will become pure Betty Kenward. Finally Frank throws me completely by saying, 'Well, if you are writing about me and Bilbao, *I* will write about *your* next building'. Dear Editor, if you want a witty piece from the world's greatest architect, find me a lovely job.

The Guggenheim Museum, Bilbao, opens to the public 21 June 1997.

Frank Gehry polishing. All photos of the Guggenheim building are by Piers Gough.

Nicolas Granger-Taylor, Seated Figure, 1996, oil on canvas, 20 x 14 ins

Nicolas Granger-Taylor

is represented by

OFFER WATERMAN & CO. FINE ART
20 Park Walk London SW10 0AQ
Tel: 0171 351 0068 Fax: 0171 351 2269

Venus Breaking Cupid's Bow, oil on canvas, 183 x 168 cms., by Simon Casson

SIMON CASSON

EXHIBITION DATES
20TH NOVEMBER – 21ST DECEMBER 1996

LONG & RYLE
4 JOHN ISLIP ST LONDON SW1P 4PX
Tel: 0171–834 1434 Fax: 0171–821 9409

KETTLE'S YARD

remaking reality

Painting & drawing by
10 contemporary artists
November 16 1996 - January 5 1997

bodyworks

Sculpture by
Caro, Paolozzi, Davies, Gormley
January 11 - March 2 1997

KETTLE'S YARD
Castle Street, Cambridge CB3 0AQ • 01223 352124
gallery open
Tuesday-Saturday 12.30-17.30, Sunday 14.00-17.30
Christmas closing: December 23-27, 30 & January 1

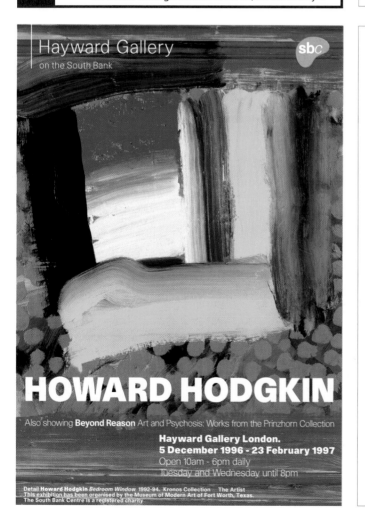

Rewriting Tillyer

William Tillyer takes **Norbert Lynton** *by surprise.*

The William Tillyer retrospective in Middlesbrough this autumn is more than an eye-opener, it's a shock to the system. It confirms a growing suspicion that we have all got him wrong. With each new show he has shifted his ground substantially. Instead of going with that, we have clung to a notion of what he is and does, that is reactionary rather than reactive. London no longer has any sort of programme of retrospectives; they are culpably rare. Our art world itself has become very mean – defensive and divisive to a self-mutilating degree. The fact is that William Tillyer's work, after thirty one-man shows in the UK (and the same number abroad: New York, Los Angeles, Chicago, Sydney, etc.), is not known to the many who should know it. But my main point is that those of us who think we know it have not understood it because we haven't known the whole of it.

I'll risk an analogy. What was going on in avant-garde Paris a century or so ago? Impressionism was crumbling. Symbolism, coming up, ranged from the sublime to the ridiculous. Some of the Symbolist painters were addicted to Burne-Jones; others eager for quick-fix mysticisms of various sorts clung to the coat-tails of writers great and small. Redon was in Paris, a natural solitary. Gauguin tried Britanny, Martinique and Tahiti, and ended up in the Marquesas Islands. Who were the other most significant painters then? Van Gogh who, after a couple of years in Paris, went down to Arles. Seurat who stayed in Paris, detached from its art world until 1886

when he launched Neo-Impressionism in the last Impressionist exhibition. He died in 1891, not having troubled Paris much. Cézanne who kept away from Paris almost completely, while Paris scarcely gave him a thought. Few noticed his big show at Vollard's in 1895. Anyway, they had him down for a clumsy painter and an awkward customer, so why bother.

In the 1960s, when I first knew him, Tillyer was a technical assistant in the print-making workshop at Chelsea School of Art: very able, very quiet, almost invisible. Chelsea was a clubbish place, full of ambitious painters hobnobbing between teaching and visits to the Kings Road bars. A lively scene, but Tillyer was not part of it. Trained as a painter at the Slade, where William Scott refused him his diploma in 1962, Tillyer was then working mainly on prints. There was something of a prints renaissance, with Bernard Jacobson publishing many of them, and though it had some effect in enlarging the public for modern art, it didn't last long. To those who cared to notice, Tillyer was a part-time print-maker who earned his bread by teaching. He was not of the company of those who became known through Situation and who showed at Waddington's, Robert Fraser's, the Hanover, the New London and Kasmin's, or even Grabowski's. He was friendly enough when spoken to, but generally withdrawn.

That hasn't changed much. In 1980 he moved back to North Yorkshire where he lives at some distance from anything but the Cleveland hills, embracing him on three

sides, and an almost infinite plain opening to the north-west. We don't notice how much he travels, working, exhibiting, teaching etc. in Europe, America and Australia. It is amazing how much this Yorkshire hermit puts himself about. But not in London: here he visits when necessary, does his business, stays a couple of nights, and is off again.

He is not part of any clique or cluster. He does not rub shoulders. He'd rather be in his studio, working. There are artists who reckon he should have stayed with print-making. They see him as an upstart, and say so. It's a way of keeping him out. Critics are influenced by art-world chat, and putting absent people down usually works; persuading the world otherwise is a slow business and unwelcome.

There are other problems. One is that Tillyer is not one to expose himself more than he must. In theory I know his work well, though some of it only from reproductions (whole sections of it have been waiting in New York to come home) and from what he has told me and others. In fact, I keep being jolted by unexpected aspects of his work, old and new. There were several moments of that sort in seeing the Cleveland show. This guardedness may be partly in Tillyer's nature, but it has surely something to do with the way we treat him, artists, art institutions and critics, even we who have written positively about his work. Perhaps he is tired of finding his unceasing process of development and innovation met with so many turned backs.

From now on there is no excuse. The Cleveland catalogue includes a vigorous essay by Mel Gooding, as well as Tillyer's own comments on some of the series of paintings done since 1980. It lacks a list of exhibits. The Cleveland Gallery is a good place but not very large, nor was every work available that was asked for, so the list could not be finalised until the hanging was done. But the general picture is clear now and has never been clearer. Tillyer is not the artist we say he is.

The most obvious mistake is to label him a landscape painter. That he is passionate about the natural world is clear, and he has never refuted the label. His living amid landscape is taken to support it. His major work has long involved generalized forms of sky, earth, plants and water: hieroglyphs rather than representations. To these he has added contrasting, geometrical forms which are not part of nature's appearance. To colours and brush-work suggesting space and movement he has added smooth, neat forms, usually asserting flatness. He has gone on to break into the physical surface, interfering with illusions of space and movement. Nature has been his main, overt thesis. To this he added successive antitheses – isolating his

William Tillyer, Eight Clouds, *1966, glass case with felt and pebbles, 57 x 91 x 43 cm.*
Collection of the artist

William Tillyer, Kachina Blue, *1994, acrylic on canvas, 172.7 x 142.2 cm*

hieroglyphs of nature, even enhancing their visibility, but denying them dominance.

When I wrote about his 'Westwood Paintings' in 1989, I focused on his juxtaposing of classical and romantic forms, natural and man-made, organic and geometrical. This duality was presented strongly and generously in paintings on canvas, and though these were clearly

modern in their near-abstractness, it could be seen as part of an honoured tradition (Cézanne, Poussin, etc.). This was more or less correct, and came out of the work and discussions with Tillyer. I should have thought it through further.

Two years earlier Peter had eloquently praised his landscape watercolours. British art needed an artist working directly with

nature again: Fuller had found him. He was not interested in Tillyer's paintings. He even ignored the several watercolours in the same series that Tillyer had torn in two to insert an anti-natural geometrical form. These did not fit the role Fuller had allocated him and so they did not exist. (I too was disconcerted by those violated watercolours, and don't know what I would have

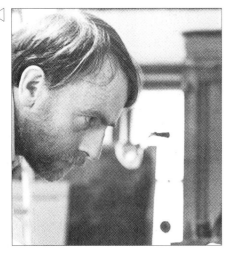

written about them then. But I couldn't have ignored them. Today they seem to me more central to Tillyer than his fluent, often delicious watercolours of observed scenery.)

In the early 1980s Tillyer had done paintings in which he had cut much of the canvas away and criss-crossed the gaps with string to hold the rest together. That was in 1981, part of what he did in Australia. Their motif is Victorian terrace houses, their windows and balcony railings and the plants growing in front of them. I knew something of these paintings from reproductions and longed to see them. I still do. Only one of them, *Jika*, is in the exhibition. It's the one the Tate thought of buying if only Tillyer would paint the revealed sections of the stretcher bars white. Of course, the vertical/horizontal emphasis of the bars is essential, stabilising but also asserting the painting's transparency. This transparency stresses before and behind while vetoing art's invitation to suspend disbelief. Large geometrical forms accompany lavishly brushed-in vegetation and light and shade. The effect should be

three-dimensional and loose; in fact these paintings are flat and tight, reminding me of Matisse around 1915–17 in their firmness. Tillyer's surfaces are much rougher, but there is a similar play of geometry against painted arabesques. There will probably be more of the Australian paintings in the Whitworth showing.

They were followed in 1983–4 by the 'Bridge' series, again cut away and tied together, displaying stretcher bars and using broad frames, so that what is visible of the solid bridge form is played against the curved cuts and plant forms and also against the straight orthogonals of the stretcher bars and frames. These paintings are more abrupt and tighter than the Australian series; Northern rather than Mediterranean in feeling. The contemporary print series, 'Living by the Esk', shows Tillyer playing various conceptual games in setting a still-life motif (vase and flowers) against the bridge form; it is witty as well as appealing, but above all intelligent.

Earlier, in 1979, he had done the 'Mesh Paintings', using for support not canvas nor boards but a diagonal mesh of strong rods. To it cling chunks of painted collage, back and front, leaving large areas of mesh visible, and there can be thick paint on the rods themselves as well as thinly coated rods and rods cut away to yield a negative form. Before any of these, around 1977, he had done more extreme mesh-based works. The 1979 'Mesh Paintings' used landscape imagery. The painted bits signalled sky and ground, sometimes a roof. The 1977 ones had nothing to do with landscape but employ Tillyer's typical still life: the vase a vertical cylinder, i.e. rectangular, the flowers dollops of colour above and beside the vase, soft forms against hard. In *Framed Oval with Blue Vase and Arrangement* the dollops are collaged sparsely on to the mesh, which makes an oval shape, here

and there reiterated by hints of framing; the vase itself is mesh, given a thin coat of blue paint and cut away on three sides to hint at three-dimensionality.

Bits of mesh and bits of board had previously come together in Tillyer's series of 'Studio Shelf' sculptures, never shown in the UK and now represented by two examples. They play pieces of mesh of varying gauges against each other, against plain forms and against a board inscribed with mesh lines. These refer back to prints made from about 1971 in which a diagonal mesh of lines, interrupted or fading away in places, serves as the visual grain by which he presents a variety of things-in-landscape images. *High Force* (1973) out of the 'A Furnished Landscape' series is in the exhibition, a screen print in tones of blue, suggesting the rather ambiguous form of a Yorkshire waterfall splashing into a pool. The titles emphasise the motifs; seeing the prints we get first the mesh, this mechnical anonymous image transcribed by Tillyer carefully on to the (mesh of the) silkscreen or on to the metal plate for etching.

Before this, in the mid-1960s, he had made a number of works that continue explorations he'd embarked on as a student. Scott could not give him a diploma in painting because they have nothing to do with painting. In the Slade studios they must have stuck out as devil's work, done to ruin the holy peace of those at their pictorial prayers. There are three fine examples in the show, never seen before. *Piano Hinge* (1966) is a square board, about 18 x 18 inches, painted white, with about twelve inches of piano hinge screwed aslant on to its upper portion. *Fifteen Drawer Pulls* (1967) is a larger square board painted white but criss-crossed with grey bands to make fifteen rectangles, each armed with a commonplace chromed U-bend handle. A hinge unhinged; unhandlable handles. No hint of landscape or anything else. Instead, two intensely focused works, somewhere between Conceptual art and Constructivism but not quite signing up to either.

Conceptual art had not taken off then. The new thing then was Minimalism – bits of activity in diverse places which American critics corralled into a movement in 1966 – but these pieces put among Minimalist paintings and sculptures would have looked like devil's work again, disturbing the high-minded, *noli me tangere* solemnity of the rest. The third is *Eight Clouds* (1966), a low glass cabinet within which a blue tray with recesses presents eight white chalk pebbles ranging in size from quite small to rather too large. A joke? A tease? The thing itself is warm and beautiful, and why shouldn't pebbles on a blue tray do what we habitually accept from white paint on blue? The fact is, they work. This is unquestionably a small, considered collection of clouds; cumulus, I'd say. They look handlable, and would be so were they not in a display case, controlling our behaviour.

If we go back before these things, we get to the late 1950s and Tillyer's pre-Slade

William Tillyer, Sea, Clouds and Beach, *1958, oil on canvas, 71 x 91 cm. Collection of the artist*

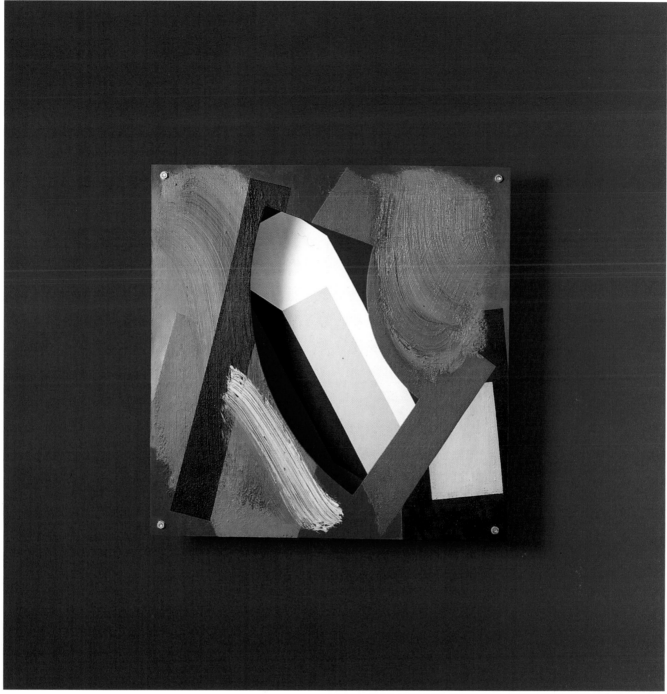

William Tillyer, Atelier Méchanique, *1996, acrylic on canvas and panel, 122 x 122 x 18 cm*

student years. There are some examples in the show and I have seen photos of others. Yes, he painted landscapes, and the paint is strong as paint. A lost seascape is dominated by foreground pebbles. He also made sculptures. One of them, illustrated in the catalogue, was a rising piece of carved sandstone, almost conical, accompanied and outreached by a spiral of copper wire. Not quite a carving, not quite a construction, but something of both and more like a Russian's project for a revolutionary monument than a piece of English 1957 art. It echoes a painting Tillyer had done a year earlier, of a Conference pear set upright on a dark surface, against a washed blue ground with a blob of white floating in it, some way above the pear. *Pear and Cloud* says the title. The cloud is tiny, or many

miles away; the pear is close to us, almost carved sandstone. Together, they make an extraordinary image: its loaded simplicity makes you hold your breath. (William Scott would have liked this one.)

In going backwards like this, from the 'Westwood' series I wrote about and the watercolours Peter Fuller wrote about in 1987, to the earliest works, we can now see or know about, I have of course been disconnecting, or almost disconnecting, Tillyer from the landscapist role we partly laid on him, partly took from what he spoke about. There is no denying Tillyer's commitment to landscape. The point is that he is equally committed to other things, conceptual matters that show more at some stages, less at others, but never go away. They have become more dominant

since 1990, with Tillyer painting on board but cutting large openings away to reveal another board behind it, repeating the ground colour of the front plane, or almost the same colour, or making a strong contrast. In *Two Standing Forms on Red Ground* (1990) the right half of the vertical painting shows not landscape forms but the brushy, colourful hieroglyphs he has taught us to accept as landscape. Tillyer's subtitle says 'Landscape with Tree' but the tree is hard to find. The left half has had a zig-zag shape cut out, suggesting two overlapping rectangles, one flat on, the other tilted in perspective, as in some of the 'Westwood' paintings. Are those 'standing forms' there or not there? Is the vase there in the 'Mesh' series? Is Mona Lisa smiling?

Of Tillyer's latest series, the 'Fluxion Paintings', there is only one example in the Cleveland show, *Atelier Méchanique*. Subtitled *Hexagon on Blue Ground* and measuring 72 x 72 x 18 inches, it is very strong, confronting us as we come in and lit dramatically. At the Bernard Jacobson Gallery in October there were more of them on show, and these made a fascinating group. But the way they had to be shown there (coming at them from the side) gave priority to their construction rather than to the visual encounter each offers. A square board hovers centrally about nine to eighteen inches –depending on the size of the painting – in front of a much larger square panel. A shaped hole cut into the front board lets us see through it to the back panel. The front board bears hard and soft areas of paint, lively hints of landscape and tacit geometrical forms. The ground colour of the front board repeats on the back panel, where a stereometric form, shown axonometrically, can be glimpsed through the opening. The mechanics of this are quite simple: the front board is supported by four threaded rods and nuts. From the side, these are too intrusive. Seen frontally and as one moves past, they are no problem, just a neat, open solution.

Nothing is neat or open in fact – experience here being more fact than how these paintings/constructions are made. As we approach, as our angle of vision changes, our reading of them shifts and needs reconsidering. Our behaviour and what the paintings reveal is in some conflict. The nameable stereometric form is made emphatically 3-D and seems to float between the front and back panels. As we move it mutates. The harder we look, the more it refutes its visual and conceptual identity. Again, a joke, a tease? The brushy painted forms on the front still signal landscape. The stereometric thing hovers in infinity, like the axonometric forms in Lissitzky's 'Prouns' of 1920–23, answering Malevich's visions of cosmic geometries of 1915+.

The 'Fluxion Paintings' series plays with processes of perception but is not a peepshow. It questions, again but more fiercely, our need to read and know simplistically, nostalgically. Has Tillyer been using landscape all these years as a sort of stooge? His passion for nature is clear.

William Tillyer, Framed Oval with Blue Vase and Arrangement, *1977, acrylic collage on metal mesh, 106 x 77 cm. Collection of the artist*

What we have to accommodate is his equivalent passion for *à rebours*, for what is against nature and against the grain, inviting misconstruction. The painter whom Peter Fuller wanted to see as 'tentative and tremulous', and thus a worthy extension of the English tradition, is armed with all the skills Fuller credits him with, but also with cunning at the service of a questioning mind.

Richard Gregory says that 'perception is a hypothesis of the world' . Perception of a work of art must then be a hypothesis of something already hypothetical. Perception is purposive. We want to make sense of a work of art too. It won't run us over if we perceive it falsely, but it will disconcert, perhaps even derange us. To cope with a visual/conceptual maze demands action as well as readiness to surrender to it. One of the functions of art has always been to free us, at least temporarily, of the trammels of common sense, to lift us out of ourselves

William Tillyer, Two Standing Forms on Red Ground (Landscape with Tree), *1990, acrylic on relief panel, 152.4 x 122 cm. Private collection*

towards, perhaps to, the divine frenzy the Neo-Platonists spoke of. In this way, the arts have always been anarchical at one extreme; at the other they reinforce convention. Much modern art has signed up to anarchism in this sense; too often it has been overcome by anarchistic gestures and conventions.

The Tillyer retrospective at the Whitworth Art Gallery early next year will have more space and will offer a fuller account of what he has done, though of course it will still only be something like a one-per-cent sampling. The Cleveland show was selected to emphasise the early years, the assembled and broken-surface paintings (cut canvases and sawn panels) produced in their different ways since the late 1970s, and then the newest work, the 'Fluxion Paintings' series of 1996, represented by that one magisterial example. *Atelier Méchanique* dominates the show but acts also as a bridge between the earliest work and the recent. The unbroken-surface paintings, from the 'Westwood' series of 1989 to some of the 'Kachina' series of 1994, are hardly represented at all, no more than the lyrical watercolours of the '80s. (In the 'Kachina' series he was using references to the American Indian figures together with his landscape signals.) I would not put it past Tillyer to surprise us all with a post-Fluxion development – perhaps a sculpture.

I do not know any other artist whose work has moved on so insistently, disrupting anything one might even retrospectively call a 'development'. Tillyer strikes me now as the most restless artist I have ever come across, probing his own work and probing art in general, and trying to prod us into going at least some way with him in his desire to construct and deconstruct at the same time, wowing us with swathes of paint and colour while breaking into our enjoyment of them by breaking into the perceptual process just as he breaks into his surfaces. Those who go to him for the pleasures expected from English landscape painting have never had it easy; it's a credit to the aesthetic richness of the work that they have hung on. The consoling elements are still there, even in the Fluxion paintings. But after the Cleveland and Whitworth showings we shall all have to admit that they are just one component in a complex programme.

In *About Modern Art* (page 151) David Sylvester refers to the main developments in modern painting. Thanks to them (Matisse, Picasso, Klee, Mondrian, etc.), it is now each work's first task to present a configuration of shapes, colours and marks:

> ...before the work conveys reality it must achieve its own reality, before it can be a symbol it must rejoice in being a fact, and the more it affirms its autonomous reality the more will it contain the possibility of returning us to the reality of life.

'William Tillyer 1956–1996: paintings, constructions, drawings, prints', January 17– March 16, 1997, the Whitworth Art Gallery, Manchester.

Matthew Collings Weighs In
(at 12 stone 3 ounces)

Hi! Here's all the things I'm going to be writing about. The Jasper Johns and Ellsworth Kelly retrospectives in New York. 'Life/Live' in Paris. Schnabel's Basquiat. Mary Harron's I Shot Andy Warhol. A film about the preposterous French popiste Niki de Saint Phalle. And a film about Nico called Nico Icon. Hey isn't it great that Nico's name is an anagram of Icon! Mine is only an anagram for athmewt, which isn't even a word! What else? The Turner Prize. Two Angus Fairhurst exhibitions. The time I bumped into Sarah Lucas in Holloway Road and nothing happened. Well I might not write about that. Abigail Lane's Friday afternoon haircut soirées in her studio. An exhibition about painting at MOMA in Oxford. Rachel Whiteread cheering up all the holocaust survivors. Then I'll probably have some thoughts about Robert Hughes's TV series. And – I don't know, whatever!

The Turner Prize

So, the Turner Prize. Blimey, what a lark. Surely Douglas Gordon is just incredibly pretentious? Except, there's no reliable formula for pretentiousness in art. For example, pretentious = bad, or not pretentious = good. In fact, Douglas Gordon has done at least two good things – *24 Hour Psycho* and another one with a man with wobbly legs from shell shock.

The Body

Just because I'm not pretentious, that doesn't mean I'm good. For example, I'm quite shallow. I'm obsessed with my appearance. And my weight, which isn't even very high now. Every morning I step on the scales, but only if I don't have any clothes on, and after removing my glasses which only weigh about two ounces. And then I have to really peer down at the LED reading, and that probably changes the reading slightly anyway. But I'm not quite six feet tall and this morning I weighed twelve stone three pounds, which is good.

What I read

Last week a letter came to *Modern Painters* from France. It said, what does Matthew Collings read? Wow, I was really flattered. Anyway, I can tell you now I really read a lot of art magazines. *Art Monthly, Freize, Artforum* – everything. Also, when I went to Paris I started Balzac's *Lost Illusions*, which I'm definitely going to go on with, at some point. And when I went to New York I started a book by Philip Roth that had *Sabbath* in the title. It was disgusting and depressing, although it was extremely well written. I admire Philip Roth because he is very observant and has a fantastic ear for dialogue, and also a sense of people's inner monologues and the angry things they're thinking. But I stopped really bothering to read him in about 1980 and this is the first one I've read since then, although I didn't finish it because I lost it at the airport on my way back to London.

Broadway Diner

I was reading it in the diner near my hotel, when I was some granola, yoghurt and fruit salad – which I thought would cause further weight loss, but when I got back to London I'd only not put any more weight on than I had when I left; so remember, granola, yoghurt and fruit salad, surprisingly high in calories – when the waitress came up and said, 'Oh why are you reading that?' And I said, 'Uh?', and she started telling me how she was on a creative writing course that Philip Roth was teaching once, and he was quite insane. So I said, 'How could you tell he was insane? Were his clothes very shabby? Didn't he wash?' And she said, 'You're very sharp. There's the issue of negligence.' And I couldn't tell if this was a point of mental health theory generally, or confirmation that, yes, he really looked deranged and he was dribbling in class. But she overrode my frowning with more of her story, which was just a stream of assertions really. She said the other college staff all laughed at Philip Roth and played him

This is not Matthew Collings being pretentious, it's Douglas Gordon, Turner Prize winner. Photo: Douglas Gordon

for a fool. And the students covered up for him because he was their father figure. But he was holding out a sword and they were just throwing themselves on it. And he gave them bad grades because they weren't pretty, and then stole their ideas and put them in *Patrimony*. And she was going to publish her memoir about him now that Claire Bloom's book about their marriage was out. Then she gave me her phone number in New York and I politely gave her mine in London. But when I was on the plane I was nervous because I thought she looked mentally ill herself.

1983

On the other hand, there really is something creepy about Philip Roth. I was in a hamburger place in Fulham Road once, in about 1983, and he came in with a really famous London artist, and they were both talking disgustingly about the waitress and women and stuff, and I was surprised to find myself feeling slightly disturbed, even though of course I'm just a normal guy mantype myself.

London, Tate Gallery

But back to the Turner Prize. Simon Patterson. Good. Craigie Horsefield. I don't like that work personally but that doesn't mean he isn't good. Gary Hume. Good. However, at the private view I bumped into the art writer and author Mel Gooding, and he said he had reservations about Gary Hume's paintings and that for him they lacked a certain metaphysical element. My eyelids started drooping but then he said he was one of the judges of the Turner Prize this year. So after that I was really careful to try and remember what he said, so I could put it in this diary. But he only said he liked Simon Patterson's big spectrum coloured wall with 'Nirvana' and 'Xanadu' and 'Cloud Nine' non-sequiturishly written on it, and I think that was only because we were standing in front of it. And then he said he was going to come to my studio and buy a photo-text artwork I

Simon Patterson, First Circle, *1996, wall painting.* ©*The artist. Photo: Marcus Leith*

made last June which described how I was kidnapped once, when I was a teenager, which is in an edition of ten.

Pensées

My favourite literary style is the fragmented Pascal style of great thoughts just tumbling casually onto the page. For example, what do you think of Rachel Whiteread? She's dreadful isn't she? Isn't it amazing the way everyone takes her seriously. It's incredible. She just casts the space under a table in plaster and because it's a positive shape of an empty space it's poetic. But that's a really literal idea of what poetry is, isn't it? Another one who's just as bad is Anthony Gormley.

Robert Hughes. He wrote one good book, which was about the history of the convicts in Australia in the nineteenth century. I read it in 1988. It's the most gripping story, fantastically well researched and finely written, all about cannibalism and aborigines and stuff. But I don't think he really knows anything about contemporary art does he? Why do they have him in *Time* magazine and on TV? It's a mystery.

What else? Bruce Nauman – good, but we don't want to hear any more about him. Louise Bourgeois, same. Damien Hirst, not even all that good, but, yes, same. Except his restaurant will probably be really good.

New York

The first thing I did on that trip to New York was go to the Angelika cinema and see Schnabel's film *Basquiat*, which I had really been looking forward to, because I like everything he does, and I like Basquiat too.

The film was quite good but there were a few problems. The artworld characters were very listless. They really needed to eat more cornflakes. This was true unfortunately just as much for the central character, played by Jeffrey Pierce, as all the others. And there was some very embarrassing writing, particularly all the lines given to Gary Oldham, who was playing Schnabel. Everything he said was grating and pretentious and it reminded you how weirdly split the real Schnabel often seems to be, between being a really sensitive, talented, funny, handsome, rocking, groovy kind of a guy, and an utter git.

David Bowie plays Andy Warhol, as is well known, and the first time the film really warms up is the first scene with him in it. And after that all the Warhol scenes are good, and gradually you start to get gripped by the story. Not just because, by the natural law of the cinema, you start to identify with the hero, however tedious and floppy he unfortunately is being. But also because there really are some genuinely good things about this film. There are some very good insights in it about artworld psychology, and how envy works, and the problems and confusions that can arise for artists when they get early success.

There's a moment when Basquiat gives a painting to the art writer René Ricard, who was Basquiat's most significant early champion. Basquiat writes Ricard's name on the painting, so that it becomes part of the general improvised graffiti, with the date and the time of day underneath the name. And then, when Ricard has left the studio, he paints it out again. At the private view of his exhibition, later on, he gives the same painting away again, this time to someone more important, the Swiss art dealer Bruno Bishofsburger, played by Dennis Hopper. Ricard pulls a very good face of pain and dismay when he witnesses this act. Until that point the writer and the artist had been kind of feeding off each other, but then suddenly Basquiat is confused about where his loyalties lie, or what betrayal actually is. Then after the opening, in a restaurant crowded with artworld types, Ricard behaves badly and nobody's quite sure why, and they don't care and they just think he's being a prima donna as usual, not realising the pain he's in. Schnabel's writing in these areas is very smart and compassionate.

Another good moment is when a self-styled sculptor, played by Willem Dafoe, who works as an electrician at Mary Boone's, solemnly says to Basquiat, who's also doing a spot of manual labouring there, that he's 40 years old and he's glad he's never had any recognition as an artist, because it's given him the freedom 'to develop'. Everyone in the cinema laughed at that one, although it made me feel a bit uncomfortable because I was 41 this year.

The Angelika is an arthouse cinema, so the audiences there are always very sophisticated. But an interesting point about ordinary cinemas in America, and New York is no exception, is that the audiences are really sickos. They talk to the screen and laugh uproariously all through the film, whatever has happened, and whenever anyone is shot, they clap and cheer.

Another good thing about *Basquiat* – something that, to me, makes it visually the best artworld film ever – is that Schnabel painted all the Basquiats in the film, and they all look stunning. Every scene that has art in it looks authentic and great, including the scenes in Schnabel's own real-life studio with his own real-life paintings in it.

Jasper Johns

The next day I went to the opening of the Jasper Johns retrospective. Here's a good formula: Jasper Johns resisting Modernism in the '50s and '60s = good. Jasper Johns giving in to Post-modernism from the '70s onwards = strangely boring. So that's another mystery, since he kind of invented Post-modernism, along with David Bowie.

The thing Johns was good at was not taking the art rhetoric of the time when he was developing as an artist – which was the early '50s – as his only reference. But instead taking all the doubts about the rhetoric too, and making them just as important. God, that was a good idea.

The first part of this exhibition, then, is extremely fine. But then when he went off the boil in the '70s, he forgot about the doubts and started really going for the art rhetoric, which by now was mostly about him, in a big way, and only making paintings for upmarket zombie scholars and curators to write about. And that's been going on steadily until today.

Nowadays he does paintings full of tantalising clues – about his autobiography, about philosophical and perceptual puzzles, about the big questions of human existence, about the mysteries of great art, modern and pre-modern. But the paintings are done in a dull, energy-less way, and they don't have the amazing Cézannian luxurious robustness and pizzaz that made his earlier paintings, where the subject matter was always from the ordinary world, so expressive and moving.

In the first part of the exhibition, the genius part, you go around marvelling at the surfaces, the graphic facility, the stuttering edges, the spring of every mark, the tension between grids and gestures, the inspired choices of ordinary world subject matter, like knives and forks, or coat hangers, the genius way he has of doing something impulsively that doesn't mean much – like a smudge, or silk-screening onto the canvas a photo of some scribbly instruction or other ('Make fork seven inches long') – and then going back and doing something else in relation to it, and then another thing, and another thing, and so on, until there's this whole amazing cathedral-like edifice, all going nowhere and meaning nothing, or so it seems, but actually being incredibly arresting and thoughtful and rich.

So, early Johns is quite rightly widely regarded as an amazing high point of post-war art. Plus also of course, he was a very good-looking man when he was young, with really good taste, and a great name that he didn't even make up.

But after that it's all Eric Clapton after Cream, and everybody still clapping even though nothing is happening.

Ellsworth Kelly

I saw this retrospective at the Guggenheim Museum and it was a very beautiful and visually enjoyable show. One room has a lot of drawings and collages and rough proto-types for paintings. This was fabulous. He gets his shapes from nature instead of just out of his head or from rulers. He has a strange Christian name and he really knows how to do those big flat areas, and he is obvi-ously a very good decorative artist. But I can't think of anything else interesting to say about him. Green. Good. Red. Good. Etc.

Peter Saul

Also in New York I saw an exhibition of new paintings at an uptown gallery by the not very well known '60s Pop artist Peter Saul. He was always very funny but not stylisti-cally quite right, and he never really made it big. In the '70s he did some funny paint-ings of Donald Duck in the style of de Kooning's *Woman on a Bicycle*.

In this new exhibition he had a painting of the art writers Peter Schejldahl and Hilton Kramer committing suicide, called *Art Suicide*. A painted caption read: 'Too stupid to look at painting they think about art', which I thought was a bit harsh. Two more captions, in the form of cartoon speech balloons coming from Kramer's and Schejl-dahl's mouths, read, respectively: 'Bad art is wrong Dead art is good' and 'Minimalism is alive Painting is dead'. All the other paint-ings had a similarly angry tone, but they were all very good, quite large, executed in a neurotic, highly labour-intensive, speckly, pointillist style, in dry acrylics.

There was a really twisted one about O J Simpson with very strange thought and speech balloons, and O J's lawyer, Johnnie Cochran, represented as a penis in a hotdog, saying 'Relax Boss'. Another caption read, inexplicably, 'Battury asid rilly hertz'.

Angus Fairhurst I

After that I went to a gallery in SoHo run by Baselitz's son, Anton Kern. The exhibi-tion there was a sleeping bag on the floor, called *Sleeping Bag*, and a hand-made gorilla suit, called *An Ill-fitting Gorilla Suit*. There was also a video. When I got back to London I mentioned I'd seen this show to Angus Fairhurst, the artist who's show it was, and he said showing the video wasn't his idea, he only meant to show the sleeping bag and the gorilla suit. When I was at the exhibition I asked Anton Kern if he was planning to show lots more young British art, and at first he was very blasé and said, in his German-international-American

Nico-Icon, *director: S Ofteringer.*
ICA Projects release

accent, 'Oh no, no, it's just boring, nation-ality'. But I tortured him mercilessly and finally he admitted the young British artists were definitely the hot ones, and absolutely no one doesn't think that.

Meg Ryan

Then I went to Dean and DeLuca to get some low calorie carrot cake, but you can't smoke in there, so I tried to go outside and sit on the stoop, but I got waved back inside because they were shooting a film in the street, with Meg Ryan and Matthew Brod-erick, called *Addicted to Love*.

London, ICA

So, yes, those other art films. *Nico Icon* is the best. It's the top film on art, except for one stylistic tick, where sometimes frag-ments of sentences that people are saying

Peter Saul, Donald Duck Descending a Staircase, 1979, synthetic polymer paint on canvas, 198.1 x 134 cm. Courtesy Fisher Fine Art, London

are suddenly captioned on the screen, as they're speaking. Don't do that, directors!

I didn't see it in New York, because its run was already ended over there, but at the ICA, and I can really recommend it. Nico started being an icon in the late '50s in Germany. She was in Fellini's *La Dolce Vita* and many magazine and TV ads. She went to Paris and had an affair with Alain Delon and a baby by him called Ari. Alain refused to acknowledge Ari as his son, but – magnificently – Alain's old mother leapt up and insisted on bringing up the baby herself. And then Alain disowned his mother! It's incredible. And he hasn't spoken to her since! In the film Alain's mother pointed out how modestly she lived. It was clear her heart was broken and she'd really suffered in life. And then a fabulous old bohemian man in a little shabby flat was interviewed and he sounded like he might have been English once, and it turned out he had been Nico's friend in Paris in the old days, and he said she didn't like sex anyway, and that Alain Delon was just a butcher, which was almost literally true as he really did come from a famous family who were in the meat trade.

So then Nico was in the Velvet Under-ground in New York and of course that was really great, with Andy Warhol and The Factory and everything. Because of that, Nico became the rock icon we now remember. But – even greater – after that she didn't want to be beautiful and blonde, so she just lost her looks and stopped dyeing her hair, and she got suddenly older and put on weight, and suddenly she looked quite frightening, like something from Polanski's *Dance of the Vampires*.

And when her old friends from The Factory said 'Gee, Nico, why are you looking like that, you look bad!', she was glad. She had chosen the route of art, and the route of negativity. So she started her endless touring – doing gigs that nobody liked much – which went on until her death a few years ago, from a brain haemorrhage. As the film went on, she looked worse and worse, with her formerly beautiful big blue eyes kind of hanging out of her head, horribly. And her singing was all droney, in a magnificent nineteenth-century doomed poet way.

Then after about ten years or so she got Ari back and took him around with her, on the tours. But by now she was a heroin addict. She first bought heroin in Paris, in Pigalle, in 1971, and she soon became hooked. Pretty soon she got poor Ari hooked too, and they used to fix each other up. Yuk! It was a disgusting story. And she lived in squalor with no heating, with a succession of addict guys, who were film makers or musicians. Addicts in attics. Oh, it was painful. But the tale is very well told in this film, and the times are very well evoked, with intelligently researched and edited interviews, and inspired use of archive footage and good music.

Poor Ari was on a life support machine at one stage, because of his addiction, and Nico went to visit him and heartlessly recorded the sound for one of her records. When we finally meet him towards the end of the film, he looks stunningly beautiful, like Alain Delon, but with long hair, like something from Fellini's *Satyricon*. He's about 30 now, with a jaded air, but it's clear he's still a poor maladjusted Eurotrash teenager at heart.

New York again

Another art film I saw in New York was *I Shot Andy Warhol*, about Valerie Solanas, who wrote the *SCUM* (Society for Cutting Up Men) *Manifesto*. This is a surprisingly good film, too. Traditionally, dramas set in the artworld are wooden and stupid, but this one has a lot of energy. The main good thing about it is all the quotes from Solanas's book, which the actress playing the lead role, Lily Taylor, reads to camera, as if auditioning. Valerie Solanas was an inspired writer and the underrated and misunderstood *Manifesto* is really rapid-fire, vivid, violent, funny stuff. If she hadn't been mad she would have made a brilliant journalist or novelist, or terrorist even. Or young British artist.

Solanas shot Andy Warhol in 1968. Lily Taylor's performance is impressive, but after a while she's a bit too cute – Oliver Twist urchin-cute. You can really believe Solanas was unhinged, but from this performance she's so cute you can't believe she wouldn't have been better cared for. In reality, although she was released from prison only a few years after the shooting, she simply drifted away, loved by nobody, and her death in the '80s was a terrible one – alone in a welfare hotel room, her body eaten by maggots.

Everybody in the film acts well – particularly the Warhol actor, Jared Harris, son of Richard Harris, who gets Warhol's streak of kindness and his genuine curiosity about the world, as well as Warhol's looks, very well.

New York, 1986

Hey I interviewed Andy Warhol once! It was a very halting and awkward affair. But when I got the audiotape back to London the art writer Stuart Morgan kindly edited it for me, and so when it was finally published it seemed not only coherent but very funny too, and kind of clever of me to have thought of interviewing him at that time, which was a few months before his death. But the reality was that, when I went to do the interview, I just thought he was a sell-out and a has-been, and he hadn't been good since about 1965.

So I turned up at the place where Warhol's studio and the offices of *Interview* magazine were, which was just called The Studio now, not The Factory, and I met Brigid Polk, and she told me to wait, so I did, and there were a few Basquiat collaboration paintings knocking about, and then Warhol came in. I wasn't as observant then as I am now and I didn't even really stare at his wig – I don't think I even knew it was a wig – let alone check what shoes he was wearing. But

Chris Ofili, Captain Shit and the Legend of the Black Stars, *1996, 243.8 x 182.8 cm*

I think it was the usual get-up, with new jeans and black top and '60s-style Chelsea boots and wig and everything. I was quite disdainful, I suppose, in my ignorance, and I just asked him a few questions about Americanism and European art and if he had his own ideas or if Brigid had them all, and he was quite straightforward and intelligent and witty. And when it was clear I obviously hadn't done my homework about him, he wasn't sarcastic or impatient. And he tried to be reassuring when I started to get nervous, when I realised I was out of my depth.

New York now, again

I went to see a film at another arthouse cinema about Niki de Saint Phalle. I was full of good expectations, but it was a very disappointing film. Niki de Saint Phalle used to make artworks in the early '60s by shooting a rifle at balloons filled with paint, and letting the paint spatter and run down found objects stuck to a surface of white

Glenn Brown, I Lost my Heart to a Starship Trooper *(detail), 1996, oil on canvas, mounted on board, 65 x 50 cm*

plaster. She documented the shootings – which were often performed with famous artist friends – and exhibited the resulting objects as assemblages, which was the funky style of the time, like Johns and Rauschenburg. They looked great. She was great. But then she started doing big painted fibreglass sculptures of cartoony big-breasted goddess women, and they were bad. And she went on doing that more or less all the time. This documentary film about her that I saw – I can't remember the title – is very tedious. She does her own commentary and it's all rubbishy clichés that don't communicate anything.

So that's another failed formula: documentaries about art = good, dramas about art = bad. In fact documentaries can be bad and dramas can be good.

But still, the film has something going for it. Her life was thoroughly documented from a very young age, and it's fascinating to see anyone's life unfolding on screen like that, from young to old. Also it ends on an up note. Her husband Tinguely died a few years ago, and after that she was a bit depressed and got asthma badly and was on an oxygen cylinder all the time. So she went to live in La Jolla in California, and now, in her 70s, she's a new woman and does hang-gliding and she paints the whales at Seaworld.

Studio 54

Also in New York I found myself at a dinner in a restaurant with the art writer and author Anthony Haden Guest. He kept running downstairs to phone LA to check if an important million dollar deal had come through. And he responded to anything I said in a slightly different timing to the one I was using, as if his dialogue had been incorrectly synched in post-production. So I felt quite intimidated by him. He said his forthcoming book of artworld recollections, called *True Colours*, was going to be good because 'I was at all those events, I was at the opening of Studio 54, I got laid there, I shot up there'. I listened respectfully, of course, but after he'd gone I thought I should have questioned him more closely on that line. Hey, what was it like? Are you an addict now?

Museum of Modern Art, Oxford

'About Vision'. This is an exhibition sponsored by Absolut Vodka of young British painting. All the paintings look a bit boring except Chris Offili's. There's really a lot going on in his stuff and you can go on looking at it. The show is incredibly vulgarly hung, without any intelligence, but also a lot of young British painters are just boring aren't they? The young British artists who don't do painting are better. One part of the exhibition is all abstracts. The other part is all figurative, except Fiona Rae. Only in a way she's figurative too because she does representations of abstractions, so maybe that's the one sophisticated part of the hanging.

At the private view there's a lot of vodka going round. Glenn Brown's incredibly skilled copy of a Rembrandt is called *I lost my heart to a starship trooper*, which was a song by Andrew Lloyd Webber's wife when she was in *Pan's People*, as I remember, but when somebody told me this title I thought they said, I lost my moustache to a starship trooper, which made sense for me in that moment, because I thought the Rembrandt was a youthful self portrait, which I thought I remembered as having a wispy moustache. So I was talking at drunken cross-purposes with Glenn Brown for a while, until he realised I thought one of the Post-modern things he'd done was to remove the moustache, whereas in fact it was a very famous painting of a woman.

In the abstract room there's two very big black paintings by Jason Martin with pretentious titles, *Geronimo* and *Shamen*. Maybe *Geronimo* isn't pretentious, just plodding. But I don't think you can get away with *Shamen* nowadays.

Paris

'Life/Live' is an exhibition of young British art not confined to any one medium but open to them all, including film. One film is by Steve McQueen, whose name is easy to forget because it sounds wrong. This is an excellent film, although it doesn't sound like much when you describe it. I'm having a block now, trying to think how to describe it.

I don't know, maybe it wasn't excellent. Patricia Bickers, the editor of *Art Monthly*, said it was, when we saw each other in the room where the film was showing, and I was so impressed by her confidence in her own judgement I've been kind of going along with the thought ever since, going around saying 'Steve McQueen, excellent'.

Another film in the show is *English Rose* by the writer and curator Carl Freedman. This is another difficult film to make sense of in writing, but for different reasons. Steve McQueen's film is very simple, the camera pointing upwards at a black man, walking along, the frame showing only a head bobbing up and down along the bottom edge, and a lot of white sky. The frame is enlarged to take up the whole space of a wall, with the effect that the head is bobbing up and down, coming in and out of sight, on floor level. The soundtrack is something sensitive and unidentifiable, like Eric Satie. It's just a really good film, like a good sequence from a Spike Lee film but with all the rhetoric and heavy underlining of thoughts that Spike Lee has to do, because he's Spike Lee, removed, and something slight but poignant left behind.

But *English Rose* is quite different in mood. It is a kind of office Christmas party satire, a pantomime of young British art, with three young British artists all playing each other in three separate sequences. Gillian Wearing plays Tracey Emin, Tracey Emin plays Georgina Starr, and Georgina Starr plays Gillian Wearing. These are all

Jared Harris in I Shot Andy Warhol, *director: Mary Harron*

very good artists. They dress up and do improvised gags and they're very funny and silly, and the jokes are all unbelievably insulting and savage. But to run through them here I'd have to explain the references and it would be really exhausting, so that's my only problem with that film.

'Life/Live' is about the young scene, but there are some oldsters in it too, like Gilbert and George, David Medalla and Gustav Metzger. David Medalla has suddenly popped up again recently, doing a lot of performances. He was already around before, in the '70s, and then you didn't see him so much. Then the other night I saw him doing a performance in Great Titchfield Street, and he was saying how marvellous young British art is, as part of the performance. That was really desperate, I thought. But I shouldn't knock him. He's all woolly and positive and cuddly and '60s, in a harmless way.

In one of the chambers of the Musée that has a Dufy mural describing the discovery of electricity I think, there's some videos showing short films by artists. They're all quite bad except for one with Gilbert and George, where they're just intoning their rules of what art is. Everything they do is good.

All the other spaces are allocated to various independent British galleries, like City Racing, Bank, Cubitt Street, Transmis-

Gillian Wearing is Tracey Emin in English Rose, *curated by Carl Freedman*

sion and so on, so the exhibition is like a three-dimensional map of the alternative London and Glasgow art scenes, with each gallery putting on its own little show. That makes the show as a whole quite lively, since you're never quite sure what's going to be around the next corner – whereas with most young British art shows you always know exactly what's going to be around the next corner – but also, unfortunately, quite scrappy and unmemorable. I can only remember the stuff I've been writing about because I knew I'd be having to write about it. One artist who was there was Donald Parsnips who publishes a newspaper every day and hands out copies to anyone who will take it. That's a good idea.

Angus Fairhurst II

I went to an opening at White Cube in Duke Street St James, and Jarvis Cocker was there, and that was groovy. The exhibition was by Angus Fairhurst, and that's a coincidence because I was just writing about him. There was a video showing an animated gorilla being split into separate parts, with the parts turning into fizzy abstract patterns on the screen, like interference on a TV set, or computer graphics. And then in the next room the same were on some paintings which, Angus Fairhurst said, were done by trained monkeys.

Westbourne Grove

Guy Healey. He is very handsome and a good hairdresser. When he was cutting my hair today he said he goes to the young British conceptual artist Abigail Lane's haircutting *soirées* every Friday in her studio, where he does haircuts for artists. You get your hair done by Guy and then you can get a certificate by Abigail Lane that looks like that 1920s or '30s collage by Marcel Duchamp, that looks like a souvenir from a roulette game. So in a way that's saying that every haircut is a gamble as well as conceptual art. □

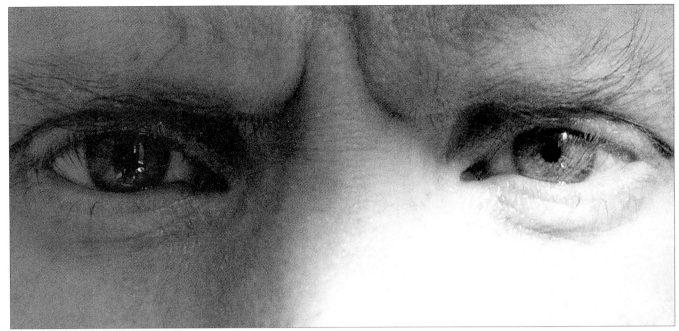

Robert Mapplethorpe, Self Portrait, *1988*

Robert Mapplethorpe: Squandering Beauty

Looking beyond the scandals, **Lisa Jardine** *considers whether the 'bad boy' produced 'good art'.*

In June 1984 wealthy New York socialite Sam Wagstaff, Robert Mapplethorpe's one-time lover and long-term patron, sold his entire magnificent photography collection (except his Mapplethorpes) to the Getty Museum for 4.5 million dollars. For ten years or more Wagstaff had spent all his collecting energies, and much of his considerable wealth, on building up a unique collection of early photography that had largely contributed to raising the medium from popular to high art status. Once a collector of modern paintings, he had become a major influence in persuading the élite connoisseur community of North America that photography was the art – and above all the art market – of the future.

With the money from the Getty, Wagstaff immediately began again from scratch in pursuit of his latest passion: he started to collect late nineteenth- and early twentieth-century ornate American silverware. His stated ambition was to raise the status of this currently unfashionable commodity (and the price of items he had acquired before the 'vogue') just as he had that of photography over the course of the late '70s and early '80s. And, as with photography, Wagstaff's interest in silverware developed into something close to an obsession. Pieces flooded into his penthouse apartment, acquired in haste through agents all over the United States. Wagstaff read up avidly on silver, pursued unusual items determinedly, and spared no expense to ensure that he personally owned anything regarded by specialists as 'important'. Shortly before he died of AIDS in 1987, he spent 80,000 dollars on a single bizarre piece which one of his agents had tracked down, and which he wanted as the centrepiece for an exhibition of his silver at the New York Historical Society.

Robert Mapplethorpe was already indignant at Wagstaff's defection from photography to silverware. He threw a violent scene when he discovered the cost of the centrepiece – a silver bowl supported by four elaborately caparisoned elephants. Mapplethorpe stood to inherit a substantial portion of Wagstaff's fortune and was outraged at his benefactor's death-bed squandering of vast sums of money on what he regarded as vulgar and 'hideous' pieces of non-art. But of course he was also angry at the implied suggestion that his own artistic reputation might have been 'made' by Wagstaff in a similar kind of way – that the conscientious investor in a particular art market could raise the status (and price) of particular artists' work at will.

Nor did this seem to some a far-fetched proposition at the time. Shortly before Mapplethorpe's own death in 1989, Holly Solomon, one of the art dealers who contributed to establishing Mapplethorpe's reputation as a major artist, recalled the crucial part Sam Wagstaff had played in that process.

> Sam was considered the great photography collector. He had many people who believed in him, especially me. I wouldn't have touched Robert without Sam, and there were others like me who felt the same way.[1]

When Mapplethorpe and Sam Wagstaff met in 1972, Mapplethorpe was 25. He was a single-mindedly celebrity-seeking participant in the art scene in New York, sharing a loft with the equally exhibitionist Patti Smith (his lifelong friend and kindred spirit). His interventions in the world of avant-garde art and underground culture had been calculated to shock and to provoke, and had included (in 1970) the starring role in Sandy Daley's short movie *Robert Having His Nipple Pierced.*[2] His artistic reputation was largely self-concocted and contrived; his financial situation was precarious. Sam set him up in a new apartment, and within six months of the beginning of their relationship

Mapplethorpe had his first exhibition – of polaroid photographs at the Light Gallery on Madison Avenue. Their sexual passion for one another cooled (Mapplethorpe was, in any case, pathologically promiscuous, and incapable of sexual fidelity, even where it might be materially to his advantage). But Wagstaff continued to support Mapplethorpe financially, and to promote him vigorously as an artist of genius, for the rest of his life.

It is easy, then, to construct a scenario which suggests that Mapplethorpe himself might have been elevated from attention-grabbing taker of pornographic snapshots and assiduous social climber to celebrity artist by Wagstaff's by no means disinterested enthusiasm, influence and cash. However, I do not think that such an explanation is any longer plausible, nor do I believe that the extraordinary impact the exhibited work now makes can be ascribed to any crude process of 'special pleading' on behalf of sexually explicit art against the reactionaries.

So what is it that makes Mapplethorpe's work, so convincingly, 'good art'? The answer to that question is certainly complicated. Arthur Danto has argued that there was only a brief moment in 1988 when it was possible to assess Mapplethorpe's work impartially, before it became 'notorious' and critics were forced to take sides (significantly, Danto's important 1988 review in *The Nation* of the Whitney Gallery exhibition claims real artistic significance for Mapplethorpe). But I think that in the seven years since his death it has become possible to look in a less strained manner at the relationship between the image-making in which Mapplethorpe undoubtedly indulged – his self-publicised role as ultimate artistic bad boy – and the quality of the work he produced over a period of 25 years of artistic experimentation.

The Mapplethorpe exhibition at the Hayward Gallery in London this autumn was almost unbearably beautiful. It also had an energy and an urgency about it which was difficult to resist – which was, indeed, I think, irresistible. After many years of tut-tutting over reproductions of Mapplethorpe photographs (including the infamous 'X portfolio', reproduced in its entirety by the Journal of the College Art Association of America) I was astounded by the impact these same pictures made, framed and hung as their creator intended. Confronted with the original compositions – brilliantly selected by Germano Celant of the Guggenheim Museum, New York, and intelligently hung by Claudio Silvestrin – any simple suggestion that Mapplethorpe is overrated, or that the impact of his work depends upon the shock of some of his subject matter and the scandal surrounding his personal behaviour falls to the ground.

It is important, I think, for someone like myself – someone with no vested interest at all, no identity-politics connection of any kind with Mapplethorpe's kind of art – to affirm, on the evidence of the Hayward

Gallery show, that Robert Mapplethorpe is a great original artist. I was frankly predisposed to find the Mapplethorpe exhibition 'voguish' and contrived – some kind of awkward retrospective testimony to the artistic permissiveness of the '60s and '70s, a permissiveness which has all but disappeared under the combined pressures of AIDS, concerted lobbying in the United States by the forces of moral rearmament, and the decimating of public funding of the arts in Britain and North America. I had intellectualised the whole issue of Mapplethorpe's work on the basis of the notorious 1989/90 controversy around art, pornography and censorship which the cancellation of the 'Perfect Moment' exhibition at the Corcoran Gallery of Art in Washington precipitated. I had persuaded myself that the 'Mapplethorpe phenomenon' had been artificially constructed out of a volatile cocktail of political correctness and notoriety. But if there is a 'Mapplethorpe phenomenon', then, on the basis of my response to the exhibition at the Hayward Gallery, I am bound to admit that I have succumbed to it.

So I began to think about that phenomenon, and when I did so it was natural for me to start by looking for Mapplethorpe's patron. For in the course of my work as a historian looking at Renaissance art purchasing and taste I had come to believe that all taste in fine art emerged out of commercial ventures, trade and exchange of goods, with wealthy patrons playing the key role in establishing the 'worth' of collectable items. The antique cameos and contemporary engraved gemstones for which collectors like Pope Paul II and Cardinal Francesco Gonzaga paid substantial sums of money in Rome in the mid-fifteenth century acquired inflated value and status as covetable possessions, largely as a consequence of their enthusiasm: half a century after their deaths, Isabella d'Este in Mantua was trying to purchase items from their collections for her own, in what by then had become an inflated market (her agent warned that there were people around who were prepared to pay 'a fortune' to get their hands on them).

But my work on Renaissance patronage had taught me something more. Renaissance collectors were obsessively hungry for the objects of their desire, just like Sam Wagstaff. A good deal of what they collected no longer interests us. Much of it has disappeared or disintegrated through neglect and the passage of time. Those precious objects to which we continue to give attention, however – the panel paintings and canvases, the bronzes and marbles which fill our museums – are now invested with a preeminent aesthetic value which matches, or possibly even exceeds, any cash value we might like to attach to them. They have achieved, in other words, an assured status which defines contemporary educated taste. Our taste is defined and shaped by these very objects.

Was it possible that this is what had

happened to Mapplethorpe's work? The key point to notice in the Renaissance case is that the selection process over time involved a significant element of wastage – a metaphorical discarding or jettisoning of whole segments of the taste of earlier periods, to leave a kernel of the 'timelessly' beautiful. Was there any sense, I asked myself, in which something similar had happened or, possibly, was happening, in the case of Mapplethorpe?

After my visit to the Hayward Gallery, buoyed up by my sense of having discovered a transcendent beauty in the Mapplethorpes exhibited there, the first thing I did was go back to the published books of his photographs to check my sense that these 'reproductions' had failed to do justice to Mapplethorpe's work. I quickly discovered – or rather, rediscovered – what a keen sense of tact and timeliness had evidently guided Germano Celant's choice of items for the Hayward Gallery exhibition. For you only have to glance (and, speaking for myself, I can only glance) at the rough stuff Mapplethorpe included in an unsettling published volume like the *Black Book* (1986), or the art photography publication of the 'X portfolio', to realise what kind of work Celant chose not to hang, and what a difference what he left out made. Not, I hasten to add, because of any kind of deliberate censorship, but rather in the interests of a kind of tense, instructive logic which the juxtapositions and running sequences of hung composite and single photographs set out to convey – what Arthur Danto has called, with reference to an earlier Mapplethorpe occasion, the exhibition's 'syntax'.[3]

The work Celant has chosen for the travelling exhibition – which has now moved on from the Hayward Gallery to Dublin – strives strenuously and self-consciously for artistic 'meaning' in Mapplethorpe's work. This is clear, for example, in the way pornographic images, portraits and formal flower photographs are hung as matched runs (similarly printed and framed), as if to say: it makes no difference, the perfection of the image is the same. Or in the way that Celant chooses to retain the now rather dated '70s frames – silk panels, velvet borders – for some of the photographs which one might associate with something like a 'gay aesthetic', as if to pinpoint the moment – the period of fear-free sexual confidence – to which those images belong. Above all, Celant never crosses some indefinable threshold between what the 'ordinary' art-lover can contemplate with (relative) equanimity and the darkly dangerous.

By contrast, books of Mapplethorpe photographs select flagrantly for audience – books of flower photographs, portraits, gay icons, S & M. The flowers and portraits take on an aura of (for me) almost suffocating archness and glossiness in book form. The sexualised, erotic photographs acquire somehow, in the privacy of the relationship between image and viewer on the printed page, a possibility for prurience or salaciousness, for complicity, which is unsettling for those of us who do not customarily scrutinise pornographic pictures. The contrast between their compositional brilliance and the disturbing nature of the acts they without reservation represent simultaneously attracts and disgusts. They remind me of those photographs of dead and mutilated bodies – casualties of innumerable worldwide acts of inhumanity and violence – which *Paris Match* used to go in for, and which as a child I both did and did not want to look at, flicking through the magazine on my parents' bedside table. But that is not all. The photographs we (or at least I) do not want to look at are additionally troubling precisely because they remind us of what is not shown, but is consciously alluded to in the exhibited photographs.

For when we return to the gallery, we carry those reproduced, art-book images with us. On both occasions I was there I heard earnest fellow gallery-goers exclaiming: 'Oh yes, I've seen that one before'. Meaning, that they had seen it in reproduction – which meant that they had seen other, more devastating images than the one they were currently scrutinising on the gallery wall. That additional 'background reading' informs the way we look at any of the 'great' Mapplethorpe photographs we are seeing in large-format platinum print on high quality paper, linen or canvas, and Germano Celant and Claudio Silvestrin know that and exploit the fact.

Take *Mark Stevens (Mr. 10 1/2), 1976*, which has become something of a classic. Mark Stevens is bent forwards, almost protectively, over his sizeable penis, which is stretched out – displayed – on a textured pedestal. The photograph is closely cropped so that the subject is only seen from forearm (coyly tattooed with a tiny devil) to leather-clad thigh; the pedestal occupies almost half the composition. The shadows cast by the figure create triangles of intensity directing the viewing eye back to the centred penis. And in the end you can't help smiling at the evident vanity with which Stevens sucks in his muscular stomach so as to set his genitals off to even better advantage. But once you have seen a book-reproduction of the Mapplethorpe diptych of a penis and balls bound and trussed into a purpose-made wooden board – intact on the left, bloodied on the right – there is no escaping the fact that *Mark Stevens (Mr. 10 1/2), 1976* persistently recalls those images. It calls them to mind; it exists as the controlled, manageable version of the dangerous others. It reassures us that we inhabit a world whose aesthetic does not require that we damage or inflict pain in order to find erotic pleasure (but which can derive added pleasure, a further frisson, from knowing that the other world is there, not far away).

The same point can be made by looking at 'related' works shown in the exhibition. The carefully juxtaposed photographs of Eva Amurri and Susan Sarandon (both taken in 1988) are at once

Robert Mapplethorpe, Leo Castelli, *1982, gelatin silver print, 50 x 40 cm*

compelling and troubling. A naked Susan Sarandon gazes wide-eyed directly at the camera, her nostrils slightly dilated, her lips sensuously parted. Her hair is tousled. She clutches a length of velvet to her breasts, her fingers spread to protect her modesty. The infant Eva Amurri is also naked. She gazes at the camera with an expression uncannily similar to Sarandon's. Her hair is tousled. Her clasped hands cover her genitals, with her right elbow angled in a tiny reminiscence of Sarandon's. With an inevitability that I personally find terrifying, little Eva becomes saturated with Sarandon's sexual knowingness, by proximity and association. In this case we are instructed to make the connection: the works are hung side by side. We 'know' that Mapplethorpe was not interested sexually in children, and that he never posed his

Robert Mapplethorpe, Man in Polyester Suit, *1980, gelatin silver print, 50 x 40 cm*

child subjects (he said they were impossible to control). Yet we know with equal certainty that Eva Amurri *becomes* a sexual subject.

The meaningfulness of Mapplethorpe's pictures is constantly intensified, modulated and magnified by the visual connections between the images seen and the images unseen, between the formal photographs (including portraits) and the sexualised photographs, between the images we want to acknowledge as 'art' and those we would rather not. Because we 'know about' Mapplethorpe, because we have scanned the rough and dangerous images (even, I suspect, if we haven't seen them, but know that such dark images exist), *Watermelon and Knife, 1985* becomes a visual metaphor for the consented-to mutilation of flesh – becomes related indeed to the series of 1983 self-portraits of a leather-jacketed Mapplethorpe, brandishing a flick-knife, and beyond the self-portraits, to that troublingly unforgettable *untitled 1978* image from the 'X portfolio' of a squatting, pierced man with initials carved on his body.

At the comic end of this scale of association, there are irresistible visual links between the memorable *Man in Polyester Suit, 1980* and Mapplethorpe's portrait of prominent art dealer Leo Castelli in 1982. Notoriously, *Man in Polyester Suit* is a photograph of a man in a cheap beige three-piece suit. The figure (actually Milton Moore) is cut off at the neck and above the knees. The man's hands are awkwardly to his sides. Between them, hanging to precisely his finger-tips, and framed by the inverted V of the buttoned waistcoat, his large, slightly engorged penis protrudes from his fly, highlighted by an edge of shirt. In the portrait, Castelli wears a light-weight suit, somewhat crumpled around the crotch. His hands are also slightly awkwardly at his sides, holding apart the edges of his single-breasted jacket, caught open in an inverted V by one button, so that the V frames the fly of his trousers. That fly, of course, is closed. But the mildly amused, quizzical expression on Castelli's face seems to suggest that the closed fly registers an *absence*, an omission.

This may be a joke at Castelli's expense. The exhibitions director of the ICA in London, Sandy Nairne, agreed to be photographed by Mapplethorpe in 1983, when the gallery mounted a thirteen-year retrospective of Mapplethorpe's work. He was determined not to allow himself to be manipulated by the artist, but found himself overpowered by Mapplethorpe's sheer force of personality. 'I was suddenly part of the process', Nairne recalls, 'and I felt myself becoming stiff and formalised. Robert was sculpting me into a Mapplethorpe photograph as surely as if I'd been a piece of stone.'[4] It was one thing to consent to be photographed by Mapple-thorpe. It was another to imagine that the bond of trust between photographer and subject would prevent (or even inhibit) Mapplethorpe from incorporating that subject into a larger scheme of creativity, tailored to his own complicated, perverse and above all profoundly narcissistic agenda.

Is it possible that what we are experiencing here is close to that intensifying effect over time of wastage which I referred to as a crucial part of the Renaissance's establishing of our European taste in art? There are certainly closely analogous cases in the history of art. We no longer want to consider a graphically sadistic work of Titian's like his *Flaying of Marsyas* as part of the painter's classic oeuvre, nor do we want to take overly seriously the more overtly pornographic of his nudes, like his *Venus and the Organ Player* (though Renaissance cardinals particularly appreciated them). Those best forgotten paintings, however, stand behind a masterly piece of controlled high art like Titian's *Danaë*: the power of the painting's erotic impact, together with the complexity of the composition owe them a great deal. We 'read' the great works, we appreciate them aesthetically, in terms of those other, discarded traditions and images.

But I think we can take this argument one stage further in the direction I suggested earlier. The Italian churchman, Cardinal Farnese, whose Titian nude, commissioned after he saw the *Venus of Urbino* at Guidobaldo da Montefeltro's summer residence in 1542, was reputed to have made that Venus look like a frigid nun, spent as lavishly, as diversely (in terms of the types of art object he purchased), and, tastewise, as indiscriminately as ever Sam Wagstaff did on his paintings, his photographs or his silver. The soaring artistic stature of what we nowadays associate with the high art of the Villa Farnese, is the reputation of what survives – not of the mass of collectables which has been lost or conveniently forgotten.

I am suggesting that Robert Mapplethorpe's work is a prime example of the principle of artistic wastage – that work which achieves artistic greatness over time depends upon a buried corpus of rejected or discarded work. Or, in the case of Mapplethorpe, of work deliberately squandered. Mapplethorpe poured his creative talents and energies into areas of work to which he was deeply committed because they fulfilled his deepest desires and fantasies. He belonged to a brief moment in recent history when it was apparently possible to pursue one's sexual fantasies to the edge of self-destruction. Except that there turned out to be no edge. If we have turned away from that moment in horror it is because we know all too well what came afterwards. If we have not had to come to terms with Mapplethorpe's most aggressively pornographic

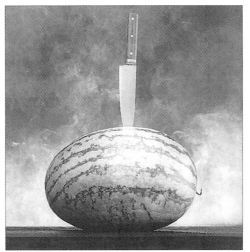

Robert Mapplethorpe, Watermelon with Knife*, 1985, platinum on paper, 66 x 66 cm*

and explicit artistic work it is because the world changed, exempting us from the requirement to try to cope with what we could not conceive of as part of our own lives or pleasures, let alone part of our high culture.

Which brings me back to patronage. The crisis which was precipitated by Robert Mapplethorpe's 1988/9 exhibition, 'The Perfect Moment', broke immediately after his death. This is not an accident. For with Mapplethorpe's death the financial arrangements between patron (Sam Wagstaff) and artist were dissolved, and the National Endowment for the Arts entered into partnership with the estate of Mapplethorpe to finance the exhibitions. The issue around which the 1990 obscenity trial charges centred (charges of which the show was acquitted) was the issue of public funding of such exhibits. It was argued strenuously that it was unacceptable for public funds to be spent on 'art' of this kind.

The outcome of the whole affair amounted to an acknowledgement by the

Robert Mapplethorpe, Self Portrait*, 1983, gelatin silver print, 50 x 40 cm*

public funding bodies that they were indeed not in a position to take the kind of risks that a patron was entitled to take. Of course, I simplify, but I believe that this is the lesson to be learned from 'The Perfect Moment' affair. An individual like Sam Wagstaff is entitled to buy whatever he chooses; he can spend his private money on any kind of material goods he cares to. If some of it is squandered, or goes to waste, that is a purely private matter. As it happens, we were able to see what the inevitable consequence is of a recognition of the requirements on public funding to operate a 'good housekeeping' policy in art purchasing – buying wisely, wasting nothing, keeping even the scraps and left-overs – at the Hayward Gallery, alongside the Mapplethorpe exhibition. Upstairs (admission purchased for the price of the Mapplethorpe entrance ticket) was an exhibition entitled 'Ace!', of recent art purchased for the Arts Council Collection. It is an exhibition of dismal ordinariness. Even the obligatory Rachel Whiteread, Damien Hirst and Wilson twins pieces are quiet, muted and uncontroversial. As for the rest, they could comfortably hang in the average living room. Prominent among them is a series of small oil paintings of pet hamsters.

Taste in art has never been formed by backing politeness. Taste is the residue of fine material objects which patrons over the centuries have purchased, against the grain of the generally acceptable. When I look at the Francis Bacon *Screaming Pope* at the centre of the Sainsbury Collection at the University of East Anglia, I wonder what the Sainsburys' dinner guests thought of it, hanging above their heads as they sipped their coffee. Wagstaff's friends and colleagues were frankly appalled by his passion for Mapplethorpe's raunchier photography, including pieces like *Made in Canada, 1973* which we now regard as masterly. The enduring purchases from collections like these are the foundation for our future artistic heritage, the blueprints for future generations' aesthetic sensibility. Much of the rest of what they bought will fall away and be forgotten. But long may such patrons continue to squander their cash on the inconsequential and the bad – on anything, so long as we're not subjected to Arts Council ordinary until the end of time.

1. Patricia Morrisroe, *Mapplethorpe: A Biography* (London: Macmillan, 1995), p.172.
2. Until I read Mapplethorpe's biography I had no idea that this Robert was Robert Mapplethorpe.
3. Arthur C Danto, *Playing with the Edge: The Photographic Achievement of Robert Mapplethorpe* (Berkeley: University of California Press, 1996). Danto used the phrase of the 1988 exhibition of Mapplethorpe's work at the Whitney Gallery in New York.
4. Morrisroe, *Mapplethorpe*, p.278.

Robert Mapplethorpe, until the end of January, 1997, The Gallery of Photography, Dublin, Ireland. Catalogue: £35.

Julian Mitchell *applauds a new play, but laments a general want of 'art' in contemporary theatre.*

Art, a new play by the French writer Yasmina Reza, is packing them in at the Wyndham's – indeed it's standing room only for this old-fashioned West End comedy about a Parisian dermatologist (a man interested in the surface of things?) who buys a minimalist white picture which upsets his relationships with his two best friends. The three men are played by Albert Finney, Tom Courtenay and Ken Stott, and there's nothing gay or arty about them – far from it, they have sensible jobs and make traditional jokes about mothers-in-law. (You can't imagine how they became friends in the first place, but never mind.) The play is about theatre, not art, though minimalism comes in for the expected middlebrow bashing, and there are a few mild digs at those who buy name artists for social reasons.

Perhaps the scene the audience enjoys most comes right at the beginning. Finney, as the representative of bluff common sense, struggles not to say what he thinks of someone who's just spent 200,000 francs on a white painting; and fails. He has the audience wholly with him. It says a lot for Courtenay, the dermatologist, that he is able to bring the audience round, if not to his side, at least to thinking of him as something more than a mere sucker. But then the whole point of this sort of entertainment is to watch actors exercise their craft. Stott, not yet as famous as the other two, soon will be. He has the best speech, and delivers it superbly. In the old days we would have called *Art* a feast of good acting.

It reminded me, in fact, of a big '50s hit also translated from the French, *The Little Hut*. That was about three people stranded on a desert island – a neat metaphor for star performers on a West-End stage, the stars in that case being Robert Morley, David Tomlinson and Joan Tetzel. Robert Morley (who'd have been Finney in *Art*)

used to improvise so broadly that a play's running time could vary by ten or fifteen minutes. But then the audience went to see him, not the play. Finney, Courtenay and Stott will no doubt soon get bored with their success and start improvising too. The evening will become even more successful. Who wrote *Art*, did I say? Christopher Hampton did the translation, and very good it sounds too, but.. Who wrote and translated *The Little Hut* then? Sorry, I..[1]

There is absolutely no point in getting heavy about *Art*. It succeeds brilliantly in doing what it sets out to do. There's a slight sag in the middle, which even Mathew Warchus's deft direction can't quite conceal, but the set is perfect. It has to be three different apartments, two of them for a single brief scene each. Mark Thompson solves the problem by making all three characters live in what looks like the corner of an empty art gallery. One panel of the wall swings round to show what the Finney and Stott characters have on *their* walls: Finney a pretentious pseudo-Dutch landscape through a window, Stott a nice bright still life of fruit which turns out to have been painted by his father. It's on this panel that Courtenay finally decides to hang his picture. Its whiteness has no particular significance, alas – it's not even a mirror for each character to see himself. The picture is there to be laughed at and argued over, as though white pictures were somehow new and outrageous. (In fact they're at least as old-fashioned as the play – Ad Reinhardt was doing all-white and all-black pictures at just the time of *The Little Hut*.) Half an udderless cow might have been more apt.

But *Art* is a translation, not a transposition, and perhaps Paris is behind the times – not that there's anything very Parisian about the production. Courtenay, Finney and Stott, with their different British provincial accents, do not attempt

any sort of Frenchness. In fact references to off-stage French life come as rather a surprise. But during the slight sag I found myself thinking – what if the producers had been bolder and had Finney playing Paul Johnson? The British audience would have enjoyed that, surely, even if it left the tourists puzzled. Stott, the intermediary figure who just wants the others to be nice to each other, could be one of the Sunday paper fence-sitters, too scared to say what he really thinks (always supposing he ever dares think at all). And Courtenay could be a friend of the Tate, who once had dinner with Doris Saatchi, and is anxious not to be left behind. But that would be another play, which might make the audience think about itself and its attitudes to art. It wouldn't be so popular.

In any case, the current London art scene is almost beyond satire. It needs a new *Tartuffe*, crossed with *The Way of the World*. *A Bad Trip*, perhaps? The leading character would be the fabulously rich Maharajah of Sarota, who comes to London accompanied by a train of praise-singers and critics to receive an honorary degree from Silversmiths' College, where the Doctoral robe is so exquisite it's invisible. After the ceremony he is taken for a cruise down the Thames to the humble artists' working quarter in the East End. Hidden among the sailors is Bridget Swell, a poor (but honest) artist, who hopes to seduce the Maharajah into putting on a show of her high-pitched video self-portraits. As the steam-yacht sails past Bankside there is a firework display organised by Filbert and Forger, a vivid evocation of their dysentery after a visit to the Maharajah's palace. The explosions are loud, but not loud enough to drown the cries of Bridget, whose disguise has been penetrated, in several senses, by a psychopathic member of the catering staff, whose disappointed lust has led him to exchange his meat axe for a chain saw. He threatens to cut not merely Bridget but the boat in two from stem to stern. But do not fear – the Arts Council helicopter (customised by David Hollywood) is on its way!

I can just see *A Bad Trip* on the stage of the Olivier. Or rather, I can't. One part of the British arts establishment would never dream of upsetting another, and the 'Royal' National Theatre (avoided at all costs by the Monarch), which wanted in its early days to put on a play attacking Churchill, has become a staid, respectable museum, devoted to reverent revivals, with Churchill's daughter as its recent Chairperson. It is a dreadful disappointment to those who supported its creation in the hope of boldness, danger, innovation. It's safe, commercial, star-studded – exactly like the West-End producers' theatre of Binkie Beaumont to which it was supposed to be the alternative. Indeed, it keeps reviving old Binkie hits – I expect *The Little Hut* in the Lyttelton any time now. If only it wasn't reviving Binkie values, too.

An Inspector Calls is an example, precisely the sort of popular play that people were agitating against in the '50s and '60s when a National was seen as our only hope for a serious theatre. It's gentle but not disturbingly left-wing, Jolly Jack Priestley – Bradford, pipe-smoke, the Brains Trust – wagging his finger at the uncaring middle classes. The reps have been doing it for years. So why should the National decide to revive it in the 1990s? Because the National is run by and for directors and designers, and a particular director and his special designer had ever such a clever idea for doing it. Goodness gracious, they'd literally explode the middle-class house! They'd put the sub-text on the stage! They'd leave the audience with nothing whatever to do but sit back, as though they were at home in front of their tellies! And of course the audience loved it. After cheering it at the National, they're still cheering it in the West End, and in New York, once the critics had told them it was all right, they stood and whooped. Because there was no interval, those who loathed it had to sit and grind their teeth. All right, we should have got up and shouted. But who wants to be sourpuss when so many people are having a good time? Anyway, the National looks so like a major police station, who would dare?

An Inspector Calls is an example of how our subsidised theatre, instead of showing the way forward, has gone back a hundred years to spectacle and superficiality. There were real deer in the Forest of Arden in *As You Like It* in those days, and it was against just such silliness that Granville-Barker and Shaw produced their seasons at the Royal Court from 1904–1907. They wanted to make the theatre a place an intelligent person would at least not be ashamed to be seen in. Famously, the Royal Court is now the home of the English Stage Company, founded by George Devine in 1956 as a writer's theatre, very much with Granville-Barker and Shaw in mind. And who is the

Left to right: Tom Courtney, Ken Stot and Albert Finney

new head of the English Stage Company? Why, the director of *An Inspector Calls*. And did he celebrate his appointment with a wonderful new play? No, he revived Arnold Wesker's *The Kitchen*, removing most of the theatre's seats in order to create a highly realistic restaurant kitchen. It was a statement. Ours is a visual culture, it said; audiences reared on TV have to have naturalistic sets and everything made simple. And the audience duly oohed and aahed. Unkind people say that Stephen Daldry's ideal is a theatre so full of set there's no room for an audience at all. They can only stand outside and watch the flats going in and out of the fly-tower.

A theatre in which design is king is no sort of theatre to me. In *John Gabriel Borkman*, another recent hit at the National, the designer wanted to emphasise the coldness of the house (not just psychologically – it's Norway, and snowing outside) by siting the stove upstage centre. Fine. But he also wanted such a steep rake that the doors to Mrs Borkman's drawing room, in order to be practical, let in a deadly pneumonic draught. Did the director query this absurdity? Clearly not – and he was Richard Eyre, Artistic Director of the National. It wasn't supposed to be taken literally, I'll be told. But if not, why did Mrs Borkman continually go to the stove to warm her hands? This may seem a trivial example, but it's symptomatic of a deep disorder in the current theatre's priorities.

John Gabriel Borkman is stuffed with stars, just like a Binkie Beaumont production. Directors and designers were highly regarded then, of course – Cecil Beaton more than most, though modern designers would shudder at his sets. But at least Binkie did put on new plays, it wasn't all revivals. At the director-led National, the play's not the thing, it's the interpretation. Directors are like dealers: they prefer an old, established artist to a new one. Critics feel the same. You don't know where you are with the new, you have to show your hand, you may make a fool of yourself. And

with a new play, it's the play, not the director, which attracts attention. But a new *Hamlet*, a new *Cherry Orchard*, a new *Hedda Gabler*, above all a new *Death of a Salesman* – there a director can show his wares. Or he might like to have a go at one of those ridiculous old melodramas by Hugo or Schiller – shove in some stars and see if he can't wreak a little magic. (No, he can't actually.) Thus we have revival after revival but scarcely ever a new play. When it started, the Cottesloe, we were told, was to be for new work – and for a time it was. Now, the National relegates new plays to its studio, where they are 'workshopped' for weeks, with a director and actors, then disappear. This is as though critics were allowed into an artist's studio to repaint the canvases, then decide whether they're worth a show. Just occasionally a new play is allowed on to the public stage, but usually only if it's by one of two or three very well-known favourite National writers. Sorry, but things were actually better before the National was born.

It's proved not only a conservative but a highly destructive institution, sucking the audience for serious theatre away from the West End to which it will probably never go back. For one thing, the National (except for the Cottesloe) is somewhere you can sit in comfort. The seats in most West-End theatres, designed for a smaller population, are now no longer acceptable to people with normal knees. You can park at the National, whereas getting to and from the West End is such an effort, people are discouraged before they start. And anyway, where are the stars? They're at the National, doing revivals. It's only two or three nights a week, not the greatest money, but plenty of time to earn a serious living with voice-overs. The old idea of eight performances a week is anathema to these coddled darlings. And as for going on tour – please! Like all institutions, the National has become a home for its inhabitants.

That's why the arrival of *Art* in a commercial West End, even more given to conservatism and revivals than the National, is surprisingly cheering. People defend directors' theatre as more intelligent than actors', but I don't see much difference. (A genuine writers' theatre is a mirage.) But here an actor – Sean Connery, whose wife saw the play in Paris and got him to buy it – has put it on for three other actors. Warchus, one of our best young directors, has agreed to stage it, even though it isn't a revival. It's as though a group of artists hired their own dealer to put on their show, and sold every picture. That it's not a great play doesn't matter. It's a play, about the only new one in the West End. Next time, who knows? Perhaps a play about art.

1. Andre Roussin and Nancy Mitford

Art by Yazmina Reza, translated by Christopher Hampton, directed by Matthew Warchus, booking until 9 March, Wyndhams Theatre, 0171 369 1736.

Brief Candle

William Boyd *reviews Julian Schnabel's film,* **Basquiat**.

The bio-pic is a difficult genre, perhaps as difficult as it comes in the film world, and the longer and more familiar the life to be filmed, the tougher the challenge. Films are rarely over two hours long; at two and a half hours you are probably at the maximum length for these times of ours, stretching the tolerance of studio, exhibitor and – possibly – audience as well; and to encompass an entire life, public and private, and do it some justice (let alone produce an interesting or watchable or memorable film) within that frame is a daunting challenge.

The modern exemplar of the bio-pic – in my opinion – is Martin Scorsese's *Raging Bull*. Scorsese was initially fortunate in that his subject was virtually unknown outside the fight game. Secondly, the area of Jake La Motta's life that he chose to treat was comparatively short – the rise and fall of a professional boxer, a decade or so. And third, Scorsese showed real astuteness in opting to eschew traditional narrative chronology. The film is a series of vignettes, punctuated by flash-forwards to the bloated, ageing Jake in his premature dotage as a nightclub raconteur. The style of the film is fractured and eclectic: sometimes naturalistic, almost *cinéma verité*, sometimes stylised (particularly the fights), but as a portrait of a man and his life it is remarkably successful. It could only have been bettered in that most fluid, capacious and malleable of art forms, the novel, but, in Scorsese's hands, film – and I don't mean this as faint praise – takes on a rare depth and texture (Robert de Niro has a lot to do with this, it goes without saying). It is nuanced, it resonates, it is both banal and passionate, it is full of complexities and ambiguities – we do not understand everything. It resembles, in short, life.

All this is by way of preamble to Julian Schnabel's film *Basquiat*. A bio-pic also, and one that shares many features with – however paradoxical this may seem – *Raging Bull*. Basquiat is comparatively unknown: certainly, outside of an art-world coterie, the details of his life are unfamiliar territory. Furthermore, his life was short, dramatic and controversial. Schnabel's film needs only to concentrate on the few years – approximately 1981 to 1987 – that chart his discovery, sudden fame, exploitation and ultimate drug-propelled downfall and death. Wisely, too, the style of the film is fractured and impressionistic. Basquiat's story is presented in a series of episodes, often concentrating around encounters with

Director of Basquiat, *Julian Schnabel*

friends, or girlfriends, artists, dealers, etcetera, who move in and out of the story at random. One of the film's most memorable shots is visionary: Basquiat, contemplating Manhattan's vast roofscape, sees the sky replaced by sea, with a solitary surfer riding a creaming breaker, high above the skyscrapers. Is this a vision of happiness? Of mere wishful thinking? Or simply the kind of aesthetic epiphany that can visit any artist, however down and out?

These ambiguities complement the film's tone and atmosphere well, and Schnabel is excellently served by his cast too. Jeffrey Wright is superb as Basquiat: understated, befuddled, endearing, he can move effortlessly through the range of emotions from sweetness and charm to the manic, spoilt selfishness of the drug dependent. One's

L–R: Jeffrey Wright, David Bowie, Gary Oldman and Dennis Hopper on the set of Basquiat

sympathy is thoroughly engaged, rarely the case with addicts, and Wright's fraught depiction of a desperate soul on self-destruct rivals Ray Milland's great portrayal of an alcoholic in *The Lost Weekend*.

The supporting cast solidly buttresses Wright's central position. The luminously beautiful Claire Forlani as Basquiat's girlfriend is touchingly, edgily vulnerable. Benicio del Toro for once keeps his mannerisms under control as Basquiat's friend from his graffiti-spraying days. Christopher Walken, playing a journalist, manages to invest a two-minute interview with such an amazing freight of off-beat menace and downright weirdness that it almost steals the show. Dennis Hopper and Gary Oldman, old reliables, do not let the side down. Special mention must be made of David Bowie as Andy Warhol. This expertly pitched performance is kept well this side of caricature (very hard to do with a white fright-wig on your head). More importantly, you see a version of Warhol that for once makes sense. Warhol emerges, not as some spaced-out party-animal, but as Basquiat's only real, unconditional friend in the sea of sharks that is the New York art-world. The friendship is played as manifestly genuine, without a trace of *quid pro quo*. And Warhol's death, when it comes, provokes a vicarious sense of loss. And one understands vividly why this may well have been the factor that pushed Basquiat over the edge.

The film further benefits from an easy, unforced authenticity. Julian Schnabel knew Basquiat well, and has thrived and suffered (to a degree) in the same world. Tellingly, in the production notes to the film, Schnabel describes that world as an 'arena'. In which artists as gladiators are pitted against a succession of wild beasts, perhaps?

As an oblique demonstration of biting the hand that feeds you, or of fouling your own nest, Schnabel's take on the art scene of the '80s is unsparingly harsh. One wonders if it is fuelled by a personal bitterness, or perhaps a retrospective wisdom, but whatever the motivation, his portrayal of the gang of asset strippers that gathered round the frail personality and modest talent of Jean-Michel Basquiat makes other sinks of iniquity – Hollywood, the music business, oriental sweat shops – seem positively perfumed.

And this provides the material for the searching sub-text that runs beneath the film. At another level it can be seen as a Hogarthian satire, a dire moral warning to the unsuspecting artist. And here we encounter the vexed question of Basquiat's reputation, both while he was alive and posthumously. Basquiat died at the age of 27, a year older than Keats was when he died, but Basquiat is no Keatsian figure. Basquiat's own idols were doomed, drugged musicians like Jimi Hendrix and Charlie Parker, and perhaps there the parallels are more valid, but not entirely. One would hesitate to call Charlie Parker the Basquiat of the jazz world. The inversion is revealing – it tends to diminish Charlie Parker – for what it tells us, both about Basquiat's 'gift', whatever that may have been, and the world he moved in, where it became a commodity of huge value.

The fact is that Basquiat belonged to that category of artist who traded in, for want of a better term, one smart idea. It is a recent phenomenon, this, perhaps only prevalent in the last four decades or so, and posterity is already marking down the dividends sharply. Artists of this category offer a quick fix of appreciation and that quick fix can be relied upon to pack many a gallery and fuel many column inches for a limited period of time. I do not deny that the frisson such work generates may be genuine, but it is like a firework rocket, refulgently, gloriously *there* for a short time, and then darkness, and then the faint distant thump of the wooden stick and scorched cardboard falling back to earth.

Scenes in the film of Basquiat frenziedly producing his huge, vivid, scribbled upon canvases are excellently done and fascinatingly revealing (canvases on the floor, paint slapped on, scribbled words and phrases randomly added). Basquiat was unusual – young and black in a white, highbrow world. He would have liked to have claimed to have come up from the street, but his origins were bourgeois. He had a certain wit, a certain worldly cynicism and an artful enough faux-naif style. And that was it. But it was enough to provoke an engineered feeding frenzy amongst the dealers and their patrons, the critics and the gallery crowd.

In his notes on the film Schnabel happily bandies about the term 'genius' as applied to Basquiat, but the idea is utterly risible. Basquiat was not a modern snake-oil salesman, not quite; but the currency of his talent, his ability, his 'knack', was on the lightweight side, and I suspect – and Wright's deeply sensitive performance encourages this conclusion – that amongst the demons that hurried him on his way to his premature death were those that were whispering 'fraud' and 'sham' in his ear. One of the loudest messages this film broadcasts is that there is no medium or long-term substitute for talent, hard work, elaboration and exploration of technique, intelligence, hard work, empathy, thought, virtuosity, hard work and so on. This is the serious artist's lot – his or her via dolorosa, if you like – and the froth and spume of celebrity, of radical-chic acclaim and lots of easy money cannot drag you away from it. One smart idea may buy you all this, for a

Jeffrey Wright as Basquiat, with Schnabel's Basquiats

while, but unless you cultivate a redoubtable cynicism (and bank your loot) it will not stand you in any further stead. Plenty of other flim-flam men and women are coming along behind you with all their smart ideas. Soon you will be old hat.

Perhaps Basquiat saw old-hatdom beckoning, perhaps he couldn't think of anything else to do apart from his graffiti stuff? But, in any event, the indictment is not his to bear alone, but must rather be the burden of the world and its denizens who fell upon him and pushed him into the lucrative glare of the limelight.

Basquiat was vulnerable from the start because he held the wrong concept of what an artist was, believing that 'Your life was the price you paid for your talent'. Such ideas of 'being an artist', a poet *maudit*, a tormented genius, or whatever, demonstrate a fanciful romanticism of the most puerile sort (which is why they are more often found amongst very young rock musicians, or very deluded actors). No serious artist can afford to believe in this notion of afflatus, whether God-given, spontaneous or drug-induced. The art-world may be indifferent, or reluctant to make such a judgement, but the world of the real artist is ruthlessly self-regulating. The Stoics' famous rejoinder, 'Be silent – unless what you have to say is better than silence', casts

a long, minatory and humbling shadow over all artists' endeavours.

Julian Schnabel has made a fine film and he can be proud of his début as a director, but it seems to me that what emerges is something different from what he may have set out to achieve. Schnabel has said that 'Jean-Michel's work mocks categorisation. It wasn't enough for him to be a great black artist, or a graffiti artist or even a young artist. He placed himself among the great artists of all time.' Good God. Well, if he did, he paid a heavy price for his hubris. But this is not what the film conveys: there is a marked absence of vainglory, of preening self-congratulation. As Basquiat is fêted and wooed by his well-heeled acolytes and hangers-on, his mood appears rather to start as one of gratified bafflement, shading swiftly into cynicism, self-disgust and ultimate despair. Basquiat, it seems to me, is not so much Icarus or Narcissus but a sort of latter-day, low grade, Manhattan Faust. Too young, too gullible, too insecure, too easily led, he made his own Faustian pact with the art-world – he did the Faust deal – and got royally burned.

Basquiat, directed by Julian Schnabel, distributed by Guild Films, will be on general release at the end of March, 1997.

Wilson's Eye

Edmund Wilson *brought an acute visual sense and descriptive flair to a surprising range of subjects, artistic as well as literary, as* **Jed Perl** *demonstrates.*

Edmund Wilson believed that his classical verbal precision was equal to any occasion, and he made his point with a shelf full of books that are so clear-headed and wide-ranging that they leave us exhilarated. By the end of his life – he died in 1972 at the age of 77 – Wilson knew that people regarded him as America's greatest man of letters, and he knew that he'd earned the title not only because he wrote beautifully and brilliantly but also because he'd spent decades seeing how many different kinds of writing he could do. Everybody has probably heard of *Axel's Castle*, the pioneering exploration of modern poetry and fiction, and *To the Finland Station*, a series of biographically oriented studies of the thinkers whose ideas inspired the revolutionary acts of Lenin and Trotsky. In recent years there's been a good deal of attention focused on Wilson's posthumously published journals with their elaborate descriptions of sexual encounters (the last volume, *The Sixties*, appeared in 1993). But Wilson also published lots of other books – novels, plays, poetry, literary chronicles, political and travel reportage, even a pamphlet on *The Cold War and the Income Tax*.

Considering the magisterial egotism at work here, it's not surprising that readers have always been tempted to respond to Wilson's omnivorousness by poking around for the areas that he's slighted or overlooked. And that's by no means the end of the story, for Wilson, ever the intellectual competitor, wanted to stay a few steps ahead of even the most demanding readers by locating and repairing the gaps in his own ambitiously comprehensive view. In 1963, when he wrote 'Every Man His Own Eckermann' – a mock interview, really a comic playlet, for the fledgling *New York Review of Books* – he was casually displaying his grasp of exactly the subjects that people felt were not up his alley, such as nineteenth-century comic illustration and Stravinsky's chamber music. Here was a man who was even at home with the material he wasn't supposed to know.

As this dialogue begins, a fictional visitor, associated with the new magazine, presses Wilson to give his opinion on 'all the arts... That's what I wanted to ask you about. You've written so much about literature but not much about painting and music. We wondered if you wouldn't contribute some opinions about graphic and musical subjects'. Wilson is testing the limits of his intellectual reach, so with mock modesty he responds, 'Gladly: I know nothing whatever about them'. But the visitor is quick to point out that the eminent author hasn't completely overlooked the other arts. 'In the twenties you used to do articles on concerts and exhibitions.' That, Wilson replies, was when he was a 'cultural man-of-all-work for the *New Republic*. I wrote about everything from burlesque shows and circuses to Stravinsky and Georgia O'Keeffe. I'd never dare to write such stuff today'. But here he is, 40 years later, writing 'such stuff'. Actually, he has quite a lot to say about the visual arts.

'Every Man His Own Eckermann' is one of Wilson's self-consciously amused self-portraits as a bookish old man. Yet even as he's deliciously casting himself in a role, he manages to speak with some passion about his affinity for the graphic arts, which he dates all the way back to the engravings by Callot that he bought in France when serving in World War I. Wilson then launches into a list of graphic artists who interest him. He says he likes

> picture books in general of the comic or fantastic kind: Gilray, Rowlandson, Fuseli, Spitzweg, Cruickshank, Phiz, Edward Lear, Beardsley, Toulouse-Lautrec, George du Maurier, Phil May, Max Beerbohm, Sem, Max Ernst, Marc Chagall, Peggy Bacon, Saul Steinberg, Leonard Baskin, Edward Gorey – to mention people of very different magnitudes.

He describes his passion for the turn-of-the-century caricaturist Sem, and makes a point of comparing Sem's interpretations of various late nineteenth-century figures with those of his friend and contemporary, Proust; he observes that the delicate story-telling in the illustrations of Henri Monnier anticipates elements in Flaubert and Maupassant; and he speaks at length of his enthusiasm for George Grosz.

Wilson likes pictures with a strong narrative or anecdotal dimension, and that's to be expected in a literary man. His taste in music also runs to works with words and plots; in the self-interview he focuses on opera and gets into a discussion of the relationship between Mussorgsky and Pushkin. It's disappointing to find him taking a greater interest in the clever anecdotes of Tchelitchew than in the graphic elaborations of Picasso, but Tchelitchew is an enthusiasm that he shares with Lincoln Kirstein and a number of other people who ought to know better. Too much can be made of the idiosyncracies in Wilson's taste; what's really impressive is his endless curiosity. In 'Every Man His Own Eckermann' he even has ideas about the work that he doesn't care at all for, so that you feel him bringing the same front-and-centre attention to art and music that he'd at one time or another brought to foreign cities, popular culture, and a lot of other things.

In spite of Wilson's somewhat dismissive remarks about his journalism of the '20s – some of which was written for *Vanity Fair*, where he was managing editor in 1920 – he never lost his early appetite for pictures and music. There are a number of fascinating twists to this interest in the non-literary arts, not the least of which is that the protagonist of his most important work of fiction, *Memoirs of Hecate County*, is an art critic whose life in many respects parallels Wilson's. The narrator of *Hecate County* is not an Edmund Wilson self-portrait; this is a portrait of a man who would like to be the kind of writer that Wilson was, but lacks the focused energy necessary to pull his artistic and economic interests together into a Wilsonian whole. Yet there are pages in *Hecate County* where one feels that Wilson is enjoying seeing things through the eyes of this aesthete – recording the way that a connoisseur mentally catalogues the Canova and Daubigny and Corots in one suburban home, or analysing the art-historical inspirations behind the various dresses worn by

Book jacket, Edmund Wilson's Night Thoughts, *designed by Ronald Clyne, 1961*

Pavel Tchelitchew, Nudes, *c. 1931, black ink and wash on paper, 25.4 x 20.3 cm*

Imogen Loomis, the Princess with the Golden Hair whom the narrator pursues through the central story in the book.

Wilson, the man who wears so many literary hats, can't resist imagining himself as a critic in an entirely different field. In an unfinished novel, written before *Hecate County* – it's slated for publication in the near future under the title *The Higher Jazz* – the narrator is a music critic rather than an art critic, and you feel Wilson rising to the challenge of yet another form. Here he describes the critic's feelings at the beginning of a performance of Schoenberg's *Pierrot Lunaire.*

> Schoenberg had always gotten me and he still did. It was partly the Wagner that was still behind it, though all reduced to moonlight and blackness, discolored and flattened out – the old thrill of the Germanic music theater, the shiver and the shudder and the longing ache.

The expansive yet precise language is

George Grosz, Self-portrait for (Charlie Chaplin), *1920*

vintage Wilson. No matter what the subject, he's himself. In *Hecate County*, when the narrator reflects on the inadequacy of Clive Bell's formalism, we can see that Wilson is spinning a variation on his basic point of view, which is that it's always useful to set literature in a broad cultural context. In both *The Higher Jazz* and *Hecate County*, Wilson is drawing on his experience at *Vanity Fair* and it's clear that his early immersion in the everything-is-new days of modern art had implications that went way beyond the confines of literature, and stayed with him for a very long time.

In the 1958 book *The American Earthquake*, which Wilson subtitled 'A documentary of the twenties and thirties', articles about Alfred Stieglitz's gallery and some recent compositions by Stravinsky are printed one after the other. In the Stieglitz piece, Wilson writes admiringly about Georgia O'Keeffe's flower abstractions, comments on works by Dove, Marin and Hartley, and concludes with a beautiful description of Stieglitz's recent cloud photographs, the *Equivalents*. In the Stravinsky article – actually two notices joined together – he describes the *Piano Concerto* of 1924 and *Petrushka*, and touches on work by Schoenberg, Varese and Satie. These pieces – together with a review of a George Bellows exhibition at the Metropolitan Museum of Art – evince an extraordinary ease and authority in writing about arts other than literature.

In the Stravinsky review, Wilson speaks about the echoes of Handel and Bach in the new *Octet* and *Concerto*, saying that in the *Piano Concerto* 'the Bachesque development is finally broken up by momentary ragtime rhythms and fragments of sarcastic parody, just as Eliot interrupts his Elizabethan blank verse with bar talk and popular songs'. The comparison isn't noteworthy in itself – it's a fairly standard observation about the tension between avant-garde and classic in the late 'teens and '20s– but there's something about the unforced, I'm-making-this-just-in-passing demeanour of the writing that underlines the directness of his response to a non-literary subject. His emotions on hearing a piece of music or seeing a photograph can be as immediate as his feelings about a book. I wonder if anybody has ever bettered his description of the Stieglitz cloud studies:

> Stieglitz, in pushing his mastery of the camera further and further from mechanical reproduction and closer to the freedom of plastic art, has lately left the earth altogether and taken to the shifting clouds, where he seems to have found a material of maximum variability. The textures and shapes of the sky are infinitely irregular and strange, and they never are twice the same – so that the artist can have practically whatever he likes; and the person who looks at the picture is never distracted from the artist's intention by familiar objects, familiar subjects of photographs. One finds effects of a feathery softness or of a solidity almost marmoreal. Certain of these prints, I suppose, are among the artist's chief triumphs. Especially impressive are cloud-masses – somber and grand in their darkness – which lift themselves as if in grief.

Sem (Georges Goursat), Head Waiter and Guest – Penguin and Flamingo, *from* Sem à la Mer, *1912. Collection of Lionel Lambourne*

The marmoreal clouds, by the way, reappear in the chapter on Valéry in *Axel's Castle*.

When Wilson gathered some of these early non-literary pieces in *The American Earthquake*, he wrote postscripts to both the Stieglitz and Stravinsky articles, in which he saluted the two men, pointing to them as heroic figures. After noting Stieglitz's steely control and unwillingness to brook disagreement, Wilson adds that he 'commanded respect. To think that he had been working for "modern" art – in an age of convention and commerce – since the time when I was ten years old!'. The '20s had been, as Wilson reported in later years, a complicated time for him, exhilarating but also exhausting and demoralising, closing with the crisis that he described as 'a kind

Marc Chagall, At the Easel, *from the series* My Life, *1922, drypoint, 24.7 x 18.9 cm. Museum of Modern Art, New York*

Pablo Picasso, Portrait of Igor Stravinsky (after a photograph)*, Paris, 24 May 1920, pencil on paper*

of' nervous breakdown. From the vantage point of the '50s, he remarked that 'it touches me today to think of [Stieglitz] running counter to the pressures of that era and trying to make beauty of – in Paul Rosenfeld's words – the "strange brazen human emptiness" of the city in which I then lived...' As for Stravinsky, if in the mid-'20s Wilson sounded a bit lukewarm about the recent work of a composer who was in mid-career, with what is generally regarded as his greatest work behind him, succeeding decades led the critic to revise that judgement.

> I have come to respect and prize him even more highly than I did thirty years ago when he was still a novel excitement. His intensity and variety, his persistence and craftsmanship, continue to delight and to fortify the worker in any craft.

These views on Stravinsky are repeated in a slightly different form in 'Every Man His Own Eckermann', where Wilson praises the 'sustained career' and how Stravinsky is

Walker Evans, Fireplace, Tenant Farmhouse, Hale County, Alabama, 1936

'always himself and always doing something different, but always doing everything intensely with economy, perfect craftsmanship and style'.

A fellow critic and close friend of Wilson's whose words and thoughts are woven into these writings on both Stieglitz and Stravinsky is Paul Rosenfeld. Wilson had begun to read Rosenfeld's music criticism 'with avidity' even before he met him in 1922 – the year of *The Wasteland* and *Ulysses* – and for Wilson, Rosenfeld held a key to the American Renaissance, for he was close to the Stieglitz circle and wrote about all the arts. In later years, Rosenfeld came to represent for Wilson the part of the '20s that hadn't been about drinking and wild parties but about a questing artistic and intellectual spirit. Rosenfeld personified 'the new era of American art [that was] just beginning to burst into life between MacDougal Street and Irving Place'. It is from him that Wilson borrowed the phrase about Stieglitz's relationship with New York, and both in the 1925 piece on Stravinsky and in the postscript, Wilson quoted an interview that Rosenfeld had conducted with Stravinsky and published in the *Dial*, in which the Russian announced that, although there was much to envy about the situation of the musician in Bach's day,

> I feel we in our day are working with our material in the spirit of Bach, the constructive spirit, and I feel that what we give, though it is perhaps smaller in comparison, is in its concentration and economy an equivalent for the immense structures of Bach.

For Wilson there was something immensely attractive about the range of Paul Rosenfeld's interests – he was against narrow specialisation, a believer in intellectual versatility. Like Wilson, he was not a card-carrying member of the modern movement but a dedicated observer, whose avidity enabled him to bring the modern news to a growing public.

Wilson, who is sometimes thought, and not without reason, to have been a sort of Edwardian figure, had a keen eye for the musical and visual expressions of the new century. He could evoke modern taste quickly and wittily, as in this 1927 description of a fictional Greenwich Village apartment, with its precise, bare-bones decor.

> On the white walls above the row of bookshelves, were brass candlesticks with red candles in them, an oval daguerreotype of a rugged Wyoming grandfather, a black bowl of red holly-berries, an Alaskan illustration that Rockwell Kent had given her and two portraits of herself – one a charcoal drawing and the other a painting that presented her with green skin and half-shut eyes and made her look like a corpse.

This is the apartment of a character named Jane Gooch, editor of a magazine called *Vortex*, which is planning, we are told, 'a big hydraulic number'. This, Gooch explains, will focus on

pipes and oil pumps and plumbing fixtures – and all those things. We've got some photographs of bathrooms by Leo Kleist that are the most marvellous things you ever saw. There's a series – of washbasins at different angles – that looks just like the tomb of the Medicis.

This is a wonderful send-up of the kind of wilfully abstract photography that was already becoming a cliché in the '20s. That Wilson's parody is so perfectly on target reflects an insider's understanding, and elsewhere in his writing he himself uses for serious literary effect the very eye for abstraction that he's joking about here. He grasps the transforming power of simplification and exaggeration; it was a technique that was being passed back and forth between the writers and the painters all through the 'teens and '20s. Take, for example, his description of the apartment of the Dimiceli family in Brooklyn, in a piece of reportage from the early '30s that's called 'A Bad Day in Brooklyn'.

> The Dimicelis' flat is extremely clean, and it is furnished with an unexpected vividness that contrasts with the discolored streets of Flushing. The walls of every room are decorated with bright religious prints in green, blue and red – the Bleeding Heart and the Holy Family, the Virgin with flowers in her arms that presides above the bed in the bedroom, the Last Supper over the kitchen table. The whole apartment, in fact, has the brightness and the clear outlines of one of those simple prints: bedroom walls in green, kitchen oilcloth in blue and white squares, kitchen curtains in green and white, kitchen table and sink smooth white, and three yellow canaries in yellow cages.

Wilson's description represents the same hyper-refined – aestheticised – documentary sensibility that we know from the photographs which Walker Evans was beginning to take around the same time. In their essential spirit, both men hark back to what, in *Axel's Castle*, Wilson called Flaubert's 'aesthetic Naturalism'. But his use of primary and secondary colours also gives the writing some of the daring, immediate simplicity that painters achieved early in the century by avoiding half-tones and shadows. He almost turns the Dimiceli home into an interior by Matisse. Wilson has a modern feeling for the free-standing descriptive power of words. Think of the title of one of his collections of travel writings – *Red, Black, Blond and Olive*, his studies of Zuni, Haitian, Soviet and Israeli culture. He sends those names of colours, with their complicated metaphoric implications, into the world with all the stark mysterious elegance of Rimbaud's 'A noir, E blanc, I rouge, U vert, O bleu...' And of course, it's with Rimbaud that *Axel's Castle* concludes.

Even the design of Wilson's books, with their distinctive size and superbly elegant typographic covers, underlines the feeling that the modern movement gives words a new kind of lucidity and power. No other twentieth-century American writer imposed so firm a design sense on a range of publishers over a long period of years. I think there can be little doubt that it's Wilson himself who inspired the equally brilliant dust-jackets done by Ivan Chermayeff for *The American Earthquake* at Doubleday and by Ronald Clyne for *Wilson's Night Thoughts* at Farrar, Straus, Cudahy. And then there's Edward Gorey's comic but elegant design for *The Duke of Palermo and Other Plays*. Wilson's feeling for typographic clarity unites two styles that dominated the book arts in the 1920s. In these extraordinarily designed covers there's a merger of the sophisticated traditionalist approach of the '20s, with its return to an eighteenth-century severity and simplicity, and the very different but equally vigorous constructivist graphic style that was being developed by modernists in Germany and Holland.

Wilson had a wonderful eye, and it gives descriptive power to everything from his snapshots of the shabby Finland Station, all 'rubber-gray and tarnished pink', in the closing pages of his 'Study in the Writing and Acting of History', to a description of Punch and Judy puppets, with their brilliant colours, in his travel diary from the 1963–4 trip to Europe. His descriptive gift is grounded, as is the psychological genius of his portraits of writers, in an insistence on seeing everything whole and clear. All of Wilson's intellectual powers gain concrete form through the beautifully regular rhythm of his prose, with each word presented exactly, precisely, so that we seem to take its full measure before we pass on to the next word. It's thrilling when this dense, eloquent voice, apparently so well suited for discussions of books, takes on subjects as unexpected as the architecture of Thomas Jefferson and the prints of John James Audubon in a chapter on poetry in *Patriotic Gore*. Wilson speaks of Jefferson's University of Virginia, and with how

Alfred Stieglitz, Equivalent, Mountains and Sky, Lake George, *1924*

> sure a touch [he] has situated his charming creations on the hospitable little hills in such a way as to involve the landscape in a personal work of art. The bubble domes, the candid facades, the variety of the classical cornices in the 'pavilions' that enclose the university 'lawn' and in which the professors live, the delightful white octagon rooms, with French windows that open on level vistas, have humanized the Palladian style into something eclectic and lovely.

What a surprising adjective, that 'candid' is. In Audubon's studies of quadrupeds Wilson admires 'his genius for personalizing and dramatizing his subjects and, by the imaginative use of landscape, embodying them in balanced compositions'. Here is 'the magnificent striped plume of the mother skunk defending from the vantage of a hollow log her still groping babies inside it'. And 'the violet rosettes of the star-nosed moles that delicately vibrate to their prey in the darkness of the burrows or streams where they hunt' and make 'a strange contrast with the free-skimming sails on the river in the distance behind them'.

You might think that by the time of

Patriotic Gore – it was published in 1962 – after the decades of politics and reportage, Wilson would have little appetite for the visual flexibility that's needed to make such delicate discriminations within the work of an architect or a watercolourist, yet in the lines on Jefferson's architecture and Audubon's animals he shows the same acute visual sense that he'd brought to Stieglitz's gallery decades before. It's an amazing passage in *Patriotic Gore* – there's a sense of looking up from the thick rows of nineteenth-century memoirs that loom so large in Wilson's Civil War work, up to the landscape, and that expansion of the horizon somehow recalls the way that Stieglitz, in his cloud studies, looks up from what's ordinary to take in a wider, immediately surprising view. The elegant severity of Wilson's mind did not allow for a more consistently expansive exploration of interconnections between the arts, but this did not mean that he was indifferent or unsympathetic to such associations. On the contrary, much as in the '20s he had admired Rosenfeld's willingness to take the

risk of interweaving the arts, in his later years Wilson was praising writers, especially André Malraux and Mario Praz, who felt equally at home in literature and the visual arts.

Wilson published a review of the first three volumes of Malraux's extended exploration of art history in 1951. And when he reprinted the essay in *The Bit Between My Teeth* in 1965, he added a long afterword, discussing the volumes that had flowed from these early ones and which together struck him as forming a lavishly illustrated 'kind of huge philosophic prose poem'. Malraux's spiralling narrative comes out of the studio atmosphere of early twentieth-century Paris, where the artists had been eager to relate their work to the heretofore ignored or misunderstood masterpieces of Romanesque and African and Asian civilisation. Malraux threads his opulent, almost stream-of-consciousness approach to the history of art through pages full of beautifully lit, dramatically cropped photographs, photographs that are in some respects related to the unexpected close-up

Mario Praz's home, from his autobiography The House of Life

views that Wilson was parodying in the piece on Jane Gooch and her *Vortex* magazine. Yet he takes immediately to Malraux's layered vision, to the way that whole epochs and continents are interwoven and cross-cut in order to get at the feeling of open access to the past that you so often feel in the studios of modern artists, where reproductions are tacked to the walls and books are brought out to give visitors a broad context for what the artist is doing now.

Malraux, he writes,

> skip[s] all over Europe from one cathedral to another, and from these to illuminated Psalters and Books of Hours and the works of art in palaces and mansions, and this involves an adroit play of mind which must dart here and there in both space and time to show analogies and point up contrasts.

Wilson goes into Malraux's spinning, cycling universe with some of the avidity that he'd given to another product of modern art's ripeness, Joyce's *Finnegans Wake*: his review of Malraux has some of the combination of overall enthusiasm plus strong reservations that he'd brought to his discussions of the later Joyce. He compares the book to Gibbon, Tolstoy and Marx. In response to those who would criticise Malraux for attempting too much, he asks,

> Is not Malraux himself an artist who, whether working in terms of the history of art or of fiction based on current history, has by the force of imagination, been recreating for us our world?

Wilson was on friendly terms with Malraux; they had in common the experience of literary men who'd been immersed in the political hopes of the century, and at the end of the day they both perhaps were coming back to the way that they'd felt in the beginning, when the free-standing integrity of a work of art was the most important thing of all.

By saluting Malraux's history of art Wilson was also reaffirming his sympathy for the modern collaging of many historical styles that we find in Eliot and Pound and Joyce, even if he had expressed some reservations about what he described as their 'veritable literary museums'. Another enthusiasm of Wilson's later years, for the writings of Mario Praz, brought with it precious mid-century echoes of the *fin-de-siècle* colorations of those other figures out of *Axel's Castle*, Yeats and Proust. We know that the first and last pieces in Wilson's literary chronicles have each been chosen very carefully, and have a particular personal significance. *Classics and Commercials* – the chronicle of the '40s – ends with Wilson's fine-grained memoir of Paul Rosenfeld. *The Bit Between My Teeth* – covering the years 1950–1965 – ends with a long article about Praz, the Italian writer who was as interested in the visual arts as

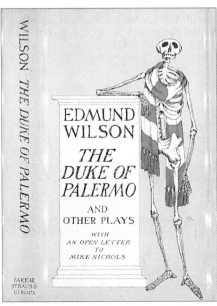

Book jacket for The Duke of Palermo *by Edmund Wilson, designed by Edward Gorey, 1969*

he was in literature. Earlier in *The Bit Between My Teeth* is a review of the book of Praz's that's still best-known in America, his study of the influence of de Sade on the Romantics called *The Romantic Agony*. The essay on Praz with which *The Bit Between My Teeth* concludes, much larger in scope, is an attempt to give American readers a sense of the whole range of Praz's concerns.

Wilson focuses on Praz's autobiography, *The House of Life*, which takes the form of a room by room tour of his apartment on the Via Giulia in Rome – thus the title of the essay, 'The Genie of the Via Giulia'. This autobiography is in part the confession of an obsessive collector of Neo-classical and Empire antiques: but each object that catches Praz's eye, whether it's a dark mahogany bookcase with bronze fittings or a watercolour of a Neopolitan interior or a series of porcelain plates depicting scenes along the Thames, inspires such a stream of asides and memories that the whole book takes on a Proustian psychological fascination. Wilson speaks of his visits to Praz's home, where he was 'made to feel that there were presences lurking about me'. And he goes on to say that

> These presences – artists long passed into eclipse, craftsmen no longer famous, vanished families, faded myths – have somehow been brought to life, refreshed, by proximity to Mario Praz.

The House of Life is, like Malraux's symphonic writings on art – and, for that matter, like Paul Rosenfeld's salute to the American Renaissance, *Port of New York* – a work in which an avidity for images energises a literary imagination. Wilson understood exactly what these writers were up to. When he responded with such whole-heartedness to *The House of Life* – he called it Praz's masterpiece – he must have felt with a shiver of excitement as if he were revisiting the tastes and enthusiasms that he'd explored decades earlier among the Symbolists of *Axel's Castle*. The richly figured surfaces and elegantly echoing distances of Praz's *House of Life* cannot but bring to mind elements in the writings of Pater and Huysmans and the Goncourt Brothers. All of this would have been obvious to Wilson. During their 1963–4 visit to Europe, Wilson and his wife Elena had dinner at Praz's apartment. In his diary Wilson noted that Elena was made 'uncomfortable' by the proliferation of Praz's ponderous Empire furnishings; as for Wilson, he was delighted by this apartment overflowing with strange and rare and beautiful old things. Here was a nineteenth-century universe that had somehow survived, and Wilson was glad to turn away from the hard-edged brilliance of the modern movement that he'd begun to report on decades earlier, when he was a young man only recently home from the war.

Edmund Wilson: Centennial Reflections, a collection of essays and memoirs by numerous writers, with an introduction by Lewis M Dabney, to be published by Princeton University Press in 1997.

A Tota£ Me$$

*After 20 years as director of Oxford's Museum of Modern Art, **David Elliott** has left Britain to run Moderna Museet in Stockholm, Sweden's national collection of modern art. He explains the reasons for his defection.*

I leave with great regret, but I am going to a country where the government, as well as the public, cares about supporting the art of its time and century.

Moderna Museet was founded in 1956 and since then has built up a strong collection of classical modern art. The Swedish government has also devoted more than £40 million to the construction of a new building for the museum, designed by the award-winning Spanish architect Rafael Moneo, which will open in 1998. The Swedish Ministry of Culture – no Department of National Heritage there – is actually prepared to invest in collecting modern art as well as constructing the buildings in which to house it. In the UK, you not only have to drive the truck yourself, you have to service the engine and build the motorway.

We didn't have much funding for MOMA in the past two decades. In the early years there was always enough left over to have something to spend on art itself. In the '70s we had the first ever retrospective of Alexander Rodchenko's work, more or less taken out of Russia in a suitcase, followed by the Eisenstein and Mayakovsky shows. We showed Jackson Pollock's drawings and Frank Stella's reliefs. We introduced the Mexican muralist Orozco to Europe, put on British stars such as Howard Hodgkin and Richard Long, and brought Sol le Witt to Britain to create the large-scale Wall Drawings in the museum.

I remember a time when an unquestioning passion for art and the desire to mount exhibitions were the sole qualifications for a director of MOMA. Now such qualities have to be strained through an education that would parallel that of a Harvard Business School graduate. Subsidy used to represent 78 per cent of our turnover; now it is 43 per cent. In order to survive, the museum director has to build up a business administration comparable to that of a medium-sized company. Art becomes a hobby.

Britain is in danger of drifting towards the US model, with the director as a highly paid but ignorant fund-raiser. Art becomes the province of that troglodytic breed of curators whose contact with the real world of money is equally remote. Thus art, life and finance are separated: curators are treated like children, administrators like gods. This is the story of the health service rewritten for the arts.

The quest for cash impedes the progress of art. MOMA is now forced to postpone and even cancel exhibitions during the search for sponsors. Imagine the repercussions for spontaneity and experiment, never mind merit. A perilous four months before our Carl Andre show last May we were still haggling with other European museums over the costs, unsure whether or not the exhibition would ever happen. It did, by the skin of its teeth. There is a spring exhibition, 'Through a Glass Darkly', including photographs by Cindy Sherman and Christian Boltanski, for which MOMA still haven't raised all the sponsorship. How much should be spent on planning a replacement show? Constant cliff-hanging is financially inefficient.

The funding of the visual arts in Britain is a total mess. It is confusingly split between the different autonomous bodies of the Department of National Heritage, local authorities, the ten Regional Arts Boards and the Arts Councils of England, Scotland, Northern Ireland and Wales. With no clear lines of demarcation, buck-passing has become an art in itself. At a recent select committee hearing, the Arts Council explained that it gave a risible 2.8 per cent of its turnover to the visual arts because they were also the responsibility of national and local authority museums. Not a terribly convincing argument. Many theatres with local authority funding receive much greater Arts Council support.

Actually the Arts Council spends more on the visual arts than it says it does. But the way its finances are laid out reflects its own bureaucratic structure. The Hayward and the ICA in London, for example, appear under the budget of Combined Arts rather than Visual Arts, because they are incorporated into arts centres. No one really knows how much funding goes to the visual arts. But it isn't much.

The central problem is a dreadful lack of infrastructure – places in which artists' work can be seen. In the past the funding system used to support the institutions it had helped create. The '60s and '70s were a golden age, when the Arts Council's 'Housing the Arts' fund stimulated the construction of theatres and concert halls across Britain. The visual arts missed out then. Perhaps they peaked too soon? The nineteenth century was the great era of museums – the V&A, the National Gallery, the Tate – and though old buildings can be converted to house contemporary art, the investment to maintain them has never materialised.

The demise of 'Housing the Arts' in the '80s ruled out any hope of capital funding. Of course building programmes did take place, and there was some new income – wheezes such as Enhancement Funding and Incentive Funding were devised by the Arts Council and the government to stave off potential bankruptcies. But organisations survived, hand to mouth, in spite of, rather than because of, the system. In the 1980s, that dark decade, the culture of the Arts Council changed from that of an endearing, slightly old-fashioned amateurism to a new managerialist fundamentalism. Business theories and market indicators were spouted to 'clients'. In MOMA's most recent appraisal, an expensive marketing campaign was solemnly touted as the thing that would solve all our financial problems, despite the fact that there wasn't enough in the coffers even to put art on the museum walls.

It was painful to watch the ayatollahs of the Arts Council study the religion of management. They decided to devolve museums to the regional arts boards. The theory was that the national Arts Council would wither away, to become a kind of holding company for those boards. This didn't happen. Some galleries were devolved, others were not. Those that were regionalised were destroyed: funding went from poor to abysmal. But the most sinister aspect of the whole development was that marketing and entrance figures were elevated above everything else. The left, staring-eyed, messianic, talked of 'empowering the audience'. The right, cooler, more measured, just spoke of 'satisfying the demands of the consumer'. Art, it seemed, had become an embarrassment.

Costs grew; grants shrank. Over the past nine years MOMA has had no subsidy to devote to programming at the beginning of each year. Extra income has to be raised just to cover overheads before the museum can even begin to pitch for exhibition sponsorship. As a regular source of income, sponsorship is sporadic and unreliable.

Contemporary British art is now more highly regarded, purchased and supported by the rest of the world than ever before. Yet at home, its funding continues in a chronic state of crisis. The gravity of the situation may at last have been recognised by the Arts Council, which is now examining the implications of national underfunding, in consultation with other bodies. This comes not a moment too soon. But it comes too late for me. □

This is an edited version of an article which appeared in the *New Statesman*, 4 October 1996.

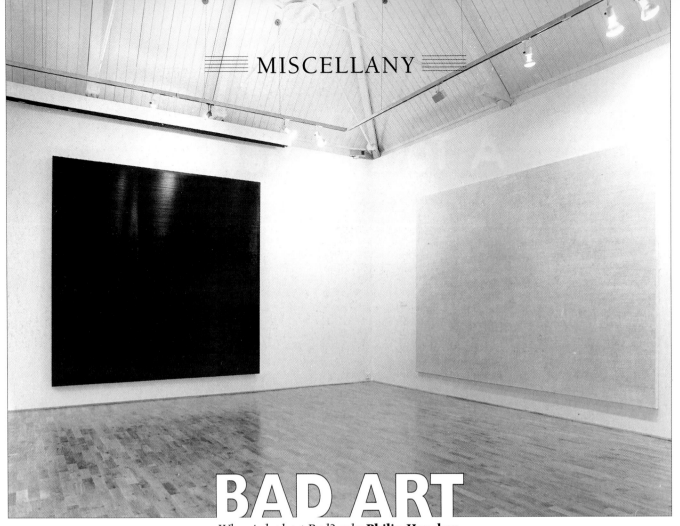

BAD ART

When is bad art Bad? asks **Philip Hensher**.

Some are born bad; some achieve badness; and some (mostly semi-willing art critics and gallery goers, it must be said) have badness thrust upon them. Bad art has been practised for years, of course, in back bedrooms and garden sheds up and down the land, hopefully submitted to local art shows and disappointedly collected, cack-handed pastels of the Queen, simple political allegories or tidy, ugly landscapes with horizontal lines for horizons. But now it's suddenly quite fashionable, and no anthology show this year has been complete without a painter whom the sceptical gallery goer might prefer to call 'not very good', but who is eagerly getting up a whole confident movement; bad painting has gained the upper case and become Bad, with the street-smart connotations of glamorous black slang. It's Bad, man, and, if nothing else, it must be admitted to be a first-rate pre-emption exercise in striking back against criticism. Over and over again, this year, one has stood in front of some revolting canvas and thought, 'My God', only to think, 'Well, it can't be bad, it's Bad'.

The question is, is Bad any good? And, a secondary question, who is Bad, rather than just plain bad? The whole thing really rather resembles those got-up campaigns by tabloid newspapers. Children are bitten by dogs all the time. One month, a tabloid newspaper decides to start writing 'Dog Bites Child' stories. Parliament passes a law against dogs

biting children. Dogs continue to bite children, at roughly the same rate as before. The tabloid newspapers find something else to write about. Similarly, bad art has been produced always; it's just that, now, the critical focus has settled on it, and there seems to be a view that it might be worth taking seriously.

I wonder. At this year's John Moores show in Liverpool, a lady called Liz Arnold exhibited a group of paintings of remarkable Badness. They were paintings of giant anthropomorphised insects, taking part in some half-begun or half-finished narrative

Marcus Harvey, Dudley, Like What You See?
Then Call Me *(detail), 1996, acrylic on canvas.
Courtesy the Saatchi Collection, London
Above title: 'About Vision: New British Painting in
the 1990s', Piper Gallery Installation View
featuring: Jason Martin,* Shaman, *1996 (left) and
Simon Callery,* Archive, *1996 (right)*

of undeniably Gothic import. They were quite revolting pictures to look at, painted in flat, clashing colours, and executed with a neatness which did nothing to mitigate the limpness of the drawing. But those criteria are not relevant any longer: we may not appeal to any notion of ineptness or quality. Rather, the viewer must contemplate his own distaste at looking at a work which gives so powerfully the impression of aiming at something which it then fails to accomplish. There is a certain school of writers of teach-yourself-to-paint books which focuses on the fact that art is produced from one side of the brain; these paintings looked like the product exclusively of the other side.

Of course, it is disquieting for a critic to look at paintings which so forcefully inform him that there is no appropriate critical vocabulary for dealing with these works, that the criteria on which he has based his judgement of paintings are no longer applicable. It might be, in fact, that the value of this art is precisely that – that it doesn't fulfil the values of critics; and an art which lives up to what a critic would like to see, and never surprises or irritates the prejudices of critical response, would be a pretty thin one. But I think there's something damaging in the way a lot of this art seems tailored to such response, to have planned itself precisely around the evasion of the ordinary critical response, and, placing it in the context of art which has evoked a comparable response in the past, it seems as if there's a new thinness, a new lack of seriousness in much of it which can't be equated, quite, with the inadequacies of criticism to perceive something so new that it's quite out of its ken. Rather, much of the art seems to have taken the prejudices of its audience, and pitched its tent firmly upon them.

To an extent, we might like to put it in the context of a few previous attempts to reconstruct the role of skill and talent in the artist's artillery. Dubuffet, for instance, united the art of madmen and children, the outsiders, the innocent and the primitive with a very sophisticated and painterly technique; his seismic canvases may be seen as an assault on the traditional notions of ability, without themselves abandoning an exceptionally virtuoso technique. He is comparable, in some regards, to Klee, who similarly glued elements of ostentatious simplicity and naivety to a framework of astonishing intellectual sophistication.

But the extent to which these artists can be compared to *art brut*, or to naive art, is very limited: it is the abandonment of ambition which is so striking when we look at these new painters. The body of work which might be seen as a more direct fore-runner of Bad art is, I suppose, late Philip Guston, which provoked one of the most famous explosions of critical disdain of the century on its first appearance. With its broad lines, its strange, inert composition and broad, ugly colouring, late Guston is some of the most puzzling painting ever produced by a major artist. But if we ask why late Guston is so exhilarating, it's difficult not to conclude that the fascination lies in the *je m'en-foutisme*, the careless and accidental flouting of every prejudice. Nothing like Guston's last paintings had ever been seen before, and, a quarter of a century on, they retain their power to shock and appal in their sheer dreadful novelty; indeed it must be said that much of their appeal lies in the novelty.

To have a look at what remains in this sort of painting when novelty has been removed from it, the reader may be recommended to take a trip to Oxford to have a look at David Elliott's departing show from the Museum of Modern Art. 'Absolute Vision' is a trip round a bunch of young British artists, not all of whom can readily be placed in any kind of school. But a number of them might be seen, at whatever risk from the libel laws, as Bad. There are some who hover on the edge; Peter Doig's *Lump/Olin MK IV Part II* is certainly not very good, with its lumpy colouring and inert, tidy composition. Is he Bad, or just bad? More unmistakable are Glenn Brown's exceptionally horrible copies of classic art, given whimsical titles and generally mucked about with; the ugliest of them may be concisely be described as the unlovely residue of a wrestling match between Grenze and Baselitz. Difficult to imagine anything uglier, but Marcus Harvey's smeary, random pictures come close.

The striking thing about all these

Philip Guston, The Street, *1977, oil on canvas, 175.2 x 281.3 cm. Metropolitan Museum of Art, New York*

painters is the intense pleasure they take in the manipulation of paint. It is as if the concentration on failed technique forced an interest, and a struggle with the raw materials of the art which is, in essence, profoundly painterly. Personally, I don't find it as interesting or rewarding as some explorations of the surface of paint elsewhere in the show. Jane Harris's beautiful and subtle investigations of the movement of brushstrokes through tiny gradations of colour, for instance, or Jason Martin's engaging *trompe l'oeil* circus trick, creating mounds of paint in two dimensions.

But the texture of paint is the key to the most interesting and successful of the painters who may be thought of as Bad. Gary Hume is currently everywhere, and his frank, fresh style, which draws on a laddish don't-care quality quite as much as on the Pop styles which are so near the surface of his most celebrated pictures, has

Peter Doig, Lump/Olin Mk IV Part II, *1996, oil on canvas, 295 x 200 cm. Private collection*

made him the most currently visible of young British painters. His Badness resides in a few, quite separate features, his hapless technique, which at any moment is prone to lapse into embarrassingly limp failures of illusion, or a gormless copy of Petrus Christus which, like an unsuccessful pupil, offers itself for any kind of praise. There is the daftness of the subject matter – two enormous rabbits in *Innocence and Stupidity*, or the heroes of the half-wit media, like Tony Blackburn or Kate Moss. Hume's willingness to make a prat of himself is one of his most appealing features, and both in an early one-minute video, *Me as King Cnut* (Hume in a bath tub wearing a Burger King paper crown), and his attempt to explain the meaning of his celebrated pictures of hospital doors ('A door is about moving in and out of the present into another place'), we have a sense of the importance of the failure to explain, not just as an adjunct to the picture, but inherent in the picture itself.

The most strikingly Bad element of Hume, however, is the texture of the paint. The use of gloss paint is not new in art, but few artists have so seized on the naffness, the low-rent niceness of gloss paint to paint pictures of startling, embarrassing prettiness. Hume takes care to let his paint drip off the sides of the canvas, to splash smooth areas of paint with little accidents and sad small disasters, but this is simply a superficial guideline to alert us to the meaning of the strange banal gorgeousness of the rest of the paintings. Hume is certainly a Bad painter, if there is such a thing, his meanings, though, are so surprising and peculiar, engage in such complicated ways with good and bad taste, that, unlike almost everyone else fascinated by their own incompetence, he might turn out to be not that bad after all.

'About Vision: New British Painting in the 1990s', until 23 February 1997, Museum of Modern Art, Oxford, and then touring in the UK and abroad. Sponsored in Oxford by Absolute Vodka.

Assemblage No. 21
Found objects on painted board in perspex box, 79 x 73.5 x 8.5 cm

REED'S WHARF GALLERY

BILL BRANDT
(1904 - 1983)

THE ASSEMBLAGES 1967 - 1974

6 MARCH - 11 APRIL 1997

Reed's Wharf Gallery, Mill Street, London SE1 2BA

Gallery hours:
Monday to Friday 10am - 6pm, Saturday 11am - 3pm
Tel 0171 252 1802 Fax 0171 237 3665

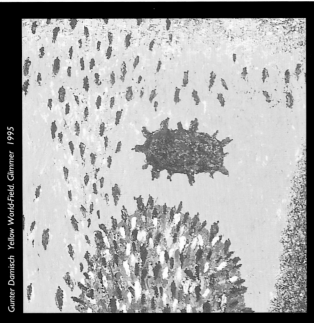

Gunter Damisch Yellow World-Field. Glimmer 1995

Shame 1996

Austrian painting since 1980
and
Austrian Video Art
Until 12th Jan 1997

Patrick O'Reilly
Recent Sculpture
6th Dec 1996 - 19th Jan 1997

Hugh Lane
Municipal Gallery of Modern Art
Charlemont House, Parnell Square North, Dublin 1
Tel: 00353 1 8741903 Fax: 00353 1 8722182 E-mail: HUGHLANE@iol.ie

HIRSCHL CONTEMPORARY ART

presents

Karl Ghattas: Images of God

2 - 14 December, 1996 at The Gallery in Cork Street, 28 Cork St., London W1X

Also at stand 4, ART'97, exhibiting works by: Karl Ghattas, Therese Oulton and Hughie O'Donoghue

"Logos", 1996, Monotype, 24 x 24 cm, £450

"Iqra", 1996, Monotype, 24 x 24 cm, £350

"Cabala", 1996, Monotype, 19 x 38 cm, £450

Suite 3 • 7 Sheffield Terrace • London W8 7NG • Tel: 0171-727 4401 • Fax: 0171-792 9173 • **By Appointment Only**

HART GALLERY

Jean Macalpine *Subterranean* 1995,
57 × 46 cm, Hand-coloured photograph

JEAN MACALPINE

Vertical Rock

January 1997

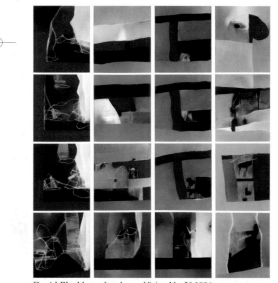

David Blackburn *Landscape Vision No. 20* 1996,
64 × 67 in, Pastel on paper

Hart Gallery will be at ART MIAMI '97 exhibiting work by
BLACKBURN, DRAPER, WHITTAKER, and WOOD
and at ART '97 LONDON exhibiting work by BLACKBURN, BOWEN, DOIG,
DRAPER, FREEMAN, HARTMAN, WEST, WHITTAKER, WOOD, WRIGHT

113 Upper Street, Islington, London N1 1QN Tel: (0171) 704 1131, Fax: (0171) 704 1707
Also at 23 Main Street, Linby, Nottingham Telephone (0115) 963 8707

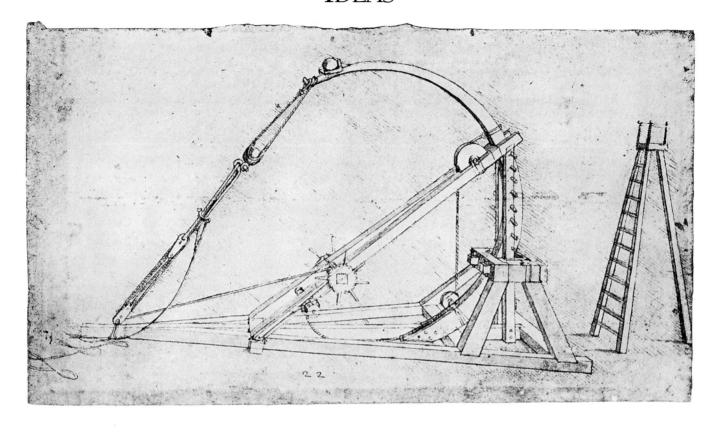

Beauty is Truth, Truth Beauty

John Haldane *seeks to patch up the relationship between art, science and truth.*

The last few summers in the east of Scotland have been uncharacteristically hot and muggy. Such weather further strains the concentration of those disposed to aesthetic intoxication in the theatres, galleries, church halls and streets of Edinburgh. Festival is not Carnival, but it is a time of abandonment to the muses – and a source of considerable income to the canny folk o' the toon. But what if the muses have grown old and tired? That is unthinkable: no art, no Festival, fewer visitors, less money!

It is easy enough to see off town folk's protests about grotesque images, dramatic indecencies and stand-up blasphemy, but when an international sage questions the value of the Festival, never mind the arts expressionistically conceived of, there *is* a problem. That difficulty has hung around Edinburgh like a bad smell since George Steiner appeared to doubt the point of the exercise when giving the Festival Lecture – the opening event of the 50th season.

> To know when to stop is a rare but vivid mark of honesty within excellence. Too many worn-out ghosts of past or altered cultural ambitions and ideals litter the scheme. It is precisely when it is still doing well, when its box-office is healthy, that an institution should draw a dangerous breath and ask: 'Is my continued existence truly representative of my initial aims?'

Not at all the birthday address that might have been hoped for; rather as if, aged 50, one were invited to consider early retirement and encouraged to follow it up with suicide.

One response in the press and in the broadcasting media has been to question the character and function of the Festival. Such discussion is part of what Steiner sought to achieve and it is no bad thing that it should go on. Indeed, while it continues, the further issue should be raised of the value of the Fringe as presently constituted. The vast number of 'new' and 'alternative' comedians hoping to be born in this setting gives it something of the character of a noisy, hot and demented maternity ward.

Also the lack of serious attention to the visual arts in both the Official and Fringe Festivals is a culpable omission. The large-scale exhibitions are often more decorative adornments than food for the educated eye. Richard Demarco is one of the few people determined, year in year out, to promote the cause of contemporary art. This year he ran twelve exhibitions including a documentation of the work *Manresa* by the late German avant-garde artist Joseph Beuys, and a set of new sculptures *In Praise of the Human Spirit* by Jimmy Boyle. Edinburgh must follow this example and offer more for the eye, from different ages and traditions.

George Steiner's reflections, however, had a deeper source than doubts about a civic cultural jamboree, or the particular representation of this or that art form. He was wondering out loud in the presence of priests and faithful whether the God to whom the feast was dedicated might not be dead, or at any rate in a long-term coma. This cultural-cum-philosophical thesis deserves more than the press attention it has received. Steiner's argument ran as follows. The Festival was established in 1946 in part with the aim of healing the scars of war. It sought to draw upon the rich artistic tradition of Europe to demonstrate the values of a humane, aesthetic sensibility and to celebrate the highest achievements of the human spirit. But, as subsequent knowledge of Nazi and Communist tyrannies showed, art is no antidote to viciousness and depravity; on the contrary it has been used to celebrate evil. How is that possible?

Steiner's diagnosis is that art is in decline and that the detached aestheticism it serves is itself a block to serious engagement with human needs and interests. In particular, art has turned its back on knowledge which is now the preserve of science. Art is retrospective, science is prospective and progressive. Moreover, while science is objective and reality-disclosing, art and its advocates now appear to be confined within various forms of relativism and subjectivism, lunatics howling that there is nothing outside the text. This last charge echoes a complaint of others. In his popular account of contemporary evolutionary science, *River out of Eden* (1995), Richard Dawkins expresses irritation at those cultural theorists, and others of relativist persuasion, who liken science to a tribal myth, regarding it as the 'mythology favoured by our Western tribe'. Dawkins responds:

> Show me a cultural relativist at thirty thousand feet and I'll show you a hypocrite ... scientific beliefs are supported by evidence, and they get results. Myths and faiths are not and they do not.

Amoral or decadent, detached and effete, self-destructively subjectivist – how might art be defended against this onslaught? One reply picks up on Steiner's positive suggestions. In his lecture he remarked that the advocates of science need to find attractive styles of presentation so as to bring together truth and beauty; and he suggested that among the best sources of pleasure and fascination available at arts festivals are master-classes and workshops in which the skills of performance and craftsmanship are on display. These two points suggest that Steiner's complaint is less with art *per se* than with the forms that surround us today. More precisely, his target is a certain philosophical idea of art that remains current and influential. This

Jimmy Boyle, In Times of Conflict,
Above title: Leonardo da Vinci, Catapult, c.1490, pen, 12.2 x 21.6 cm. Codex Atlanticus, Biblioteca Ambrosiana, Milan

is the notion of art as the domain of highly individual subjectivity; art as the product of eccentric and radical creativity; art as *expression*. But that idea is not a timeless one. On the contrary (and like the philosophies that gave birth to Nazism and Communism), it is a product of eighteenth- and nineteenth-century romanticism.

Accordingly, the advocate of art has no special reason to defend this view of the subject. Indeed, it is relevant to point out that Steiner's two suggestions recall an older view in which art was conceived as a

medium for the presentation of truth and goodness and in which emphasis was placed upon craftsmanship. For 'science' read 'religion', and for 'master-classes' read 'masters' workshops', and what is recommended is the role and conduct of art-making as it was conceived of in the medieval and renaissance periods. Look in that direction and a nobler and socially responsible idea of the making of works of quality appears through the fog of Western romanticism.

Furthermore, it is an understanding in which the ideas of truth, goodness and beauty are united. In his *Commentary on the Divine Names*, Thomas Aquinas develops an ancient tradition, writing that 'there is nothing which does not share in goodness and beauty, for according to its *form* each thing is both good and beautiful'. A 'form' for Aquinas is the organising principle of a thing, that which makes it the sort of thing it is. In contemporary terms the form of an animal might be held to be its genetic structure. Familiarly, such structures are the objects of science; so Aquinas seems to be saying that what science studies is also a proper subject for aesthetic attention. It will come as a surprise to some that Steiner's rejection of twentieth-century ideas of art is prefigured in the philosophies of antiquity and the middle ages, but the common idea is simple enough: *if it is to avoid degeneration into fantasy, art has to be keyed to objective truth.* ☐

Gallery
by
Karen Wright

Rarely am I moved by people's pleas to be included in 'Gallery', but Heather Davies's eloquent letter prompts an exception in the case of her daughter Ashley Davies. Ashley has her first solo show in the Mermaid Theatre Gallery until 18 January. This sensitive oil, *Lecanora*, shows her to be another talented graduate of the Royal Academy Schools. They do turn out some good painters.

The Tate St Ives shows Christopher Wood until 20 April, then sends the work on to the Quimper Museum, Normandy, another 'local' venue for this artist. You can't beat the predictably boaty Woods. Here is *Boat in a Harbour, Brittany.*

'Aerial Creatures', Paul Nash's war paintings, including *Battle of Germany* (1944), are at the Imperial War Museum until 26 January, and travelling to the Oriel Mostyn in Llandudno. These are war paintings at their most chilling, leaving so much to the imagination.

Ken Kiff shows recent work, graphics, oils, acrylics and water-colours, at Marlborough until 31 December. Pictured is *White Tree*. (Any guesses as to what the eyeballs are doing to me at Universal House?)

Francisco's Goya's last etchings, 'The Disparates', go on show at the Wakefield Art Gallery, 25 January–23 February. Goya was in his 70s and recovering from a serious illness when he made these extraordinary works. Don't expect to be cheered by visions like *Disparate pobre (Poor folly).*

One of the most promising shows through the chilly months is Tony Cragg's at the Whitechapel, 10 January–9 March. Featuring recent pieces like *Spyrogyra*, and including work in progress, this should be a good one.

For those who missed Bacon in Paris, there's a second chance to see his work in Munich. If you're there, don't miss Hughie O'Donaghue's show at the Haus der Kunst. Or, if you stay in London, you could catch the show when it comes to Purdy Hicks's new Bankside space, 24 January–1 March. It's really not fair to judge huge works like *Red Earth V11* from a postage-stamp format: so go and see them in the flesh, please!

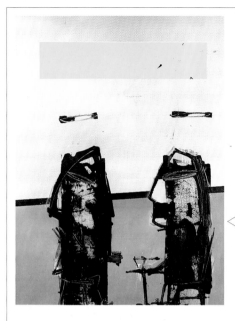

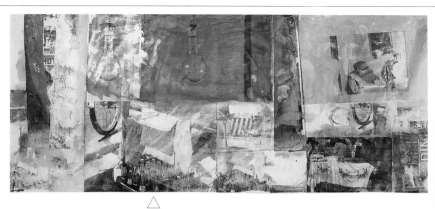

Paul Regan shows in the Front Lounge bar/café, Dublin, until 19 January. All proceeds from sales of the boldly colourful works, including *Two Pioneers*, goes to the charity for the Prevention of Cruelty to Children and to Childline.

Robert Rauschenberg exhibits new work at PaceWildenstein, Los Angeles, until 18 January, 1997. These translucent 'Anagrams' are vegetable dye transfers on paper, and 'the newest element in Rauschenberg's expanding universe', as the catalogue has it. A long way from home, but by all accounts a wonderful show – here's *Fusion,* 1996 (from the Whitney's Collection), and all of 5 x 12 feet huge – so get with the wanderlust.

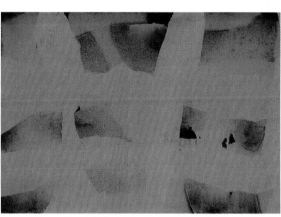

The Thaw Collection of ravishing Master Drawings continues at the Royal Academy until 23 January. I am sure we have all known teachers like this pedantic character in Honoré Daumier's *The Schoolmaster and The Drowning Child.*

Ian McKeever's 'Paintings 1990–1995' will be found at both Angel Row Gallery and the Bonington Gallery in Nottingham, 9 January– 8 February. This lovely veil of intense colour is *Hour No 32, 1994—95.* McKeever is a painter's painter, so don't miss out.

The Ted Powers collection, on show at the Tate till 16 February, shows a collector 'ahead of his time'. I love *The Handsome Pork-Butcher*'s coiffure by Francis Picabia.

Inspired by the Hayward's Howard Hodgkin show, which runs until 23 January, why not buy an original print to keep forever? Wiseman Originals shows Hodgkin prints, 1 February–31 March. Alan Christea also shows Hodgkin in a mixed show, 'Colour Etchings', until 18 January. Here is *You and Me* (are we?), or if you prefer, purple and green.

Laurent Delaye shows Milo Garcia's plywood 'assembly' pieces until 21 December. In the words of the press release, 'Passionately trivial subject-matter serves the purpose of dismissable but irreducible reference: a boy pissing in a bush witnessed by a dog, a man masturbating in a toilet' – which leaves me at a loss for further comment.

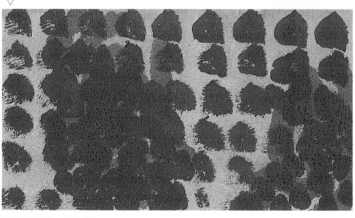

Edward Totah's death left quite a few painters gallery-less. One of them was Stephen Farthing, who dedicates his latest show to Totah. Recently at Anne Berthoud in London, it has reopened in Paris – until 15 December, at Hôtel de la Monnaie les Salons, 11 Quai de Conti, Paris 6. All the works in 'Absolute Monarchy' are headless portraits, including this one, which I dedicate to Roger Scruton: *As If Hunting.*

Women by Themselves

by BLAKE MORRISON

For men, exhibitions of women's art can be a daunting experience. On the day I visited 'Inside the Visible', at the Whitechapel, someone had scrawled 'Sex?' above the urinals in the men's lavatory – a piece of graffiti which I took to be not a proposition but a confession of identity crisis, or even an accusation: are you sure you're in the right place? Certainly, male visitors to 'Inside the Visible' (37 women artists spanning the century), or to the touring exhibitions 'In the Looking Glass' (Contemporary Self-Portraits by Women) and 'Rubies and Rebels' (Jewish Female Identity in Contemporary British Art), may feel a sense of trespass. The ambience is welcoming and inclusive enough. The curators and their advisers, far from haranguing, seem almost to apologise for the gender-specificity (Griselda Pollock says it's 'almost incidental' that the Whitechapel show is all-female). None the less, if you're male and even the teeniest bit attentive, it won't escape your notice that some of the assembled women, or some of those who've assembled them, feel antagonistic towards patriarchy and/or its canon. And however much the new man in you may assent to this, it's hard not to feel complicit. Which makes a tour of the gallery walls a bit of a guilt trip.

Women visitors can afford to be more take-it-or-leave it, less on the defensive. But even among women, there are mixed feelings about such exhibitions. Aren't they ghettoising, and self-defeating? Shouldn't women artists be battling it out with and among men, as their equals, at the Tate and Hayward and elsewhere? Positive discrimination – and it's hard for such exhibitions to avoid the taint of this – looks needless and rather old-fashioned in the age of Bridget Riley (who once said women artists need feminism like a hole in the head), Paula Rego, Rachel Whiteread and Maggi Hambling (a welcome but rather surprising contributor to 'In the Looking Glass'). It's no wonder that those campaigning for a Museum of Women's Art have met some of the fiercest resistance from their own sex.

But shows such as these (and even the MWA) do have a place if they teach us something we didn't know – if they revive a lost talent or make connections that

Claude Cahun, Self-Portrait, 1929, *gelatin-silver print, 13.4 x 8.9 cm. Courtesy of a private collection, New York*

wouldn't otherwise have been made. Gender is only one of the ways of looking at painting, perhaps no more important than, say, the use of allegory or changing representations of landscape. But it can, at best, be instructive – especially where it forces us to think about possible differences between men's and women's art.

Consider, for example, self-portraiture, which figures largely in all three shows. If the female self-portrait is flourishing now,

it's been argued, that's because of the new-found self-confidence women have attained, which in turn reflects their growing economic and sexual independence. For a woman to paint or draw or photograph herself is an act of self-assertion: the answer to those (men) who've tried to render her invisible or to distort her with their desires and misconceptions. Women no longer have to sit for the (male) Other in order to be authenticated or made flesh; they can do the job themselves.

There's force in this argument, but a couple of major problems with it, too, the first of them historical. To see a great leap forward in female self-assertion, you can go back over four centuries and compare Sophinisba Anguissola, circa 1550, whose self-portrait depicts her standing impassively while being painted by her male art teacher, Bernard Campi (as if she only exists by virtue of his efforts), with Artemisia Gentileschi, who in an equivalent self-portrait 70 years later is shown working energetically, right hand raised, eyes concentrating on the canvas and not a male painter in sight. Women have not had to wait until the late twentieth century to depict themselves as strong, defiant, unconventional, independent, self-contained.

But in any case, these aren't adjectives that spring to mind in the current shows. Vulnerable and anxious would be more like it – which makes the paintings far more interesting than if they were programmatically self-assertive. When Judith Collins asks the ten artists from 'In the Looking Glass' what made them turn to self-portraiture, the answers are various. Because 'my life was in a muddle', says Maggi Hambling. 'I was unhappy because I was getting divorced', says Frances Blane. It's cheaper and/or more convenient than using models, say Lucy Jones and Shani Rhys James. In order to paint herself as thin, at a time she was suffering from anorexia, says Julie Held; and in later work, at a time of darkness and depression, to keep her head above water and imagine herself in warmth and light.

Held's swimming costume paintings, Hambling's floating, semi-figurative eye, and Shani Rhys James's and Lucy Jones's large, red studies of themselves at work are assertive (and successful) as paintings, but not as statements of ideology or psychic health. Far from strength or solidity, the overall sense this exhibition gives is of isolation, fragmentation and even (in Isobel Brigham's *Self-*

Jean Cooke, Not Waving Just Painting, 1996, oil on canvas, 45 x 45 cm

Portrait with Detached Arm) amputation. Jean Cooke paints herself with a black eye, and Elizabeth Wilson, Frances Blane and Jagjit struggle to realise their identity through heavy layers of oil. Only Mary Mabbutt, with her Art Nouveauish symmetries, is content to render herself in a calm domestic setting.

Confidence, after you've left this low-key but attractive exhibition, begins to seem like a 'masculine' quality – the quality to be found in Robert Mapplethorpe's most notorious self-portrait, the bullwhip-up-the-anus, with its glee and bravado: look-what-I-can-do. Women artists have a different and (in present times) more likeable kind of gift: their touch is surest when confessing to insecurity, and their nerve holds when depicting neurosis. If they perform – and 'performance' is a word used a lot at the Whitechapel show – there's something fragile and provisional about the act. Mirrors, when they use them, as self-portraitists must, don't give back simple images, let alone allow narcissistic pleasure, but are a site of illusion and troubled reflection. Even when they show themselves naked, we don't feel we're getting the unadorned truth.

Take Nadine Tasseel (b.1953, Belgian), at the Whitechapel, whose *Untitled: Self-Portraits* is a series of six photographs, ambiguous enough in their postures to suggest both classical paintings of goddesses and early pornographic photos of prostitutes. Always masked and sometimes veiled, draped in cloth or framed by windows, the body conceals more than it reveals. Or there's Claude Cahun (1894–1954), whose self-portraits from the 1920s show her in a variety of poses, at one moment boyish, the next doll-like, rouged and coquettish. There's no 'real' Cahun here: instead, she plays at being whatever she fancies, or colludes in being what others imagine her to be, while never disclosing any consistent or continuous identity. Disappointingly, there are only three of her self-images in the Whitechapel exhibition, but the catalogue includes several more, including a terrifying punkish, shaved-head version from 1930 which seems to disown the earlier masquerade of womanliness.

Along with Louise Bourgeois, and several more artists, Cahun and Tasseel appear in the first part of the Whitechapel show, offputtingly entitled 'Parts of/for' but the strongest section of this otherwise rather wayward assemblage. Upstairs, in the fourth and last section, there's Francesca Woodman (USA, 1958–81), who before her suicide at the age of 23 produced a series of photographic self-portraits in which her body – the face always out of shot – is distorted, transected, squeezed or splayed. There's a pain, intensity and violence about Woodman's images which seem partly to do with a frustrated search for identity: there she is, naked, and yet we're not getting her, and nor is she. A similar bitness can be found in the photographs of Natalie Hervieux – shadowy studies of a single human body, which

Shani Rhys James, Lead White, *1996, oil on canvas, 122 x 91.5 cm*

repeatedly refuses to declare itself – and a more literal bitness in Mona Hatoum's haunting installation *Recollection*, which uses rolled-up balls of her own hair and a miniature loom. Whatever personal history (if any) Hatoum is recollecting, she transcends it by setting off larger echoes, such as the Jewish Holocaust and the part which weaving has played in the lives of millions of women down the years.

Even at its worst (for example Martha Rosler's conflation of war atrocities with the oppression of the middle-class American housewife), 'Inside the Visible' stands as a useful corrective to the stereotype of women's art as domestic and small-scale. So, too, does the all-Jewish/British/female 'Rubies and Rebels', which includes Lynn Leon's photograph of two scarfed, almost conjoined Magrittish heads (one Jewish, one Palestinian), which caused a fracas when exhibited in Haifa, and Barbara Loftus's painfully protracted documentation of Nazis removing the family porcelain. The great risk of such an exhibition is piety. In the

context – the Holocaust, emigration, the Middle East, the treatment of women in orthodox Judaism – piety seems forgivable, but several British writers of the same generation have shown that other approaches are possible, including humour, a quality notable for its absence here. It's the most didactic of the three shows, and in the end, brow-beaten by all the identity politics, I was grateful for the presence of a couple of Jewish women artists – Jessica Wilkes, Sarah Raphael – who were less insistent on their Jewishness and womanhood than on their art.

'Inside the Visible', until 8 December, Whitechapel Art Gallery, London; 14 February–10 April 1997, Gallery of Western Australia, Perth. Catalogue £24.95.
'In the Looking Glass', 17 January–1 March 1997, Aberystwyth Arts Centre; 8 March–20 April 1997, Glynn Vivian Art Gallery, Swansea; 8 May–22 June 1997, Graves Art Gallery, Sheffield. Catalogue £8.95.
'Rubies and Rebels', until 10 January 1997, Leeds University Art Gallery and Leeds Metropolitan University Gallery. Catalogue £14.95.

Max Beckmann: A Big Mistake

by TOM LUBBOCK

Is it possible for an artistic reputation to be completely mistaken? It sounds unlikely. W H Auden said that though artists are sometimes unjustly forgotten they are never unjustly remembered, and the maxim holds because it makes a judiciously minimal claim. It doesn't say that posterity's positive estimates are always sound, only that they're never absolutely unsound. It tells chiefly against severely revising critics who would have it that some fame is based on nothing, all puff, a cloud of smoke to be blown away. It says that everything that survives has something going for it. Nothing lasts for no reason at all. No smoke without at least a little fire. The thought might give one pause. But if you believe, still, that there has been a complete mistake, you'd better offer some good reasons for its being made.

Take the case of Max Beckmann. He has certainly lasted. It's nearly 50 years since his death, and that's time enough to fade, and he hasn't. So Auden's rule should apply. We should presume an achievement of some kind. Beckmann's reputation, though, is a curious phenomenon. It cannot quite find its level. Never unregarded since his Weimar years, he has never got a settled place in the modern canon. Over the decades he has been highly praised, but with the recurring sense that he has not yet received his due. He's an artist whose talent continually awaits full recognition; about whom it's still as interesting to say, now, as it was in the '40s, that he is really very good.

So it's hard to know whether the show at the Guggenheim's downtown outlet – 'Max Beckmann in Exile' – means that he has finally arrived. He has arrived so often before, only to arrive again. But it looks like one more relaunch. The gallery's Director, for instance, declares Beckmann 'unquestionably one of the century's great masters', and that wouldn't need saying if there really were no question (you wouldn't say it of Léger). And the show itself seems designed as an argument for Beckmann's greatness. It focuses on his later work, from his leaving Germany (1937) to his death in America (1950), the period when his style freed up and his ambitions mounted. But it presents only paintings, and then only paintings of the grander sort. There are none of his landscapes, still-lives, nudes, portraits. There are some self-portraits. But mostly it's his human subject pictures, the narrative and allegorical works, including seven of his ten large triptychs. Through size and genre alone, these are pictures that ask to be major. Here, they are the master's masterpieces.

And this is baffling to me. It's not the mastery of these paintings I quarrel with, it's the idea that they have any value at all. What I'd want to say about the Beckmann of this show is that he has indeed nothing going for him. He is simply no good, no good at any level, and no good in a way that is prior to liking or disliking, overrating or underrating. For example, I may not much admire Chagall or Ernst, I may confess that Braque generally leaves me cold, but I think I know how the arguments about them go, what people see in these artists or why they value them. But as for these Beckmanns, I'm stumped. I can't imagine how anyone who had actually looked at them could find anything in them, their no-goodness seems both so utter and so obvious. Yet evidently it is not obvious to some. Thus there are two problems. One is to explain why Beckmann is thoroughly no good. The other is to explain how this extraordinary mistake could have been made. I'll do the second first.

Come at it this way. Consider a very general and more or less neutral description of these pictures. Here is a painting that is unquestionably modernist, but packed with subject matter; it's a work of modern myth-making, centred on human protagonists, combining social and spiritual themes; it is history painting for the twentieth century. Now surely, you're getting interested already. You like the *idea* of it. It's the kind of painting you would like to exist. It really ought to exist.

What's attractive in the idea of Beckmann's work is that, for one thing, it

Max Beckmann, Double Portrait, Max Beckmann and Quappi, *1941, oil on canvas, 194 x 89 cm*

answers to our feelings about our century. The twentieth century, one feels, should have produced an art that measures up, powerfully but complexly, to the century itself, with its public terrors and private anxieties. The twentieth century, moreover, is in need of a mythology. The old religious ones are dead. The new ideological ones are nightmares. We want something humanistic, something between tragedy and absurdity, expressing the horror and the heroism of modern life. And having lost our faith in every other authority, we look to the artist to provide this.

And what's attractive also in the idea of Beckmann's work is that it overcomes one of our big doubts about modern painting generally: the way that it suffers from excessive specialisation. Take a brisk tour around the figurative art of his contemporaries, and note how strengths always involve severe limitations. The School of Paris: formally advanced, but not very ambitious when it comes to content. Surrealism: rich in complex imagery, but only psychological in scope. Expressionism: vigorously anguished but inarticulate. *Neue Sachlichkeit*; a hard look at modern society, but distinctly low-minded. Socialist Realism: heroic, public spirited, but frankly commy. And where is the painting that will do the full works?

Now the stage is set for Beckmann and his 'greatness'. He knows no artistic specialisation. He belongs to no confining school or movement. He rebukes our textbook categories (which we always feel a little guilty about) and offers another way. He takes what he wants where he finds it. He borrows the formal freedoms of Paris and Expressionism, not in pursuit of stylistic adventure, but so that he can accommodate any subject, story or symbolism he chooses. He makes a grand synthesis of the scattered strengths of modern painting. And doing this, he does something else. He produces the large visions the century is crying out for, tales of quest and lust, torture and triumph, an imagery both ancient and modern, a range of subjects that is not specifically political, nor personal psychodrama, but a sturdy mythic mixture of the two. And in triptychs!

But of course what we are talking about is a hypothetical art, an art whose worth is established in advance of it's being looked at. What this account delivers is only a prospectus: painting described at the level of a blueprint, a checklist of desirable features – which is then matched up with another blueprint, an artistic job that badly needs doing (synthesising modern painting, mythologising the century). The errors involved are plain. No art can be judged just on its ingredients. No art becomes important through the importance of the project it undertakes. But this is a common critical hazard: coming along with a cause, and happily believing it instanced in some actual work – and then the work must be made to rise to the occasion, and if the cause is a great one, so must the work be.

Max Beckmann, Actors, *1941–2, oil on canvas, Fogg Art Museum, Harvard University, Cambridge, Massachusetts*

You know how it goes: where are our war poets? Or: where is modern history painting?

And this, I think, is the basis of Beckmann's reputation, the source of his appeal: a job description. He offers to fill a position that would otherwise be lamentably vacant in modern art, and his admirers are ready to take the will for the deed because the deed itself would be so valuable. But now look at the work itself. It's awful. It's obvious. And if it isn't obvious, it can be pointed out.

What's wrong with these Beckmann pictures, fundamentally, is that they themselves are all too happy to take the will for the deed, at every level. Their procedures are perfunctory and indifferent. They use their form and content as alibis for one another. The picture doesn't work – but look, it's got all this subject matter in it. The human story falls flat – but look, it's meant to be modernism. Beckmann's fans are right in a way to overlook what he's actually doing, because that is what the pictures are always asking you to do.

To specifics. Composition. Beckmann's compositional principle is the pile-up. He goes on putting things in until the frame fills like a sardine tin. The space is very shallow. There are no large contrasts of tone or colour. There is rarely an interval anywhere. There is only an accumulation of flat elements, each emphatically demarcated with the same black outline (the way he keeps things separate). Sometimes there is some rudimentary scaffolding, other times utter shapelessness, but either way

no pictorial drama can emerge because there are no major sub-divisions, just a crammed whole.

The effect is sometimes called powerfully claustrophobic, and in the earlier Weimar paintings, where there is more deep space and solid modelling, it can be. But here, where everything is flattened, where anatomy can be flexed anyhow and objects represented on any scale, bodies and objects offer no resistance to their enclosure. There are crowds, but no pressure builds. Just occasionally there is an interesting tangle.

Human figures are Beckmann's chief subject. He is without concern for them, either as shapes or characters. Nowhere is there a striking configuration of the body. Their faces are dumb masks, heavily kohled. Their limbs are stock stiff or fillet limp. Their hands are always a bunch of carrots. Their actions are vacant. They are incapable of the pains and pleasures and motives which their situations suggest. To see them as tragic puppets or strangely ambiguous is simply to make a virtue of inarticulateness.

The flatness puts line at a premium. The stark black outlines make it unignorable. But Beckmann's drawing is unspeakable, without tension, or grace, or even violence. It is merely rough, heavy and prolific. Likewise his colours are merely colourful. He puts lots in, with no eye for harmony or clash, with little variation in intensity. This is his powerfulness: sheer insistence, sheer load.

All of which neutralises whatever interest his imagery might have. There are

one or two potentially memorable emblems, involving bondage and torment – men tied to the sails of a windmill, a couple lashed together body to body, with one standing upright and the other upside-down – that is, another artist might have made them memorable. But, as a rule, Beckmann's mythological repertoire is all too largely mythic: kings and warriors, pierrots and *fatale* tarts, swords and trumpets, malevolent birds and iffy fish. And it's always a general idea, never a particular image. But it might be a strange world still, if it wasn't effectively de-estranged by Beckmann's baggy pictorial procedure, in which he gives himself complete freedom to put in anything just as he pleases, where nothing is allowed its own presence.

Interpreting these pictures is a thankless task – a task of course eagerly taken on and at great length by iconographers happy at the opportunity, and happy again to find ambiguity in the under-described. But I doubt whether the most admiring viewer thinks they can learn anything from Beckmann. What beguiles is only the idea of allegory, and the idea is what Beckmann offers, and what earns him the title of painter-philosopher. Nor is it hard to see how he passes for an artist of strong personal conviction and independent vision. It is the way he carried on regardless – regardless of anything that might give his paintings life or interest. Clearly what he's doing means a lot to him. It is the conviction and independence of a crank.

Attacking Beckmann, though, one must not fall into an opposite but equivalent error

Max Beckmann, Fish-Ride, *1934, oil on canvas, 134.5 x 115.5 cm*

to his admirers, and say that what he was attempting was inherently impossible, that its failure was inevitable, because he is trying to synthesise things that cannot be synthesised. For instance, that you cannot pick up the tricks of Picasso, Matisse, Léger and Expressionism and hope to incorporate them with complex allegorical schemes: the graft won't take; the energies are mutually exclusive and disaster is bound to follow. The thought is tempting, because here Beckmann does fail completely; but it is to resort again to a hypothetical art argument, to claim that one can know in advance, just from its description, what sort of art won't work. No. Beckmann is bad, but he is contingently bad. The sort of art which his paintings gesture towards might have succeeded in other hands. Those hands never appeared. But there's no point in regretting the loss. The history of art is a lesson in the absoluteness of contingency. What actually happened is all there is. Might have been, nice idea, are nothing. Beckmann's greatness, on the other hand, his survival at all, is one great cry of 'If only..'

'Max Beckmann in Exile', until 5 January, the Guggenheim Museum, New York.

David Hepher

by JONATHAN GLANCEY

Between 1969 and 1974 David Hepher painted himself into a cul-de-sac. Almost literally. During those years, his subject was the suburban house. Not suburban houses in general, but a row of south London Edwardian semis in Townley Road, East Dulwich. Hepher lived in a flat-fronted late Georgian town house in nearby Camberwell; East Dulwich was a walk away. The paintings that emerged from his watercolour sketches of Townley Road formed a sequence of what were referred to as 'super-realist' canvases that appeared to be no more and no less than a sustained exhibition of technical skill: Hepher could represent the Edwardian semi-detached houses of south London as no one else could. No one else, that is, save someone with a galleon-out-of-matchsticks mentality prepared to spend five years of their life glued to a task at once meticulous and apparently banal.

Seen hanging together in the Museum of London, however, the paintings of Townley Road assume a surreal and oddly

sinister air. There is something in the immaculate precision of their representation, their lack of human activity and warmth, and the way in which the viewer's focal length is radically foreshortened, that makes these paintings far more than photographs in oil on canvas, and far more, too, than 'super-realist' techno-wizardry. Yet, if Hepher's Townley Road forces the idea of the banality of the suburban house (these are not homes: home is too soft and warm a word) on the viewer, it is ultimately both discomforting and disquieting. This might be what the artist intended, but it is a relief to discover that at the end of the road, Hepher put down his brush, paused, and discovered the high-rise housing estate.

It is the housing estate that he has made his own. From his beginnings as a Euston Road type of painter in the mid-'50s, through Townley Road semis to the remarkable tower-block canvases he has painted in a number of styles since the late '70s, Hepher has made the domestic urban landscape the subject of meticulous, imaginative and near obsessive skill. Skill is the right word. If the Townley Road paintings are an exhibition of imagination linked to canvas via a razor sharp brush and a photographic eye, the tower-block canvases are a tour-de-force of technical prowess. *Albany Flats* (1977–78), *Walworth Flats* (1977) and *Arrangement in Turquoise and Cream* (1978) are extraordinary creations. At first sight they are hugely powerful abstracts; second sight reveals them to be minutely detailed portraits of some of south London's most monumental local authority housing. Closer observation still reveals the texture of stained concrete represented in a mix of sand and oil, underscored by a filigree brushwork depicting the individual patterns of net curtains in several hundred identical steel-framed windows. Stand back again and these encyclopedically detailed images become powerful abstracts once more. If they share anything in common with the Townley Road paintings, it is not merely in the hawkish attention to detail, but the fact that they draw us up short and make us look again at the everyday buildings that are the kitchen-sink drama backdrop to contemporary urban life.

Hepher does not comment, as such, on the desirability or otherwise of suburban villas or high-rise estates. And, he is at pains to point this out when asked if his paintings are political statements of any kind. They are not. Hepher has painted houses since leaving the Slade and they are his subject as much as the Madonna was Bellini's or the sunset, Turner's. No one asks if Bellini was making a comment on the nature of the Catholic church when he chose to paint his gorgeous, pouting mistress as the Blessed Virgin. Of course, Renaissance artists, whatever their private beliefs, knew better than to incur the wrath of the Church (which at the time was as much fire as smoke), and Bellini was, like so many great artists of the time, using the subject of the Virgin as a means of expressing his own enquiries as a painter.

David Hepher, Study for Arrangement in Greys and Silvers (diptych)*, 1995, acrylic, plaster and PVA on canvas, each panel 31 x 61 cm*

It does not matter whether he believed that Mary was a virgin, nor even that she was mother of the Saviour.

Hepher's suburban houses and south London tower blocks have been his equivalent of the Blessed Virgin or sunsets over Petworth Park or wherever. The cool abstraction of the first series of tower-block paintings, culminating in *Arrangement in Turquoise and Cream* is an outward sign that there is no inward comment. The fact that Hepher chose not to reveal the name of the last of these tower-block paintings is, perhaps, a statement of intent: *Arrangement in Turquoise and Cream* is an abstract that happens to have a housing estate as its subject. By the time Hepher had reached this point of pure abstraction, he stopped and changed direction. The canvas is a tour-de-force, but to Hepher it was proof that he had painted himself into a corner. Where did he go now? Should he repeat himself and thus face the danger of being like the sort of artist who paints railway locomotives or war planes over and over again, trying to achieve greater realism with each new start?

It was never a real danger, although it was a real thought in the artist's mind and a real concern for him. He had already been labelled a 'super-realist', and that was not what he wanted to be, or to be thought of as being. Which is why he changed direction again and began to paint (yes, housing estates again) in a warm manner; the canvases of this period have something of the late-night and wistful quality of Edward Hopper. Hepher's nighthawks, however, do not hang out in lonely roadside diners, but settle behind the net curtains of council flats, televisions glowing, washing strung from high balconies.

These are not his best paintings: they are too soft and verge on illustration. This is not to denigrate the art of illustration, but to note that in trying to add in the 'human element' missing from *Albany Flats* and *Walworth Flats* Hepher was in danger of making a kind of social reportage that would have served well as illustrations to Sunday supplements looking at the problems of the inner city, but had lost the unsentimental and non-judgemental power of the earlier paintings. It was a short-lived phase at the end of the '70s and the beginning of the '80s.

If less successful than the abstracts of the late '70s, these cosy tower-block paintings were a respite for Hepher. *Albany Flats* (owned by the Tate) took eighteen

months to complete. The softer paintings that followed were done relatively quickly, with the artist using much broader and freer brushstrokes. In this sense they were a kind of liberation from the microscopically constructed abstracts. Or a busman's holiday.

Whatever, Hepher began painting a series of loud and colourful fantasies in the mid-'80s, based on Piranesi's prison series. Piranesi's monochrome treatment was reinterpreted in flaming reds, burnt oranges and fiery yellows, the famous prisons turned into a scorched world brooding somewhere between Heaven and Hell (it is impossible to decide which); between gaps in the prison walls, and between the interstices of stairs rising into the void, we catch glimpses of, you've guessed, south London tower blocks again. This series – 'After Piranese' – is an inquiry into rich colour and thick paint, and a release of emotions so carefully bottled up in the paintings that had culminated in *Arrangement in Turquoise and Cream*. In fact, Hepher had experimented several times before with heavy duty textures; two of these works can be seen as you walk into the Museum of London show, hung opposite his earliest Euston Road School-style paintings of terraced houses in Sheffield. They have been included to demonstrate that an artist who can control a brush so precisely has the capacity to let rip and employ raw mixed-media materials almost aggressively

(although Hepher would deny the aggression). They are interesting for this reason, but are orphans, or perhaps unwanted party guests, because the strength of this particular show lies not only in the quality of Hepher's work, but also in its concentration on house after flat after house.

Hepher's movement between a minutely observed abstract realism and a much looser and more emotional approach to paint comes together in his recent work, which happily is also his best (along with that of the late '70s).

Castles in the Air and *Home Sweet Home* (both of 1993) make convincing and powerful use of both techniques. Both comprise menacing tower blocks – things of brute beauty in Hepher's hands – bereft of people, but wounded with savage decoration: the canvases are pitted, carved and impregnated with violent and exuberant graffiti. These are accurately recorded on Hepher's walks through south London estates, but blown up on a bombastic scale on the paintings themselves. They include the usual love-trysts daubed in aerosol red, football slogans, political taunts, the incomprehensible and defiant 'tags' of rival street gangs and – the only and biggest surprise, and the subject and starting point of *Home Sweet Home* – a child's drawing, big and bold in yellow paint, of a house with four windows, a door, pitched roof, corner chimneys, garden and sun.

Of course this caught Hepher's eye, and

David Hepher, Arrangement in Blues and Greys, *1985–6, oil on canvas, diptych, each panel, 251 x 190 cm*

David Hepher, Blue Study for Lower Ground 1, *1995, acrylic, cement and PVA on canvas, 35 x 39 cm*

the irony (for that is what the yellow house appears to be to an adult) is unmissable: even a child brought up in a brutalist, concrete, late-'60s megastructure depicts the idea of 'home' in the same way as every child has before, whether from a smart house in the country, a semi-detached in suburbia or a local authority tower block.

Again, what impresses most is the fact that Hepher does not use graffiti or child's drawing to make a cheap political point. He is not telling us how dreadful these buildings are nor how alienated their occupants: he is depicting the abstract beauty of a building type that all too often we either pretend not to see or want (well, the polite middle class wants) to cover up in childish post-modern style cladding to make them look suburban and thus acceptable. The truth of the matter is that no amount of dressing housing estates in puerile architectural fancy dress will ever make them better places to live. Hepher has spent long

enough sketching these estates and talking to residents on a casual basis – they talk to him openly because he is an artist and not from the council or an architect, and therefore a friendly nutcase rather than an interfering official or patronising professional – to know that people want good plumbing and lifts that work, freedom from violence and a community that somehow jogs along. Only architects and caring, sharing, do-gooding officials want to desecrate '60s architecture with applied post-modern tat. One has to be careful here: you see how easy it is to start talking about the politics of housing and architecture when faced with a Hepher canvas? The artist himself, as we know, eschews political readings of his work, but knows full well that we, as viewers, can read any message we like into these powerful canvases. Hepher's work is more visceral and emotional now than at any time in 40 years of painting. He believes that this has been prompted by his

students (he is head of painting at the Slade), who act as his most important critics and from whom he learns as much, and maybe more, than he teaches. Although he has sold his work through Angela Flowers for many years, his teaching posts have, he says, allowed him time to paint slowly, because not only have they kept the wolf from the door, but they have been occasions for him to learn from younger talent.

David Hepher painted himself out of a cul-de-sac twenty years ago. In his latest tower-block sequence, he is painting castles in the sky that have a power to move as great as the architectural forces that make them such provocative and unmoveable monuments in the urban landscape.

'Streets in the Sky', until 31 December, Museum of London; 'David Hepher: New Works', until 19 January 1997, Flowers East, London.
Edward Lucie-Smith, *David Hepher*, Momentum, £19.95 hb., £14.95 pb.

Jon Harris:
A Singular Curiosity

by PATRICK CARNEGY

You can't begin to say anything about the work of the Cambridge painter Jon Harris without bringing in architecture, industrial archaeology, music and a host of other contingent matters. His friend the singer Jill Gomez once aptly said that his oils often appear to have been 'built' rather than painted with the brush. Whatever Harris produces springs from his own physical experience of his subject matter. He has clambered about buildings of all sorts and is himself a good enough brickie, carpenter and dry-stone waller to know what goes into their making. Every landscape he paints has been explored under boot, every building known in his mind and muscles as though he had been in at its construction.

If this suggests that Jon Harris is an architect *manqué* who happens to moonlight as an artist, do not be misled. The core of his indefatigable activity has always been painting and graphic art – it just happens that a characteristics strength is his intense instinct for buildings and revelatory insight into their life and history. To walk down any street or through the countryside with him is to have your eyes opened to a thousand things you would never have noticed on your own.

Born in 1943 in North Staffordshire (his father a naval engineer from a New Zealand family, his mother the daughter of a Scots doctor), Harris began painting as a scholar of Winchester College. The newly appointed art master revolutionised several lives. Not only the handful of Wykehamist artists that he set on their way, but architects, craftsmen, printers, art and cultural historians all acknowledge an immense debt to Grahame Drew. Having followed Drew's advice to read architecture at Cambridge, Harris's less-than-perfect facility with the mathematical underpinnings of the subject eventually led to his abandoning the course after a year, or, as he would say, being abandoned by it. His subsequent academic adventures at Trinity Hall took in modern languages, and, after two years under the exacting Michael Jaffé, he emerged with a degree in art history.

But drawing – particularly to record the changing built environment – and painting were by now the central activities. From 1965 it was teaching that paid the rent, briefly at Bassingbourn Village College and then for some years at Cambridge School of Art. The year of reading architecture, far from being wasted, had opened up a Piranesian curiosity about the ordinary fabric of the city of Cambridge at a time of great urban change: its alleys, the way time stained its native brick, the shapes of ramshackle breweries about to go under the hammer, the huge retort house as it bowed before the advent of North Sea gas. Walking round the old industrial sites of his

Jon Harris, Chimneys, *view from Brunswick Street*

native North Midlands yielded comparable discoveries. The robust originality of his drawings and paintings made an immediate impact on his circle of friends. This included many who were to make distinguished careers as architects and who began to buy his work.

Two lecturers in the Faculty of Architecture had been particularly influential on the eighteen-year-old. Edward Wright, the typographer, later at Chelsea, and the painter Christopher Cornford, who went on to the RCA, had been hired by Sir Leslie Martin to pass on their concern with the exact distribution of marks on the paper, which they taught by a series of rigorous exercises akin to those of the Bauhaus preliminary year. Both are dead now; but Harris recently acquired a beautiful Cornford drawing and says that his first contact with Wright gave him a feeling for the forms of letters and numbers and, more than that, the distinctively bold handwriting he still uses. By then he was drawing, and writing, with one of those Rapidograph pens from which his hand seems inseparable. From this time came the commitment to keeping sketchbooks and notebooks – a means of disciplining the facility and spontaneous inventiveness that characterise his drawing and watercolour work.

For his last undergraduate year he found a corner in the upper half of a tall old city-centre house in Cambridge. It was shabby and welcoming, a case of the home finding the person, because it is there that he has lived and worked ever since, sharing the front door of whatever catering business has occupied the lower floors – Coffee Pot, Omar's or Oasis Kebab House, Bangkok

City Restaurant – and contributing menu-designs and occasional carpentry, masonry and décor. What is striking from his 30-year sojourn aloft in Green Street is that the roofscapes visible from the windows, but best explored from aboard the viewing 'raft' which he can thrust out into space from the dormer window of his south-facing scullery, have been the constant study of his pen and brush. Here, as in so much of his work, he has transmuted seemingly unpromising material into images of enduring vitality.

He has constantly re-immersed himself in favoured locations, and so there are particular recurring subjects which stand as primary catalysts for his imagination. A sizeable gallery could be filled with wholly divergent paintings based on a single subject: dark, brooding abstractions, essays in shadow-tone, fantasies vibrant with explosive light.

Although an omnivorous student of the work of other artists, and admitting preoccupations with painters as diverse as Diebenkorn, Sandra Fell, Patrick George, Patrick Symons, Auerbach, Eurich, Hockney and Julian Bell (not surprising in someone whose style, as a schoolboy, was being fought over by Piper and Bonnard), he took no formal instruction after his apprenticeship with Grahame Drew.

It may be surmised that, as an autodidact to the fibre of his being, Harris would have been ill at ease as a student in the general run of colleges of art. But he acknowledges a considerable debt to debates with colleagues and students while teaching at the Cambridge School of Art.

The same eye is manifestly at work in the oil paintings as in the drawings and watercolours, but the whole approach is different. He has used canvas only about twice and has generally worked on the flat side of hardboard. The act of battening the back of the board in order to stiffen and protect it led him to invent his own configurations of wooden frames, which he also often decorates. As an undergraduate in the early 1960s, his method was to mix powdered builder's plaster into the paint on the palette with a strip of springy brass printer's one inch rule which, held between finger and thumb, spread the textured, clinkery mixture onto the board laid flat on table or even floor. Pen drawings or watercolours done *in situ* were commandeered to create moody, rainy townscapes whose patron saints might be Graham Bell or that Peter Brook whose splendid millscapes he had seen reviewed in *The Times* in 1960, and who was later taken up by the Granada Bernsteins. So the oils were already becoming what Auden would have called a 'secondary world' of their own, closely worked-out compositions derived from the subject but by no means always 'about' it.

The brass strip paintings made for close tones, muted colour and, ideally, for large-scale handling. By 1967, working smaller, he had swapped all this for the brush, with its vivid and fluid possibilities. How to register the tingle of English light on sunny – or rainy – surfaces? How to translate the luminosity of hue he experienced, working into the light in a Derbyshire sunset, on the size of board he felt it merited? He plunged into a polychromatic, textured pointillism of which the wide-angle Clifton Hall roofscape of 1973 is a good example. In this, the structure of the composition and the energetic stylisation of the dance of light are locked in resonant counterpoint.

From here it was a simple step to an even bolder geometric exploration of the interaction of colour and structure. The surfaces were now fragmented into spectra of stripes, often dislocated like geological strata-faults. A grand Pont-Aven landscape by Roderic O'Conor, exhibited in the Tate from the late 1970s, was a talisman, and it proved pivotal as he increasingly sensed the need to bring his analytic discoveries into a closer, more realistic relationship with the subject.

Although the effects of light had always been a central preoccupation, there had been a tendency in his oils (but never in his watercolours) to fight shy of the attempt to render it naturalistically – the light was often cooled or filtered into a brooding, even ominous atmosphere. Over the past ten years the play of light on walls, roofs, trees and gardens has become more translucent and more dynamic, creating a new sense of

Jon Harris, Dean Clough Mills

animation. This is particularly true of paintings where, exceptionally, the light source has been behind the artist. His preference is usually for subjects seen against the light; such paintings have become ever more theatrical. In these works the eye is drawn not to the light source but to its impact on surfaces and the depth and subtlety of the shadows.

The power of the oils should not detract from Harris's work as a watercolourist and draughtsman. The watercolour is the nearest he ever gets to a camera, which is to say no more than that this is his means of capturing a visual impression as compactly as possible. These studies are painted with extraordinary speed and concentration after sketching in a few essential outlines with the pen. I have watched him paint four different views of my cottage, each taken from an unexpected angle or perspective, in a matter of hours, the exact times of start and finish together with brief description of the subject being recorded in pen with his signature. He has always been adept at managing sketch-pad, paints and water-pot under the most adverse circumstances, as in wind and cold, on a tiny stool in long damp grass or straddling the ridge of a half-demolished barn. There are watercolour snowscapes in which traces of the feathers of ice left in a frozen area of wash can still

be seen on the paper. Commissioned by a friend to paint the London house of a mutual acquaintance as a surprise present, he got mineral water from a corner-shop rather than give the game away by knocking on the door; the topographical caption did not fail to mention that the aqueous medium had been Perrier.

Inevitably this is a high-risk process with a fair proportion of casualties, but in the survivors the sense of chosen place and time is captured with an enduring freshness by a passionately understanding eye and mind. Sometimes a subject will leap across the central reservation of the sketch-book and spontaneously become a double-spread, characteristically 10 x 28 inches. On occasion Harris will juxtapose two or even more separate images (water-colours or oils) in the same mount or frame. They are usually arranged ladderwise, the idea being that they may be read together, combined or compared, thus creating an effect of visual heterophony. We are back with his characteristic interest in conjuring a dynamic relationship between a single vision and its constituent, multiple images.

What is particularly notable in the black-ink drawings is that Harris seizes on cross-hatching and skills usually associated with engraving, but he says that his inspiration actually came from a book, now mislaid, which he found in a Hampshire bookshop around the time when, aged sixteen, he acquired his first Rapidograph: it was about drawing landscape and townscape in pen and ink, its author a Sussex doctor called J G Garrett. The work of colleagues, whether exhibited or overseen in life-classes, can be an inspiration; or he can come on a book which he has to have, even though its mastery of technique fills him 'with envy and shocked amazement': such was Anthony Mackay's book of pen-drawings, *Journeys into Oxfordshire*.

For some years after moving into Green Street he had an Albion press in the corner of the studio. A fascination with making wood-engravings developed. These were necessarily miniature, but useful for clarifying the problems of the larger drawings and paintings going on alongside, and once done they could be set up together in the press, multiple images separated by plain Edwardian wood-letter and fancy borders, then printed in experimental borders on all manner of papers. The Albion was eventually sold on to Nick Barnham, but scorpers and spitstickers lie waiting to be taken up again.

Harris has since found other ways to keep Edward Wright's legacy alive. His graphic skills and superb spatial visualisation keep him supplied with commissions from the National Trust, as well as from architects and planners. In such drawings the necessary element of instruction is leavened with fantasy and wit. The aim may be to lead a visitor through the important components of a historic landscape, or to disentangle (as at Houghton Mill, for the National Trust) a train of machinery to show – himself first, then you – how it all works. As he says, 'my drawings simply interpret what is well understood by mill-aficionados but is invisible to layfolk whose imagination can't, as my drawing can, penetrate floors'. What gives these drawings their special quality is that while characteristically accurate in their mechanical detail, they also convey a palpable sense of the sight and sound of the shafts and gear-wheels in toiling motion.

This curiosity extends to the archaeology and reconstruction of damaged ancient buildings. Whether on his own – helping to rescue the derelict manor house at Croxton nearby, working out the frame-pattern of a replaced wall and tracing the design of a missing window – or as a representative of the Cambridge Preservation Society, he has done battle on behalf of threatened vernacular or industrial buildings, using drawings to tell the tale, and even on occasion securing a listing.

Although Jon Harris has had a sizeable number of exhibitions and has long been highly valued and collected by his friends and professional associates, he has remained relatively unknown to the world at large. The director of a prominent public gallery, to whom he is well known as a regular visitor, had no reason to connect him with a couple of old drawings frequently lent out by the gallery; indeed, until enlightened by a third party, was unaware that he was a painter! For Harris is the last person to put himself forward or become entangled in any kind of promotion. In temperament he is a paradoxical blend of unshakeable dedication and self-deprecation, the latter being part of any good artist's purgatorial discontent, that will to impossible goals which drives ``remarked, lurks in every true creator. Wherever Harris leaves his mark, from his handwriting, visual wit and playful verbal inventions, his response to music, his culinary prowess, all the way through to his work with pen and brush, the style is instantly recognisable as his. The enduring value of his work – in all aspects from graffiti and ephemera to sketches and finished compositions – is evident in its singularity of vision. There is a huge wealth of personality, of appetite for physical and sensual experience, which drives and enriches everything to which he turns his hand.

'Jon Harris: A Retrospective', 14 January–9 March 1997, Fitzwilliam Museum, Cambridge. Architectural drawings and plans at the University of Cambridge Department of Architecture and History, 1–5 Scroope Terrace, Trumpington Street, Cambridge.

Anne Redpath

by JOHN HALDANE

Modern colourists – particularly abstractionists – have often been influenced by psychological and even mystical theories of the efficacy of shades and hues. But generally such ways of thinking pay insufficient attention to compositional content and other painterly contributions. Of necessity, psychological theories of colour and emotion abstract from the issue of imagery. On this account red is meant to have an effect *qua* red and not as delineating the contours of a chair, say. Similarly, such theories abstract from the manner in which colour is laid down on a surface, whether as a smooth continuous film of ink or as a storm of agitated brushwork.

No doubt there are accounts of the psychological effects of textures, and others of the impact of geometry, of scale and so on; but taken singly or together these theories miss the variable and unpredictable effects achieved by the painterly integration of colour, texture and form in the service of one another. Here the elements *are* as the elements *do*. Colour gives meaning to form, form to scale, scale to texture, texture to colour. In short, painting has the power to effect a transformation of any brute psychological impact of its materials.

That power is well exercised in the middle-period canvases of Anne Redpath, a major retrospective of whose work is showing at the Scottish National Gallery of Modern Art in Edinburgh. Born in Hawick in 1895, the second of four children, Redpath displayed a marked talent for drawing. In 1913 she began at Edinburgh College of Art and in the course of her studies was awarded a number of scholarships, the most prestigious and significant being one that enabled her in 1919 to travel

Anne Redpath (front) in the life class at Edinburgh College of Art, c.1915

to Belgium, France and Italy. How exhilarating to pass from a Scotland that regarded ornament and decoration with grave suspicion to Bruges and Antwerp, Florence and Siena, which had long celebrated the sensuous qualities of colour and texture and the embodied intelligence of line and volume.

Redpath's youthful delight in the hues and forms of buildings and landscapes is well illustrated in a small study of the *Ponte Vecchio* (1919). The central three high-arched openings built on the bridge bob above the slower engineered span through which the river flows. During the same Tuscan visit she made several studies from works by early renaissance painters. These show an attraction to decorative pattern that becomes something of an end in itself in a string of pastel-coloured paintings produced in France a decade or so later. *Villefranche* (1929) is strongly reminiscent of Rennie Mackintosh's illustrative watercolours of the same area (e.g. *Fetges*, 1925) and leaves behind the draughtsmanship of the *Ponte Vecchio* or the Utrilloesque tonal modelling of *Windmill* (c.1922).

From 1920 Redpath lived in France with her architect husband James Michie. Her three sons were born there and for a decade or so she was preoccupied with domestic responsibilities. In 1934, however, she and the children returned to Scotland and she resumed her painting career, moving from landscapes indistinguishable from the earlier French ones to post-impressionist interiors and still-lives. It is from this point on, I think, that she began to develop as a painter with a distinctive contribution to make to the Scottish colourist tradition.

It took some time for Redpath to rebuild confidence as an artist, but the works from the mid-'30s to the mid-'40s show her becoming freer and more self-assured in her brushwork and more ambitious in her use of colour. *Cottages on the Teviot* (c.1938), *The Blue Tablecloth* (1940), and what has sometimes been regarded as her masterpiece, *The Indian Rug* or *Red Slippers* (1942), and then *The Worcester Jug* (c.1946) mark stages in the development of a colour-texture medium of translation in which objects and places are given painterly equivalents. Even though her later work remained figurative, she was increasingly given to abstraction, in the sense of drawing out of, or back from, the real world. Painting became less a process of depiction and more one of alchemical transformation.

The works of the '40s are derivative of French sources. The studied and careful forms of *The Blue Tablecloth* owe much to Cézanne, while the later paintings of the decade are unmistakably Matissean in inspiration. In this connection it is interesting to compare *The Indian Rug* and *The Worcester Jug*. The former is simple in composition: a space is created by the meeting of floor and backdrop, and the eye is lead into and across the breadth of this by the angled rug of the title. The main visual interest of the scene comes from the red

Anne Redpath, The Indian Rug (or Red Slippers), *c.1942, oil on plywood, 73.9 x 96.1 cm.*
Scottish National Gallery of Modern Art

draughtsmanship, composition and coloration. The later church interiors, by contrast, celebrate a Latin liking for rich colours and textures presented as ends in themselves. Redpath writes of this period:

> I couldn't paint it smooth any more. I had to paint as if it were some kind of encrusted jewel. And while in a way they are more abstract than they were before ... they are still quite real and I don't think they ever will be completely lost in abstraction because I feel so concerned about the things I paint... They have a kind of strength about them that they didn't use to have.

Here, I think, she may have misconceived her own later work, in part through confusing orders of reality – those of objects and of representations. It is one thing to start from the world and end up with a painting that is a presence in itself; it is another for the painting to be a genuine study of the world that inspired it. Of course, a work may aim to be both; but whereas from the *Ponte Vecchio* to *The Indian Rug*, Redpath is engaged in the old struggle to find means adequate to represent our surroundings, in the later works she seems to have abandoned herself to colour and texture less as means than as ends. By steps, Redpath's colourism became an expressionist medium. Fine (and magical) though much of the later work is, I believe that her best period was that of the early 1940s when colour was more subject to the discipline of depicting appearances beyond the canvas.

'Anne Redpath 1895–1965', until 19 January 1997, Scottish National Gallery of Modern Art, Edinburgh.

chair, the patterned carpet below it, and the bridge between these formed by a pair of similarly red shoes. On the one hand, the depiction of the shoes is continuous with that of the sketchy modelling of the chair; on the other, they appear as fruit or blossoms on the woven stems of the rug's plant design. In *The Worcester Jug*, Redpath's increasing taste for the decorative is evident in her treatment of the lacework border of the cloth, the patterning of the flowerheads and the spiralling arrangement of items on and around the table. While, as in the previous work, colour is used for composition, there is now less tonal modelling and

there are intimations of a willingness to abandon the task of depicting solid objects and spatial depth.

In 1952 Redpath became the first woman painter to be elected to the RSA. Two years later she presented the Academy with a study of a small French altar and sanctuary – *In the Chapel of St Jean, Tréboul*. In subject matter this anticipated the paintings for which she was best known in later life and in the decade following her death (in 1965); but in technique and purpose it is quite different. Although unresolved as a painting, *St Jean, Tréboul* achieves a balance of interests between

Mysteries of Ancient China

by GLYNN WILLIAMS

Most antiquities we visit in our museums display the ravages of time, war, vandalism and other deliberately brutal handling. One exception to this is the artefact collections from Egyptian tombs, and another is those from the growing number of newly discovered tombs in China.

The sealed and hidden burial chambers of the rulers, nobility, kings, queens and emperors were carefully packed storage units which were a strange combination of the pragmatic and the spiritual. Death was believed to be the doorway to a journey, and provision for that journey and any of its eventualities made. This initially simple belief has deposited in a sort of time vault perfectly preserved examples not just of rich and wondrously crafted symbols of greatness but everything from the most domestic to the most magnificent. Every aspect of the dead person's lifetime needs will have been met, from food and drink containers, clothes for all occasions, games, records of

Anne Redpath, The Worcester Jug, *c.1946, oil on canvas, 86 x 111.5 cm.*
Scottish National Gallery of Modern Art

accomplishments, and of course the companionship and protection of other beings, either in the form of made or (more macabre) real people and animals. This comprehensiveness absolves us from making the necessarily broad assumptions which have to be used on many other, now fragmented remains from different cultures.

In the exhibition 'Mysteries of Ancient China' at the British Museum, one can see objects in nearly perfect condition (even woven silk materials that have their coloured designs still intact). The making and the means of making in everything are transparently clear, only the *raison d'être* of some items is tantalisingly out of reach. There is a large five-spoked, hollow, cast-bronze wheel that is certainly not functional, and too severe and simple to be decorative. Even more mysterious are the large, triangular, 'space-age' bronze plates from c.1000 BC, which look very like American Stealth Bombers. They are extremely precise and apparently purposeful and have holes, some perhaps for fixing and some that are certainly for something else. We will probably never know what these objects were made for. A large inlaid bronze 'dragon', called, simply, *Imaginary Creature*, from c.600 BC, is a securely standing four-legged animal with a decorative cluster of writhing serpents on its head. A smaller creature is somersaulting on its back, and the oddest square sectioned bronze tube emerges from the top of its left hip. The tube has a different colour of patina from the rest of the beast and has decorative studs all over its surface. It most certainly has some utilitarian purpose but I hazard no guess as to what it may be. Likewise, a large and beautiful ritual jade 'cong' from c.3000 BC is a very 'modernist', almost minimal carving of a cylinder and a cube imposed into each other and forming a Max Bill-like complex geometric vessel with delicate and subtle surface motifs – but again its use is a mystery.

I must confess to having an almost totally visual rather than historical approach, and perhaps because of this I look at objects for their sculptural power rather than their contextual or social value. Also, I am more interested in the older, somewhat archaic pieces than the later elaborately skilful displays of unparalleled craft. The skill is there in the older work but the forms are simpler, more visually quiet, and have not yet felt the call of the rich and decorative which will inevitably come. The evolutionary journeys in art movements are fascinating, and the complete conviction of the later pieces here can almost produce what old-fashioned metaphysicians would have called 'final cause', the confidence and inevitability of the later pieces seeming to pull the earlier works through their evolutionary transformation like a magnet, towards a determined destiny.

There are several early terracotta pieces, containers of varying sorts as well as small animals. They all have an affinity with ancient terracottas from other early civilisations such as South America, Japan,

Two human figures, neolithic period, Shijiahe, culture, c.2400–2000 BC, loamy reddish clay, height 9.5 cm

even Greece and Mesopotamia. There are certain forms and devices that the human hand produces when it first makes representations in clay. The knowledge that a form made from clay on any scale, if it is to be fired, is best hollow, and the representational solutions that can be found in the way the clay is squeezed, added to and cut into – nearly every ancient society's sculptural forms have started with these.

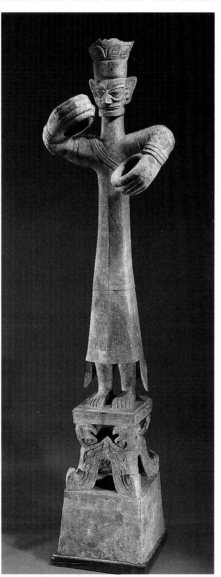

Standing figure, c.1200–1000 BC, bronze, overall height 262 cm

However, within less than 1000 years of these early terracottas, there are the sophisticated and beautifully made bronzes of 'Heads' and 'Masks', and for me the centrepiece of the exhibition is the remarkable *Standing Figure* from c.1200 BC.

The makers of these sculptures had by this time adopted an iconography of forms to deal with eyes, mouths, ears, as well as drapery and decoration. The forms have a clean-cut edge and a precise confidence in themselves. They are simplified and consolidated to convince the viewer completely. The Chinese preferences in form-making are definitely there, albeit in their more sober infancy. The repeated curves hint at an inclination to be square, and move in wide arcs often underlined by an inlaid emphasis that travels the same route some centimetres away. Within 500 years those sensitive but economic and vigorous forms will have translated into the richness of the organised visual 'fire' that flares from the decorative elaboration so characteristic of later Chinese sculpture.

The *Standing Figure* is more than two and a half metres high and has the most extraordinarily large hands. They form cylindrical containers in and through which some other object, now gone, would have been placed (it is supposed to have been an elephant's tusk). Standing empty, these huge holes have all the visual noise of great drums on this elegant and otherwise quiet figure. The figure is robed and the bottom of the robe has a little flirtation with decoration, as does the crown on the head, but otherwise the sculpture's concentrated focus is on these hands. It's a stunning piece of original work.

The *Standing Figure*, the 'Human-like Heads' and the 'Masks' have a controlled economy of form that looks so certain in its styling. Styling is the only word I can find to describe this characteristic that carries over, from one sculpture to another, the same exploration of how a form arises and ends. The *'Mask' with Ornamental Forehead and Protruding Pupils* is a remarkable example of what I can only call a restrained elaboration, an almost contradictory manifestation which I find so powerful in these earlier works.

As the decorative visual 'flaming' of the forms increases with time, a richness arrives which places the pieces into the familiar world that we recognise as Chinese art. The element which to my mind saves the highly decorated later pieces in the exhibition from being over-rich is asymmetry. The dragon-like creature described above has its power in the angular sharp twist of the head, throwing the symmetry of its four-square stance into active and attentive vigour. Even some of the bronze ritual vessels which could so easily have developed their decoration in stark symmetry have broken away from it. There is a strange bronze *Lamp Bearer* from the fourth century BC that spans a comparatively large area of ground for its small size; it moves its drama in almost episodic narrative from part to part, straggling across the surface on which it stands.

Chinese bronzes of the fourth and fifth century BC have a freedom and liveliness that is astounding. Contemporaneous sculpture from ancient Greece moved into bronze in a much more pedestrian manner. There, large bronze sculptures simply aped marble carvings, and for generations the visual aesthetic of the bronzes seemed in every way to emulate the possible poses and configurations of the carvings, and so inevitably were solid, somewhat stiff and only tentative in their exploration of the metal.

It was as if the potential of bronze's strength and its space-ranging possibilities were not imagined. Even the skilled craftsmen of Roman sculpture worked the medium as if they were making bronze versions of marble carvings. Of course, marble carving around the Mediterranean had reached the level of virtuosity; but for the ribboning freedom in space that the Chinese bronzes achieved in the fifth century BC, Europe would have to wait until the fifteenth and sixteenth centuries AD. Techniques were obviously explored through process experiment, and above all the decorative input in Chinese art would keep pushing the boundaries of how far that 'organised fire' could be achieved. The *Money Tree* (c.100 BC) is a fine example of free, open and exciting 'drawing' in space with the self-supporting strength of the bronze.

I have always been attracted by the bronze 'Vessels for Offering Wine' (the British Museum itself has some fine examples), particularly the ones whose legs end in points. They have a strange relationship with the floor on which they stand. Although completely stable, they look as if they are lifting off, or trying to tip-toe or dance on a surface that is too hot. Their forms are held high up in the object, and they are unusually robust and visually busy in their surface decoration, but the pointed legs give them a 'desire' for weightlessness. I find it a wonderfully inventive way of standing while appearing almost to defeat gravity.

There is a series of ceramic brick reliefs, on which the raised drawing and modelling is exquisite. They show dignitaries, domestic scenes, wine making and selling, and there are two very funny scenes of erotic coupling. The relief of the *Acrobats* reminded me of a Donatello relief in the Victoria and Albert Museum, in its fine, eloquent line and sense of space. It looked to me as if these relief works were made in reverse and a clay pressing taken from them to form the final brick before firing. There are no undercuts and the form of raised drawing has all the hallmarks of a negative pressing, although I could find nothing about it in the text that accompanied the pieces.

Also impressive is the jade *Death Suit* with its bullet-like array of body orifice plugs, and one of the soldiers from the now ubiquitous ceramic army of life-sized figures and horses. As one leaves the exhibition there is a large stone carved *Guardian*

Figure which, if shorn of its beard and wings, would have a lot in common with those muscular lions who are its contemporary counterparts from Greece. All in all the exhibition gives some wonderful insights and surprises, including many things never seen before in this country. I am richer for the experience. However, for me, the exhibition seemed to tail off from a half-way point. This may be entirely due to my particular affection for certain pieces, but I am not really convinced of that. It starts in an exciting way and one is led from one appetising object to another, stopping almost in worship in front of that amazing *Standing Figure*. Tasting the wonderful richness of the middle bronzes, chuckling at the humorous goings-on in the terracottas, marvelling at the jade deathsuit.... and then one is out on the other side. It is as if something has been missed. In fact, I retraced my steps twice to try and discover what it was I had overlooked. I realise that the subtitle of the exhibition is 'New Discoveries from the Early Dynasties' and it's not a comprehensive Ancient China exhibition, but I suppose I wished that it was.

'Mysteries of Ancient China, New Discoveries from the Early Dynasties', until 5 January 1997, British Museum, London. Sponsored by *The Times*. Catalogue £25.

Elie Nadelman

by LANCE ESPLUND

Walking through this exhibit of more than 40 of Elie Nadelman's sculptures and reliefs, I saw light responding to each of Nadelman's surfaces differently, but each sculpture maintained a mysterious tranquillity – an understated, aura-like presence. Nadelman's wide range of subjects includes a standing supplicant, a goddess, ideal heads, beautifully crude doll-like

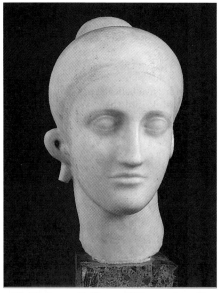

Elie Nadelman, Goddess, *c.1920, carved marble, 48.3 x 27.9 x 38.1 cm*

figurines, a couple dancing the tango, animals, busts and children. His range of materials is just as wide: marble, wood, ceramic, plaster, bronze, a *papier maché* that glows like a shoji screen, and a beautifully-rough, deep brown-almost-black, bronze-like substance called galvano-plastique (made of metal deposits, mostly copper, laid into a plaster base – a surface Nadelman often hatch-marks to the point of scarring).

I was surrounded by Bodhisattva-like beings, as if unearthed from some ancient/modern ruin, some of whom seemed to have travelled from as far away as Hellenistic Greece; others to have walked right out of a Seurat painting or the shop window of an Atget photograph; still others, out of the circus, the ballet, or the studio of Ingres or Donatello. There were also gracefully whimsical and equally surprising figures, who resembled yard ornaments suddenly blessed with sainthood. Some of them, with arms or legs outstretched, like living sign-posts, directed me to their counterparts throughout the space.

Born in Warsaw in 1882, and granted American citizenship in 1927, Elie Nadelman became one of the greatest and most influential sculptors of this century (the last in the workshop tradition of the Renaissance). He studied briefly at the Warsaw Art Academy, spent six months in Munich, then in 1904 like most artists of worth, moved to Paris, where he became a major component in the circle of artists, writers and intellectuals who ushered in Modernism.

Yet this is the first major exhibit of Nadelman's work to be held since the 1975 Whitney retrospective, which was in turn the first to follow the 1948 MOMA show held two years after his death. In a lucid catalogue essay for this exhibition, Hilton Kramer observes that at the time of that Whitney show more than twenty years ago, he incorrectly predicted in the *New York Times* that 'Nadelman's exile is over'. The fact that so many people today, especially in America, have never heard of Elie Nadelman is a travesty.

Nadelman was mostly self-taught, through visits to the Louvre, where he drew from Michelangelo, among others. He was befriended by Leo and Gertrude Stein, who collected his work, and by André Gide, who, like Gertrude Stein and Matisse, sang his praises. In 1908, Leo brought Picasso to Nadelman's studio, where Picasso saw a plaster head that undoubtedly influenced his first Cubist sculpture. A classicist in the tradition of Maillol and Brancusi, Nadelman (inducing a brawl) objected to Marinetti's 1912 lecture denouncing the art of the past and extolling the racing car over the *Victory of Samothrace*. He spent a decade in Paris, which brought him great admiration and success and inclusion in the famous 1913 Armory Show. Nadelman moved to New York in 1914, and continued to sculpt and to receive commissions, including portrait busts and a façade sculpture for the Fuller Building. Years after his death, two nineteen-foot-high marble enlargements of his figure groups were created for the lobby of The State Theatre at Lincoln Center. Nadelman brought to America's attention the importance of folk art, compiling the first and largest ever American folk-art museum, and, as an inventor, he first advocated (in 1934) that luminous paint be used on roadways to improve night driving.

My first experience of Nadelman was in the Whitney Museum of American Art, where I saw the 1919 *Tango* (on view in this exhibition, from their permanent collection), a couple carved out of cherrywood, about 35 inches tall and painted in a thin wash. Two slim figures – a man in tails and a woman in a tight, long dress – dance side by side. The female figure, the more active of the two, appears to lead. They reach towards each other with knife-like hands that can never touch, their faces trance-like, in complete concentration. They are in absolute unison yet infinitely separated. Seen from the front, the pair looks almost staged, as if they had been planted there, but viewed from the sides, their silhouetted, individually curving forms swing, sweep and interweave in a swirling mixture of rhythms – unmistakably tango. The folds in her dress between her legs appear to sway autonomously forward and backward at the same time, bringing to mind the 'Dutch Mona Lisa' – Vermeer's *Head of a Young Girl* – in which the draping head-dress makes us believe that this beautiful girl, who is either fleetingly glancing or flirtatiously looking at us from out of a rich blackness, over her left shoulder, has either just turned towards us or is about to turn back – to look away, or both. If she has just turned towards us, the piece of cloth hanging from the top of her head betrays this reading, because it has swung forward instead of back. The *Tango* dress behaves similarly and, with the multiplicity of an ancient Egyptian stance, the woman's body follows the dress's lead, moving to the side, then forward, then ricocheting backward, impossibly all at once.

The 33-inch cherrywood figure, *Standing Girl* (1918–20), is another mixture of pure stasis and movement. A pre-adolescent girl in medium length dress, with tiny feet perched in high heels, tentatively steps forward, as if she were sneaking in after curfew. Her grinning face is turned in profile to her right. Poised, buoyant arms with small mitten-hands extend forward for balance, moving gracefully like cats' tails. Her eyes, fixed elsewhere, are unconcerned with her movement. Her body, elegantly curved, betrays her child-like awkwardness, while a powerful ponytail snakes out from the back of her head, lunging forward and downward in large twisting ocean-like waves, with the strength and look of a sexy mermaid on the prow of a Viking ship.

Nadelman's figures can look most elusive when viewed head-on, when (except for their noses) their generalised faces seem to disappear. The features hover between solidity and air, like transparent layers just below and above the surface of their skins – receding slightly, then wavering forward, as

Elie Nadelman, Tango, *bronze, 88.9 x 55.9 x 30.5 cm*

if they had been glazed on rather than sculpted. This is especially true of the galvano-plastique and bronze figures, in which the darkness of the materials almost swallows the features, then exhales them, in a rhythm resembling meditative breathing.

The experience of a Nadelman face is a constant search for an evasive personality, that through changing viewpoints, and especially in profile, yields more than you could ever have believed possible. The eyes seem to sink into their sockets as if they were falling away from you. As soon as you move to one side, though, you discover, methodically, as if these sly beings were only willing to reveal themselves in their own time, that there is indeed a personality, possibly two or more.

Calligraphic loops and curls appear in Nadelman's figures like punctuation. These smaller elements are painted, sculpted and tied – in the forms of bows, hair, fingers, toes, lips, eyebrows or ears, circled into question marks, keys, handles, hooks, snails and figure-eights. They are lines drawn in sculpture – becoming form; beginning or end points, signs, demarcations or keys to

the larger nautilus shell-like curves that comprise the figures' very beings. At times, they are inserted in the necks like wind-up keys, setting the figures in motion. They are also the minute entry-ways into Nadelman's whole visual vocabulary, and act as transitions between the external and internal, between surface decoration and form, between contour and void.

Late in his life, after losing his kiln and his studio, Nadelman made hundreds of small, dry, white-plaster figurines, reminiscent of Rilke's *Elegies*. These sombre, often innocent or startled-looking, child-adult dolls extend through the full range of human possibility; Lincoln Kirstein, in his exhaustive monograph of Nadelman suggested that they 'are in the scale of chamber works'. Tiny scratched and pencilled-in eyes, belts, buttons and bows scar the surfaces of these figures like petroglyphic codes. There are eight of these jewels, all delicate and beautiful, laid out on their backs in a glass case, reminding me of ancient, embryonic statues of gods and goddesses, whose bodies, often only six inches in length, are made up of contours that seem to undulate and extend into distances as long as the horizon line.

Some of the best pieces in this show are the 'Heads' and 'Ideal Heads' done in marble and wood. These lovely, full volumes, breathe, open, compress and expand, seemingly forever, their expressions changing constantly, though subtly, even from the same viewpoints. There is a look of both contentment and awe in their faces, which is sublime, but there is also the expression of surprise, one that E M Forster describes in his *Aspects of The Novel*,

> She looks a little surprised at being there, but beauty ought to look a little surprised: it is the emotion that best suits her face, as Botticelli knew when he painted her risen from the waves, between the winds and the flowers. The beauty who does not look surprised, who accepts her position as her due – she reminds us too much of a prima donna

Much of the reason for this expression is found in the mouths and eyes which hover infinitely between open and closed. Open, they refuse to part; closed, they refuse to touch. These openings, though solid, still read as space and air. This happens as well in the galvano-plastique *Bust of a Man in Top Hat* (1923–24), where his forehead merges in an upward, concave curve with the hat brim; the intersection or merging between head, hat and air is suspended, yet form constantly reads as all three, creating wondrous contradictions.

In the galvano-plastique *Bust of Woman* (1923–24), a profile view from her left reveals her as an older, matronly, society type, reserved and, though elegant, just shy of stuck up. Seen from her right, a very different personality emerges. A mouth, pursed and sunken (in profile from her left) and hardly visible (in frontal view) reveals itself in a smile that rises upward rather quickly (when viewed in opposite profile), becoming almost wild. And as if surprised that you had awakened her from her trance, a single, painted, circular eye shoots right at you – stunned and alive. The nose, from this view, is turned more upward and feels far from stuck up, more flaring. This is not a smug, dignified matron. This is a rip-roaring-kick-her-heels-up and have-a-good-time kind of gal. She is only one of the many amalgams Nadelman conjures up through his figures.

Nadelman's ideal is as varied, wide-ranging and fickle as life itself. Blissful smiles sink sadly into frowns, then return, rising in languorous rhythms. The combinations of emotions in a single head seem endless. The marble *Goddess*, from 1920, is comprised of ever-growing, pumped-up-with-air, curved volumes, which culminate in a coiffure of three stacked oval buns behind her head. They shift direction, alternately countering each other from left to right, as if they were climbing and vying for position in a game of 'king of the hill'; as full as the Venus of Willendorf, they rise upward, shifting their relationships with the airiness of an Arp sculpture.

The 1911 lusciously-dark cherrywood *Ideal Female Head* resembles Bernini's St Teresa (post-ecstasy) and a Byzantine Madonna. Her face is made up of repeating, almost logarithmically growing arcs – beginning in a chin that feels weightless, rippling upward through the curve of the mouth, the forever rising bridge of the nose, then spreading monumentally outward and back through the eyebrows and climaxing in the wide curvature-of-the-earth-like coif, which crowns her head like a halo. Bliss radiates in all directions, and releases through a long sweeping neck which is counter-curved to the tilt of the head. In profile, her head swells backward into an unnatural, zeppelin-like cranium, pinched in at the sides and bulging, as if the pressure from her pleasure or lamentation were re-forming it right before your eyes. In a letter from 1917, as relevant today as then, Nadelman writes:

> I have 156 reasons for doing my sculpture as I do it. But even if I explained them all I wonder whether I would succeed in 'arising' the sense of plasticity, which is to-day neglected, and without which no real sculpture can be understood.
> This sense of plasticity will be cultivated, not by my words, but I hope that it will be cultivated by my sculptures.

Elie Nadelman, Salander-O'Reilly Galleries, New York. Catalogue available, $20. □

The Walter Neurath Memorial Lecture
Experience or Interpretation
The Dilemma of Museums of Modern Art
NICHOLAS SEROTA

The first coherent historical account of the changing attitudes to the way art is presented in the modern museum of art. Nicholas Serota examines the relationship between the artist, the public and the curator, and predicts future developments.

With 55 illustrations £7.95 February

The Paintings of Paul Cézanne
A Catalogue Raisonné
JOHN REWALD
in collaboration with Walter Feilchenfeldt and Jayne Warman
Revised and expanded
The long-awaited, definitive work, written by the late John Rewald, the world-recognized authority on Cézanne.

With 1212 illustrations, 58 in colour
Prepublication Date: £200.00
(thereafter £275.00) February

Bacon
Portraits and Self-Portraits
INTRODUCTION BY
MILAN KUNDERA
WITH AN ESSAY BY FRANCE BOREL

The first book dedicated to Francis Bacon's portraiture – the stylistic distortions of classicism and famous deformations that have changed the traditional genre more radically than any other artist of the 20th century. Milan Kundera writes of his personal response to Bacon's life and influences.

With 166 illustrations £45.00

Gaudier-Brzeska: Life and Art
With a Catalogue Raisonné of the Sculpture
EVELYN SILBER
PHOTOGRAPHS BY DAVID FINN

The first major study in English of this pioneering modernist, containing a catalogue raisonné of his ground-breaking sculpture, with nearly 300 illustrations, including over 150 photographs taken specially for the book by David Finn.

With 289 illustrations, 16 in colour £40.00

Thames and Hudson

Jasper Johns
Privileged Information
JILL JOHNSTON

A remarkable fusion of criticism and biography, *Jasper Johns: Privileged Information* abounds with controversial new insight into the life and work of America's pre-eminent living artist. Jill Johnston examines the development of a major painter whose work will offer more resonant meaning than ever before in the light of this brilliantly original account.

With 30 illustrations £16.95

The Sculpture of Jacques Lipchitz
A Catalogue Raisonné
Volume One: The Paris Years 1910-1940
ALAN G. WILKINSON
INTRODUCTION BY
A.M. HAMMACHER

A master sculptor of the 20th century, Jacques Lipchitz's oeuvre spans six decades. This first volume illustrates all the known works created from 1909 to 1941, focusing on the creations of bronze, stone and wood.

With 444 illustrations £40.00

Anselm Kiefer
After the Catastrophe
RAFAEL LÓPEZ-PEDRAZA

A comprehensive overview of Kiefer's entire creative expression, explored through the perspective of Jung's writings, in particular the essay 'After the Catastrophe'. Myth and history, issues central to his career of more than 30 years, are scrutinized, providing a challenging new reflection on his art.

With 51 illustrations, 36 in colour £16.95 February

Joseph Beuys
ALAN BORER

From 1945 to 1985, Joseph Beuys produced work, now acknowledged to be the most influential artistic expression to emerge from Germany since the Second World War. Published on the tenth anniversary of his death, *Joseph Beuys* reveals his versatility and profundity and includes drawings and watercolours, sculptures and objects, environments and performances.

With 153 illustrations, 77 in colour £48.00 February

Balthus
Stanislas Klossowski de Rola
Revised edition
This classic work has now been expanded and updated to present one of the widest selections of Balthus' work ever published. Stanislas Klossowski de Rola, offers insight into the life and art of this elusive man, including his magisterial works of the last ten years and recent photographs of him taken by Henri Cartier-Bresson.

With 115 illustrations, 107 in colour £24.95

WORLD OF ART
Fauvism
SARAH WHITFIELD

This concise and comprehensive reappraisal of Fauvism, discusses the artists, their relationships, their achievements and the critical and commercial response to their work. Sarah Whitfield illustrates how 'the wild beasts' of art, took painting back to its basic principles, then proceeded to produce some of the most popular works of the 20th century.

With 171 illustrations, 24 in colour £6.95

WORLD OF ART
Women, Art, and Society
Second edition revised and expanded
WHITNEY CHADWICK
'Impressive and ambitious'
– *Art History*
'Valuable for placing the question of feminist art history in a more popular perspective'
– *The Times Literary Supplement*

With 272 illustrations, 60 in colour £9.95

For details of our new and forthcoming publications, please write to: Promotion Department, 30 Bloomsbury Street, London WC1B 3QP

Bookmark by Karen Wright

Sculptor Gaudier-Brzeska was a precocious talent cut tragically short by the Great War. Thames and Hudson publishes the first in-depth study of his work, *Gaudier Brzeska, Life and Art* with text by Evelyn Silber and multitudes of photographs by David Finn, at £40 hardback.

'Scholarly' books rarely sell well. Lisa Jardine's *Worldly Goods: A New History of the Renaissance*, published by Macmillan at £25, is an exception. All those lovely pictures take on a new meaning when we learn of the bargaining behind the scenes. Pictured is Federigo da Montefeltro's *studiolo* in the Palazzo Ducale in Urbino, a luxury pad paid for by Federigo's military skills. The sentiments are sweet, however: 'Both within and without the house is glorious. But all these things are dumb; only the library is eloquent'.

John Pawson presents *Minimalism*, published by Phaidon at £60, a collection of his ideas about art and life. It's a good excuse for some arresting photographs. I do feel, however, that it is all an apologia for Pawson's theory that 'simplicity paradoxically requires an enormous amount of effort'. Sorry, I prefer muddle. Still, here is a nice Georgian fork.

If you're thinking about a book of photographs for your mother's Christmas present, perhaps you should steer clear of Judy Olausen's *Mother,* published by Viking. Vivian Olausen, Judy's mum, is pictured in a number of amusing poses like *Mother Paints the Last Supper.* Apparently they had 'fun' while making this sometimes very unfunny chronicle.

Women of Flowers by Jack Kramer, published by Stewart, Tabori and Chang, £23.99, is Kramer's tribute to the unsung Victorian ladies who spent their days doing lovely pictures of flowers. Beautifully illustrated with facsimile poems and fancies, including these rather hairy daisies by Mrs Rebecca Hey who defends the humble flower: '...scorn not one/The daisy by the shadow that it casts/Protects the lingering dew drops from the sun'.

Just Like Us

by NORBERT LYNTON

Julian Andrews, *The Sculpture of David Nash*, Henry Moore Foundation in association with Lund Humphries, £45.

David Nash: Forms into Time, with an essay by Marina Warner, Academy Editions, £21.95.

Had the Tate Gallery bought not a Carl Andre of industrial bricks but one his arrangements of timber units, English entrenched philistinism would not have been handed its favourite battle cry, and we should not be hearing it still, twenty years later. We know and love wood (we think); we're at home with hearts of oak, woods 'lovely, dark and deep', trees more lovely than any poem. Part of David Nash's appeal must be that he works with, cherishes, husbands wood at a time when, for all sorts of reasons, we often want to touch wood and find ourselves surrounded by metal and plastics.

There's no shortage of David Nash as I write. Two exhibitions, sculpture and drawings, cheek by jowl in Leeds. A great new public sculpture in Eastbourne, ancient and modern, cheering and solemn. In Antwerp a survey exhibition of his work, full of visitors. Now these two books, informative and celebratory in their different ways. And of course the sculptures themselves – outdoor pieces (I have seen them called 'outdoor installations') from Wales to Japan, and indoor pieces just about everywhere. He is now moving into his fifties. In 1977 he initiated the first of his 'Planting Pieces' (to use Julian Andrews's term), *Ash Dome*, and it needs about 30 years to mature, and there are more recent pieces in other lands that need his fostering and shaping. Pray continue, Mr Nash.

It strikes me that I am thinking of him as eternal, not just green but evergreen. That is my fault, not his, but he does have a way of turning one's responses topsy-turvy – as when he makes a wooden boulder and gives it to a stream to play with, or builds a fire in the sea, or carves a large oak bowl on a mighty oak base and makes you forget, as you wrestle with the unlikely fact that this is one piece of wood, not two, that the thing was born upside down, just like us. The overriding fact is that his work is at one with nature's cycles. You can watch most of his indoor sculptures mature, changing form and expression as they dry out, just like us, only more agreeably. Outdoors, his shaped trees will grow and in some measure collude with his intentions, but ultimately they will die, just like us. The ten standing oak trunks of Eastbourne may be an exception, sea-pickled as they have been for 25 years while they buttressed breakwaters along the shore. I see them lasting many a lifetime and held in ever-growing affection

by succeeding generations.

Julian Andrews, in the eighth of the 'British Sculptors and Sculpture' books sponsored by the Moore Foundation, wants to tell and show us as much as possible. The original idea was to publish a complete catalogue of Nash's sculpture with a commentary. But not everything he has done in the last 30 years has yet been traced, and his output of well over a thousand pieces to date would call for a more massive, and less accessible, tome than this one. What Andrews gives us is a wide-ranging but selective survey in words and photographs, partly chronological and biographical but going also by sculpture types. David Nash likes to use a tree diagram to sketch the development and spread of his ideas, from the twenty-foot tower I saw him build in the courtyard of Chelsea School of Art in 1969 to the great oak gate he made in Hokkaido, the *Ubus*, the *Crack and Warp* cubes and columns, the eggs, thrones, stacked ladles, the ladders, etc. of the last ten years, and the Platonic solids, sphere, cube and tetrahedron, that reappear at intervals to answer his more random, nature-led forms. There's much else, including more immediately ephemeral things like the switched rings of turf, his *Sod Swap*, Wales to Kensington Gardens and vice-versa, and the stoves he builds where he works, of slate, ice, snow or bamboo, of sticks and clay in a clearing, of sea-swept stones on Bute, recorded in photographs. There are the drawings he makes with the charcoal he makes of the bits left over when he 'quarries' his trees. They are all one family, just like us.

Andrews's is a warm narrative, carefully worked from discussions with Nash and from consideration of the work. One wishes it were longer and that there were even more than the 240+ illustrations. There will need to be a second volume

David Nash, Ash Dome, *1976, charcoal on paper, 50 x 50 cm*

before very long. *Forms into Time* is an anthology of Nash's work in excellent photographs, most of them in colour, prefaced by a lively and interesting essay by Marina Warner. It is Nash's own book, though this is not clear until one notices the dedication to 'my elder brother Chris' and checks in Andrews that Chris is David's brother, not Marina's. She writes mainly about the echoes she finds in this work of ancient myths and symbols, medieval literature 'about God's wonders' and ageless folk tales. Nash's work has set her quarrying her vast store of this wisdom which the Age of Reason called esoteric though it belongs to all of us. She also points out how close his work often is 'to the common artefacts of daily life and to the craft-work of ordinary survival', and this is both true and apposite. Oddly, though, it is the one bit quoted in the press release that came with the book. Are people still embarassed by any thinking that goes beyond the immediately factual and utilitarian?

David Nash, Ash Dome, *winter, 1995, Cae'n-y Coed*

A modest Nash commentary accompanies the plates. What he says is mostly practical: the situation was this, I did that. He engages deeply with what nature provides, his whole life as artist consists of working with it. He loves trees in their infinite variety, timber's many changing colours, the way fire chars wood, and so on. He likes working by himself. He likes working with people all around the world; language problems don't exist. There are a few anecdotes about officialdom and about how people have used the sculptures. Just occasionally the veil is lifted: the Buddha is quoted, Nash speaks of the Chinese potters' focus on the space in the pot, not on the skin they were giving it, and in another place he refers to the Holy Grail and Parsifal. We see him using the Greek cross as a form and within sculpture. He tells us that 'for the ancient Greeks Geometria was one of the seven hand-maidens of the Goddess Natura'. He calls some of his ladders 'Jacobs'. Like Warner, he is at home with such ideas and images.

It is known that David Nash, like Beuys and probably also Anselm Kiefer, admires Rudolf Steiner and Anthroposophy, and that he and his wife, the artist Claire Langdown, joined local friends to found a Steiner school in Snowdonia. Andrews's 'chronology' section includes Nash's account of how Anthroposophy answered their worries about their sons' education after primary school. What was already on offer seemed to dull their minds rather than develop them. But Nash also found that Steiner's philosophy gave 'form and articulation ... to vague intuitions'. We call that philosophy mysticism and relegate it to the mists and marshes that lie beyond the industrial bricks of common sense. For Nash, Steiner's belief that each material fact has its spiritual counterpart is both common sense and an invitation to think and act with similar breadth. Common sense is sometimes called horse-sense; perhaps it is tree-sense too. Those of us who listen to 'Farming Today' on Radio 4 learned some years ago of Steiner's 1920s warning that feeding meat to cattle would drive them mad.

David and Claire began to investigate Steiner schooling and found Anthroposophy in 1983. That was the year *Ash Dome* got its first fletching, the Tate bought its first D Nash, Nash was included in the Serpentine/Hayward 'Sculpture Show', and he made sculpture in Wales, England, Ireland and the USA (he worked in Japan and Holland in 1982). In other words, he was already Nash when he discovered Steiner. That is how encounters of this significance work. The child is father of the man. That dedication, in *Forms into Time*, is to Chris 'who took playing seriously and let me join in'. Steiner, too, is a confirming and enriching ally, I suspect, and a deepening, structuring influence on that Wordsworthian 'natural piety' which Nash has drawn on from the moment he began.

This is something I, for one, would dearly love to know more about, and in as much detail as possible. More books will

undoubtedly be generated by these two and by the growing interest Nash meets with on every hand. One of them should consider how this work is to be understood in the context of modern art. How does Nash relate to others who work directly with nature – Long, Goldsworthy etc. – and with Land Art, as well as with art's apparently inalienable urge to connect with nature, too often expressed in timid paintings? And what is his place in sculpture as such? How different are his 'Descending Vessels', one of them as tall as a tall pine, indeed made of one and standing where the tree died on its roots, from, say, Bernini's *Apollo and Daphne*? Yes, very, but how, how much, how profoundly? Hilton Kramer wrote in 1983 (in the *Zeitgeist* catalogue) about painting that, 'above all, it has a hearty appetite for the metaphysical and the mysterious'. Sculpture too. One hesitates to claim this as a modern development, belonging to a time when sculpture stopped being statues. But it is certainly a theme in modern sculpture – most clearly in Brancusi, Beuys and Nash – in spite of sculpture's inalienable material presence.

A Precocious Gift

by BORIS FORD

Stephen Reiss, *Peggy Somerville*, The Antique Collectors' Club, £19.95.

Infant prodigies may not be common, but there are fields, such as maths and chess, or music, where they unaccountably turn up quite often. One of the most extraordinary instances was Szigeti: born (I believe) of quite unmusical parents, he was given a toy tin violin at the age of four or five and proceeded, in a matter of weeks, to teach himself how to play it more or less fluently. Yet playing a violin

Peggy Somerville (aged 3),
Figures in a Pink Landscape, *watercolour*

involves a mixture of skills and aptitudes that are about as 'unnatural' physically and mentally as can be imagined. In the cases of Stephen Wiltshire, who could produce an uncannily accurate impression of the Doge's Palace after looking at it for a few moments, or Nadia who drew magnificent cockerels or a zany White Knight-like figure cantering along wildly on his great horse, their quite astonishing draughtsman's skills as children defy explanation; and the mystery is only increased by the fact that both of them were autistic. The parents of 'normal' children have to be content with their infants' splashes of bright colours and elementary pin-men and outlines of houses.

Peggy Somerville was born in 1918, an apparently 'normal' little girl, growing up very happily among a large family of brothers and sisters with whom she played games, looked after pets, climbed trees, and watched the gypsy encampment in the field across the stream which bounded the Old Ford Farm in Ashford, Middlesex. But at the age of three she started painting and seems never to have painted like a small child – the evidence is there to be seen, for her family kept everything she drew and painted. Before she was four years old, two of her watercolours were on view at the annual exhibition of the Royal Drawing Society at the Guildhall in London, and they were not an infant's splashes but pictures of an extraordinary liveliness and accomplishment. Her *Figures in a Pink Landscape*, for instance, has an imaginative 'realism' and depth of focus, let alone structure and colour gradation, almost incredible in a child of three.

Photographs of her at work – a pretty child sitting contentedly at her desk – appeared in the *Daily Mirror* and the *Sunday Pictorial*, and of a sudden she was famous. At the age of five Peggy was painting in oils, and three years later one of her works was exhibited at the New Irish Salon in Dublin without the judges having any idea of her age. Her *Threshing Time* (age ten) can only be described as the work of a mature artist. And at this age she had her first retrospective, at the Claridge Gallery, Brook Street. It was opened by Sir John Lavery; within a few days every picture was sold.

Today, twenty years after her premature death of cancer, her name is all but unknown. She was, of course, 'unfashionable'. And virtually penniless.

Stephen Reiss, together with Peggy's sister Rosemary and David Messum (of the Gallery in Cork Street), has worked tirelessly to bring Peggy Somerville's work back into public notice and has already written a book on her child art. In his new book he quotes from a letter she wrote to her mother in 1952:

> Looking at [these early pictures of mine] brought back a million memories – of the Old Ford Farm – my early dreams – my joys in nature. Speaking in a detached way, as an artist, I would say some of these drawings and paintings are beautiful in their

simplicity. Nothing is more pure than the first spontaneous expression of a child – its very lack of consciousness proves its closer link with God. Later there comes the conscious struggle to accept all things and still feel life as magical, as full of wonder, as one did as a child.

Pressed by a reporter to explain how she could have created such works of art at such an early age, she simply replied: 'I see the picture in my mind and then just paint it'. Apparently she almost never painted out of doors, in front of her subject, but only made a few pencilled notes and then executed the painting at her desk or in her studio; and this she did unerringly, in an astonishingly short space of time.

It may be that she inherited this acute visual memory from her father Charles Somerville, a painter, picture-restorer and teacher who was, as Reiss puts it, 'a minor player in a major movement', which might be described as the rural wing of Impressionism. He and his wife encouraged all their children to paint; indeed Peggy's elder brother Stuart had his pictures accepted by the Royal Academy when he was seventeen. But, says Reiss, 'their father ruled that they must learn for themselves by observation and memory. There should be no copying either directly from nature or from the work of others'. His injunctions are abundantly visible in her very earliest pictures, in their vitality and yet solidity.

Reiss insists that, unlike many talented child painters, Peggy Somerville did not peter out in her adolescence even if she did somewhat lose her way; and maybe this was because she never lost her capacity to transmit her child-like absorption in what she saw around her. As Matisse said, 'the artist has to look at everything as though he saw it for the first time ... one must be a child all one's life'. In fact Bonnard is the name her mature paintings most immediately bring to mind. She visited his Royal Academy exhibition in 1966 and described it as 'a glimpse of Heaven'.

It is not clear how much art Peggy had seen at first hand, for during much of her life she was too poor to travel widely, let alone abroad. For much of her adult life she lived in East Suffolk, first with her brother on the peninsula between the Deben and the Orwell, and then, for her last fifteen years, in the vicinity of Aldeburgh with her ailing mother. On the other hand, Reiss recounts that she was an avid reader and filled her sketchbooks with verses by Donne, Hopkins, Clare, Traherne, Shelley, Keats, Brontë, Christina Rossetti and Rilke – not that she was ever tempted to translate what she read into her art.

What emerges so strikingly from the comprehensive exhibition of her work at the Wolsey Gallery at Ipswich is the separation between the mind that creates and the mind that suffers. For in many ways hers was a sad and frustrated life. She had no doubt that if she had to choose between being married and having children and working as an artist she would have chosen the former. Once, when staying with her

Peggy Somerville (aged 10), Threshing Time, *oil*

brother and his family, she wrote heart-rendingly: 'It was such a heavenly morning, the birds singing, so fresh, so lovely, and I could not help wishing it were me lying up there with a little baby lying beside me'.

There were men in her life, but though they gave her enormous support, this didn't lead to marriage – indeed, they were already married. Of her collapsing relationship with one of them, she wrote:

It is simply that there are moments in one's life, and this is such a moment in mine, when there is a climax of years of self control and unuttered grief. I need a lot of strength to get me through and there are moments when I wonder if I can do it. It is not easy to live without joy – at least it has done me harm, who was born with so much capacity for enjoyment. I have tried to turn my feelings to my work, but here again it is not enough – a complete human being needs a complete life – then by being shared even the hardships and struggle can be overcome. I have tried to accept my fate and find serenity but I believe I have failed. I wanted so much to live, to give joy and happiness to others, to perhaps paint something good – but grief is killing me.

Yet there is not a hint of self-pity or black despair in any of her pictures, above all the wonderful luminous pastels that she executed at this period. They seem to be created out of a mood of serenity, 'to give joy and happiness to others'; and I am conscious that her words will seem very naive, even embarrassing, to the satraps of the art establishment. But that is their pathetic loss.

Peggy Somerville, Bowls of Fruit on a Ledge, *c.1950, panel, 24.1 x 33 cm*

Peggy Somerville's range may be somewhat restricted, and I find that some of her landscapes do not manage, altogether successfully, to transmute the dullish scene she remembered seeing. Yet from the earliest age she had an unerring eye for composition and perspective; and, in Reiss's words, she sought

> to achieve maximum density of colour without retreating into purely flat, two-dimensional design... It was an exceedingly difficult balancing act, [and in this she] succeeded through subtleties of handling and inspired colour juxtaposition.

Who would not wish to live with a glowing gem of a painting like *Bowls of Fruit on a Ledge*?

Perhaps the time has come when a beautifully illustrated account of her life like Reiss's and the comprehensive exhibition in Ipswich and then London will succeed in rekindling an interest in Peggy Somerville's art, an art which has long seemed to me exceptional, both for its sensitivity and richness, and its capacity to convey to the end of her life a sense of child-like wonder.

'Peggy Somerville', 18 January–16 March 1997, The Wolsey Art Gallery, Ipswich; 9–19 April, David Messum Gallery, London. A permanent exhibition of her work can be seen at The Gallery, 15 Lee Road, Aldeburgh.

Placing the Words

by PETER DAVIDSON

Ian Hamilton Finlay: Works in Europe 1972–1995 Werke in Europa, Edited by Zdenek Felix and Pia Simig, introduction by John Dixon Hunt, commentary by Harry Gilonis, Cantz Verlag, Ostfildern, Germany.

This austerely designed and finely produced book is a more than welcome expansion and update of Yve Abrioux's *Ian Hamilton Finlay: a visual primer*. This new publication was produced to coincide with Finlay's 1995 exhibition in the Hamburg Deichtorhallen, 'Works – Pure and Political', but it stands in its own right as an anthology of the remarkable and richly diverse pieces which Finlay has produced over the last decade. It would be valuable if only for its exhaustive listing of geographically scattered works, but it has much more than a catalogue to offer the reader. The black and white photography (by Werner J Hannappel) is of consistent excellence, serving the works themselves all the better for an intelligent avoidance of photographic atmospherics for their own sake.

Felix and Simig are to be congratulated on the meticulous documentation of place, date and collaborating artists which they give for each work, as well as for the real skill evidenced in the choice of illustrations and the space allotted to various works

within a chronological sequence. Almost every editorial choice is pertinent and actively helpful to the reader: I cannot imagine how the dispositions or the layout could be bettered.

Finlay's work is growing ever more focused as time passes: the works are ever more lucid, ever clearer in their communication, but their overtones are steadily growing more complex. It is perhaps unsurprising that such an artist has proved a stern challenge to those who are brave enough to write commentaries on his work. I feel that John Dixon Hunt's introduction, for all that it announces an appropriate conversion to the worth and standing of Finlay's work, fails to apprehend the sheer range of which Finlay is capable. It is indeed true that Finlay's own garden at Little Sparta is a work of art of the highest priority, but to reduce Finlay to the status of a garden designer alone is to do him a grave injustice. Some of the most appealing works in the book are indeed garden works: the bronze artefacts and plaques making a Vergilian garden in an olive grove of the Villa Celle, Pistoia, Italy; the Sacred Grove at the Kröller-Müller Museum, Otterloo, The Netherlands; the virtuoso reworking of English associational gardening at Stockwood Park, Luton. Yet Hunt's limiting emphasis is simply wrong: some of the most challenging pieces recorded here are urban installations, public artworks which are absolutely appropriate to an urban context. (No little part of their achievement is the precision with which each work is designed to function as a living part of its environment.) I hope to return later to at least one of these works, the giant bridge piers at the Broomielaw in Glasgow.

Mention of these leads me to my only other reservation about this book. Generally Harry Gilonis has provided an accomplished commentary on each group of works,

Ian Hamilton Finlay with Nicholas Sloan, Tree Plaque, Forest of Dean, 1988, one of three, stone

offering particularly useful thoughts on the ways in which Finlay's public works are finely judged so as to avoid the negative, directive potential of 'public art'. It must, however, be conceded that there are a very few points where Finlay has got out well ahead of his interpreter: the discussion of the Platonic text on the bridge piers misses some of the subtle variation and interplay between the Greek and English texts; the reading of the Latin text from the Max Planck Institute at Stuttgart is simply wrong (I'm afraid rather entertainingly so, in that the mistranslation generates an admirably ingenious reading of its own erroneous signification).

It seems mean-spirited to mention such small reservations when otherwise there is so much to celebrate. It is wonderful to have so much of Finlay's work available in collected form. This book sensibly documents works all over Europe (which definition, with a merciful absence of fuss, includes the British Isles), while Finlay's own garden, laboratory and command centre of Little Sparta is absent, having been treated at length in the second edition of Abrioux's book. It is illuminating to use the two books together, as some of the public works are variations and expansions of ideas already tried out in the context of the artist's own garden. Yet these are far from simple replicas in the hands of an artist who seems to have a genuine grasp of the potential and nature of any site. There are enigmas and implications in some of these related works which offer plenty of matter for reflection.

One such example would be the heroic inscription of vast stones cut in giant's lettering with a sentence from the French Revolutionary leader Saint-Just: THE PRESENT ORDER IS THE DISORDER OF THE FUTURE. At Little Sparta, the inscription is the last work in the garden sequence, placed at the point where the garden ends and the bare uplands begin. In such a context there are the words, and there are the sky and the hills, which leave you with no excuse for failing to meditate on a work which, in the present state of this island, seems at least to point a general direction for such meditation. (And yet that meaning cannot in truth be limited to the 'political', as the 'pure' is inevitably also present: the inscription functions also as a commemoration of the heroic Saint-Just and therefore as a celebration.) When the same words are translated into Dutch and placed on the lawn outside the van Abbe museum in Eindhoven, a different set of overtones and possibilities is bound to emerge: the cyclopaean stones are in a civic space; they are placed in a country with a history of notably democratic and equitable governance, where you would imagine that the majority of citizens see nothing much to complain of in DE HUIDIGE ORDE and would read a generally troubling sense of predicted disaster in DE WANORDE VAN DE TOEKOMST. In a Dutch context, the words work just as hard, but differently – as an admonition against complacency, as a

Ian Hamilton Finlay with Annet Stirling and Brenda Berman, Bridge Columns, Broomielaw, Glasgow, Scotland, *1990, stone*

celebration of the legendary, historically-remote Netherlandic 'invention' of civic freedom, as a memorial of the ambiguities of the revolutionary occupation of Holland. There is no repetition in Finlay's work, but there is infinite variation.

It is not easy to give a fair indication of the scope of the book, of the range of work which it contains. One of the most subversive and yet dignified urban works is a sequence of slabs with finely-cut definitions of uncomfortable words for the building of the Schröder Münchmaeyer Hengst Company bank at Frankfurt. There is much praise of the dignity of poverty, and criticism of the insensibilities of affluence. As so often with Finlay, the unifying idea is the aching void created by the absence of the numinous ('the secular terror') in the life of the late twentieth century. That the work should have come into being at all is extraordinary. More extraordinary is the dignity with which Finlay carries off an inherently ambiguous commission: he does not collude, any more than he falls into the indulgent denunciations of the licensed jester in the courts of affluence. The texts are definitions in the manner of a dictionary, but a poetic dictionary which offers truths about the nature and danger of wealth, with supporting quotations to reinforce moral rather than linguistic points. These definitions, clarifications, are ambiguous in their presentation (gilded, polished stone imitating the democratic medium of print in deliberately uninscriptional lettering), but they are unambiguous in their orientation. They face outwards for the public. Inside, there are simple and compelling re-workings of some of Finlay's earliest pieces. The bankers are offered the contemplation of the fishing boats coming home at twilight; the public are offered (I use the word with care) unbiased truths about the nature of banks.

On a smaller scale, there are gentle works which are poised between the public and the private. (One of the most consistent features of Finlay's work is an unerring instinct for scale: very often his interventions in place are physically unobtrusive, intellectually transformative.) Plaques on trees in the Forest of Dean command, or draw attention to, silence in the sibilants of three languages. The twin trees at the door of a handsome eighteenth-century house in Frechen-Bachem in Germany are transformed by analogous tree-plaques which identify the trees as the metamorphosed Philemon and Baucis whose story is related in Ovid, thus transforming the house, which functions as a gallery, into the temple described by the Roman poet.

The work on which I'd like to dwell in conclusion represents an intervention in the urban environment which is heroic in scale and vast in implication. Two of the rusticated piers of a redundant rail bridge, just south of Glasgow Central Station, where the track used to cross the River Clyde, have been cut in marvellous, deep, tough lettering (executed in collaboration with Annet Stirling and Brenda Berman) with a text from.* There is not space here to discuss the subtlety with which Finlay's text is an expanding transformation of the Greek, but the general sense is a clear one of the difficulty of all large works, of the perdurability of what is great and (reading on in the passage beyond the quoted words) the dangers surrounding any 'philosophical' community. The trackway has long gone, so the piers stand, monumentally, in the dark river, but in full light. The inscriptions stand one on either side of the river as though to articulate an arrival by water at the heart of the city. I don't know how the commission came about, but there is a full measure of congratulation due to whoever had the vision to bring it into being. The adroit judgement of scale is crucial: this is

no place for half-measures. But the transformative effect of placed words of such power as these, spreads out to inform the texture of life in the city. Implicitly they make a city which has suffered considerable adversity this century aware of its dignity, of its neo-classical visual heritage and of its enlightenment past. This is a kind of non-directive public art, at the furthest remove from patronising the public, which I can only imagine would really cheer and strengthen the people for whom it was made. Magnificence is added to a site which is already architecturally grand with the black grandeurs of the nineteenth century. There is also an element of the inspiredly practical – using the potential of structures already in place and deepening their monumental possibilities. It would be instructive, if frightening, to think how well Finlay's pieces function as a democratic public art where so many other attempts are either inadequate, bland with virtue or simply worrying. Finlay is not afraid of allowing his own preoccupations as poet and moralist into the public sphere, and this honesty seems worth a thousand 'big name' contemporary sculptures placed timidly at the edge of the lawn so as not to spoil the view of the Georgian façade. Finlay is always in dialogue with the past, but his integrity secures his loyalty to the present. No pastiche, no simplifications.

The achievement which this book records is unique in Europe; the best of it is that the canon which it records is still expanding, changing and deepening. □

*ΤΑ·ΓΑΡ·ΔΗ·ΜΕΓΑΛΑ/ΠΑΝΤΑ·ΕΠΙΣΦΑΛΗ·ΚΑΙ·
ΤΟ/ΛΕΓΟΜΕΝΟΝ·ΤΑ·ΚΑΛΑ/ΤΩ·ΟΝΤΙ·ΧΑΛΕΠΑ
Lit: for all great things are precarious and, as the saying has it, virtue [or 'truly beautiful things'] are difficult [or 'stern']. Finlay's lovely imitation/ variation is: ALL GREATNESS/STANDS FIRM IN/THE STORM.

READERS' LETTERS

The Editor welcomes letters from readers, but reserves the right to make cuts. Write to Modern Painters, Universal House, 251 Tottenham Court Road, London W1P 9AD

Star Letter: Who's on who?

Although it was nice to see the important critic Robert Hughes modelling blue socks on the cover of the last issue of *Modern Painters*, I felt that it was rather like seeing a trainspotter on the front of *Modern Railways*. If you decide to put photos of critics rather than painters on the cover I'd be more intrigued to see a picture of David Sylvester on André Masson or, indeed, Andrew Forge on David Sylvester.
Yours etc.,
John T Freeman
Guildford
Robert Hughes's blue-socked feet were actually 'on' Jackson Pollock's drip-festooned studio floor. Our occasional award of a bottle of champagne goes to John T Freeman for his observant wit.

'Writers just make it up'

Your magazine is called *Modern Painters* yet it is dominated by professional writers... Novelists, journalists, 'critics', etc., have usually done well in this country because literature is more appreciated than the visual arts. Certainly more trusted.

Painters are often extremely good writers. You ought to employ more than you do. After all, they are the ones who really know what it is all about. Writers just make it up.
Yours etc.,
Derek Balmer
Bristol
Artists can be wonderful writers, as Trevor Winkfield demonstrates in this issue, however they usually prefer their own 'language'. But, in this issue alone, as well as painter Trevor Winkfield, we have John Lessore, Merlin James, Matthew Collings and Glynn Williams. Other contributors, like Tom Lubbock, practise visual as well as verbal art. Indeed many of our writers are creative artists in their own medium: William Boyd, novelist; Blake Morrison, poet; George Szirtes (who also trained as an artist), poet; Michael Hofmann, poet; Julian Mitchell, playwright – to take just a few more examples from the current issue in which those who can, do, and write for Modern Painters.

An artist writes

I wish to write about being an artist and art in general. I thought I would make a start by writing a short piece on your Letters page:
For the artist anxiety is a fuel for movement. Artistic creation is an antidote.

Artistic inspiration is the veil lifting. This is clear sight, feeling sight of the world, of nature and the human spirit. Creative energy is a torrent.

Beyond technique and skill is expression and freedom.

Expression is a passage.

The journey of understanding never ends.

Arrival is an illusion
Yours etc.,
Peter Mock
Amersham

An eye for quality?

At the end of Boris Ford's article on Hilton Kramer's Fuller Memorial Lecture, he mentions comments of Peter Fuller's, which, although on a similar track, were less pessimistic. Youth seems always so much more hopeful.

In the late '60s, after one of his lectures at Bennington College in Vermont, I asked Clement Greenberg if he could comment on Bernhard Berenson's refusal or inability to go beyond .. who was it .. Cézanne? He answered by suggesting that critics over 40 years of age may start to lose it (no mention, by the way, of the culture losing it). But he went on with a story about Berenson visiting Peggy Guggenheim's one day in Venice. Although perhaps very much out of his element, it was said that he did give a nod to the Pollock that he saw there. It's the 'eye for quality' thing. To be selective. He still had it.

Robert Cronin, Sleeping Artist, *1994, oil on canvas, 111.7 x 142.2 cm*

Is the 'eye for quality' discipline now lost? What is this other desperation that puts all that aside? Or is it simply just the sweaty present?

Reflection on past history tends to tidy things up. Manet's *Olympia* was not regarded as a model of civility, either. It's rough out there. Always was.
Yours etc.,
Robert Cronin
Falls Village, CT, USA

The critic as rhino?

That William Boyd, eh, what a hero! Wading through all that dross ('Test of Endurance', Autumn 1996). Yet despite the breakneck speed of viewing some 250 pieces of artwork an hour on the selection panel of 'The Discerning Eye', he emerged 'curiously reassured' that his discernment had not been found wanting: 'contemplating an endless stream of the undistinguished, the unachieved and the unequivocally appalling made the old verities glow like jewels'.

But seriously though, I count myself fortunate to have had my work rejected by this pompous ass. Imagine getting in on his recommendation and then finding out through *Modern Painters* that he has the sensitivity of a rhinoceros!
Yours etc.,
D Kaufman
Edenbridge, Kent

Edward Bishop

I am currently preparing a book about the life and paintings of my father, the artist and painter Edward Bishop, RBA, NEAC, who is now 93 years old.
Father first exhibited in the Royal Academy Summer Exhibition in 1941 and has subsequently had over 80 paintings in Royal Academy Summer Exhibitions. Many of these paintings were sold, as were others by him at various exhibitions over the years.

I should be very grateful if any of your readers who own, or know

Edward Bishop,
The White Tablecloth, *1967*

the whereabouts of, any paintings by my father could kindly contact me as this information would greatly assist me in finishing the book.
Yours etc.,
Robert Bishop
6 East Heath Road
Hampstead
London NW3 1BN
Tel/fax: 0171 435 1496

Enfin, mon amour

This is a love letter. I received the Autumn issue two weeks ago and have almost finished with the reading of it. I'm dawdling now, so as not to finish too soon. I want more, more and more.

It's a pleasure to read an art magazine that shares my tastes and my abhorrences – finally. *Art Press* was making me feel so oppressed and vaguely sick.

I use your magazine with some of my more advanced English students, particularly Matthew Collings's 'Diary', which has a great rhythm for my students who need work on speaking and listening – some of them will subscribe soon, but I'd like to know if *Modern Painters* will be available in Paris one day. It is sorely lacking – Paris, I mean.

Also, I should be interested to know what other reviews *Modern Painters* would recommend. What does Collings read for example?
Yours etc.,
T Rolling
Paris
See 'What I Read' in Matt's Diary, page 63 of this issue. Modern Painters *is indeed rare in Paris. We're working on it! Meanwhile try Galignani (Librairie Français Etranger, No.1, 70 Taxe on CDP, 224, Rue de Rivoli, 75001 Paris, France), and ask for it in other outlets to create a demand.*

Dinner with pickled sheep

I've just finished my third and penultimate subscription issue of your magazine.
It's been swell. I can honestly say that until now I've never read an entire magazine from cover to cover before – ads and all...

However –

I feel compelled to tell you what I think about Damien Hirst...

I went to dinner the other night at the home of a gallery owner here in Tuscany and saw one (I assume there are many) of Damien Hirst's sheep on display in his sitting room. The dinner was delicious, the hospitality was warm and gracious ... the sheep was not. I was pleased to note that the condensation on the inside of the tank made the view from the top difficult and the irregular line of white sealant on the glass was worthy of a cowboy glazier from dear ol' blighty. But this was as nothing compared to the tank's contents and its perceived intent.

I mean, I get it and all: what's on either end of the fork at meal time is a 'Naked Lunch' and whatever passes off as domestic refinement at dinner is a mere bone crunch away from a more pressing reality. Nothing to boast about, believe me, but I'd like you to know that I recognise the 'art' intended by the 'artist' when he showed us his piece of meat.

The thing is, it's ugly.

I've got earlier drafts of this letter which gurn on about the divination of beauty, artistic obligations, the shallowness of irony and the intellectual shortcomings of the cheap shot but .. who cares? His stuff is ugly. Even his paintings are ugly. His sense of colour reminds me of coming down from a bad trip. His puns are puerile: *Away from the Flock – Divided*. It's almost as if he's counting on the fact that the poor boob seeing this piece for the first time will be miraculously transformed into a witty, with-it connoisseur of the arts simply by getting the joke. Without the pun it's a dead animal. With the joke, this thing becomes a serious work of art and a tongue-in-cheek yet meaningful statement on the juxtaposition of modern man and the hypocrisy inherent in his day-to-day existence in this age of ... baa-baa-baa...

A urinal on a gallery wall is equally pretentious but at least it's got a beautiful shape and somebody made it. No matter how much 'spin' you put on a severed piece of meat – religious or otherwise (after *Serious Moonlight* it's been downhill all the way) – it remains ugly; ugly as an idea and ugly as a thing, and who wants more?

Luckily, the 'contadini' who live in my valley (who have advised me on how to grow tomatoes in one instance and marvelled at Perugino's use of blue in the next) would probably see a dead sheep in a vat of formaldehyde as a sad and sorry waste of a livestock animal. But I also know that nothing any of

us will ever do – no 'thing' (alas) on the contemporary art scene – could ever rival the perfection and relevance of one of my neighbour's beautifully ploughed fields.
Yours etc.,
William Kilpatrick
Sarteano, Italy

Home goal?

In assembling a collection of essays that seeks to re-examine the canons of art history and to cast new light on well-known objects and movements in art, one does not expect to please all readers. There will be those who think art historians ought to stick to the traditional tasks of patronage studies and ekphrasis in the service of established artists. If such conservatives simply identify themselves and their passions, I am prepared to part ways amiably.

To judge from the aspects of *Not at Home* praised by your reviewer Lottie Hoare, she is one such conservative, confidently equipped with a faith in formalism and distaste for what she perceives as 'political correctness'. What is perplexing about her review is her attempt to claim also the mantle of interdisciplinarity for her attitudes. Her evidence that I lack this quality is my unwillingness to face 'the fact that the Bloomsbury group despised the outside world and preferred a tea-on-sofas-with-friends exclusivity'. Unless I am ignorant of faculties recently established in outdated gossip and over-generalisation, I feel confident that this observation cannot be assigned to any particular discipline. The problem seems to be that I am asking readers to look at old art in a new way – a way that does, in fact, incorporate the insights of new disciplines, including cultural studies and women's/gender studies.

I urge more progressive readers to investigate *Not at Home* on their own. And I urge Ms Hoare to wear the mantle of her conservatism more honestly.
Yours etc.,
Dr Christopher Reed
Editor, Not at Home
Evanston, IL, USA

Freud's freaks

The reference, in your Autumn issue, to Lucian Freud's habit of 'fanatical scrutiny' takes me back to the early 1950s. He was teaching at the Slade in those days, but that's neither here nor there. What was impressive was the way he would, while waiting for a bus in Tottenham Court Road, fix his eyes on some old Dear coming along in the distance with her shopping, and maintain the same intense gaze, leaning forward from the waist, as she passed within a few feet of him. Full-face advancing, profile in close-up, and back of the head diminishing to a dot: he drank it all in like a thirsty vampire. He was the freak then. Now he tends to look for this quality in his models. The Fat Lady used to be a fairground attraction.
Yours etc.,
John Brelstaff
Guisborough

A message for our times from Ruskin

Back in 1877 Ruskin wrote that '...the teaching of art is the teaching of all things', in other words, as I understand it, a liberal education was/is desirable for the comprehending and imaginative faculty of the mind and would go some way towards promoting enlightenment for the common man (indeed for any man or woman). Almost ten years on from the first issue of *Modern Painters* the National Society for Education in Art and Design and the Guild of St George held 'The Art of Education – Ruskin Today' conference in Sheffield... I felt that the voice of Peter Fuller was missing, or someone who could offer radical points of view that challenged rather than dictated; that gave insight as opposed to oversight.

Robert Hewison gave us a moving and uplifting account of Ruskin's views on art, design and education. But an argument for Ruskin's approach in education today was barely touched upon by the various speakers. If the practice of drawing has *ever* enhanced the life of the individual – as a member of society – then it will surely *always* do this. The conference missed the potential for a debate on the value of 'seeing' (by implication we need to be taught how to see), and to argue for the rejuvenation of a visual education for the would-be fine art practitioner. The half-baked ideas that masquerade as 'conceptualism' skipping out of the art and design institutions of this country now leave something to be desired.

Ruskin, Hewison explained, believed that enhanced accuracy of perception through drawing might lead to accuracy of thought; that sight was intended to lead to insight. 'To be taught to see ... to gain word and thought at once' – sounds revelatory!

In these days of (party political) 'morality', Ruskin's proclamation that '...the art of my country is the exponent of its political ... principals ... the exponent of its "ethical" life', sounds like a potentially modern sound bite...

So, what of the Turner prize? What would Ruskin, champion of Turner, or Peter Fuller, make of this event today? At the Sheffield conference I sought answers from the Ruskin scholars: 'Is drawing relevant to fine art education today?', and did not really get an answer. A better formulated question might have been: 'If there is a necessity for the visual and plastic arts to be visually and intellectually challenging, rather than tabloid teasing or plainly naive., is it being addressed by fine art education today?'

To end on a lighter note – at a time when the politicians' superegos are in overdrive over society's ills perhaps we need more drawing lessons in our schools to support a moral education for the 'ethical life' of our country? Gillian Shepherd take note!
Yours etc.,
Geoffrey Hands
Brighton

Still Life with a Pewter Flagon
by ANNEMARIE AUSTIN

Barely still at all, this 'still life'.
The napkin was just flung down,
a raspberry yet rolls a little
on the pewter plate, and the light –
oh surely the light has newly brimmed
the dish, touched the flagon's round
side with a bright moon, caused
the linen's white reflection in glass
and silver, porcelain – everywhere.

Goethe defined colours as 'the deeds
and sufferings of light'. Red, indeed,
is raised here in the berries and the
almost-hidden wine, a brown-green
from the vine leaves and table cover;
but chiefly the light is itself and
about its own business – bouncing,
rebounding, exalting itself in glaze
and shine and lustre, such lustre.

The word for 'beautiful' in Dutch is
schoen, also meaning 'clean'. And before
these objects were set up for their
portrait, there was laundering and
polishing to be done. An absent cloth
was grimed and put aside, an absent
woman breathed on the flagon's belly,
rubbed at it, breathed and rubbed...
Her life's also inherent here, in action.

Jan Jansz Treck, Still Life with a Pewter Flagon and Two Ming Bowls